ASIAN RIVALRIES

ASIAN RIVALRIES

Conflict, Escalation, and Limitations on Two-level Games

Edited by

Sumit Ganguly

William R. Thompson

Stanford Security Series,

An Imprint of Stanford University Press

Stanford, California

FOUNDATION BOOKS

FOUNDATION
BOOKS

Foundation Books is an imprint of Cambridge University Press, India.

Cambridge House, 4381/4 Ansari Road, Daryaganj, New Delhi 110 002

www.cambridgeindia.org

This edition has been published by Cambridge University Press India Pvt. Ltd. by arrangement with Stanford University Press.

First South Asia edition 2013
Reprint 2015

Printed in India at Sanat Printers, Kundli, Haryana

ISBN 978-93-82264-09-5 Hardback

Contents

Contributors

LOWELL DITTMER is Professor of Political Science at the University of California, Berkeley.

SUMIT GANGULY is Rabindranath Tagore Chair in Indian Cultures and Civilizations and Professor of Political Science at Indiana University.

LYLE J. GOLDSTEIN is Director of the China Maritime Studies Institute in the Strategic Research Department of the U.S. Naval War College.

S. PAUL KAPUR is Associate Professor in the Department of National Security Affairs at the U.S. Naval Postgraduate School.

SAMUEL S. KIM is Senior Research Scholar Emeritus in the Center for Korea Research in the Weatherhead East Asian Institute of Columbia University.

MANJEET S. PARDESI is working on his PhD in political science at Indiana University and is an editorial assistant at *International Studies Quarterly.*

ANDREW SCOBELL is Senior Political Scientist at the Rand Corporation's Washington, DC, office.

WILLIAM R. THOMPSON is Distinguished Professor and Donald A. Rogers Professor of Political Science at Indiana University and Managing Editor of *International Studies Quarterly.*

BRANTLY WOMACK is Professor of Foreign Affairs at the University of Virginia.

1 Conflict Propensities in Asian Rivalries

Sumit Ganguly and William R. Thompson

It is possible to argue that the past decade has focused attention disproportionately on Middle Eastern international relations. This observation is not meant to slight the significance of Middle Eastern politics but only to note that we tend to focus mightily on the regions in which the most lethal activity is prominent. Middle Eastern international relations, without doubt, have been active and prominent. Other regions, therefore, have tended to receive less attention even though, ultimately, they may prove to be more significant to the fate of the twenty-first century. For instance, an easy case can be made that Asia will prove to be relatively more important than most other regions in this century.[1] Compared to other regions, Asia contains more population and is becoming increasingly more central to the world economy.[2] It also possesses the highest potential for conflict over regional hegemony and global leadership of any region. Wars between major powers may well be a thing of the past, but if they have any potential to take place at all, Asia is a most likely venue. Hence, if for no other reason, Asian international relations should have a strong claim on our attention.

But Asian international relations represent a rather broad set of phenomena—too broad to provide a good focus. We concentrate in this book on interstate rivalries—relationships between two states in which the antagonistic decision-makers perceive each other as competitors who see their adversaries as threatening enemies.[3] Rivalries provide a good focus because they are one of the main vehicles for interstate conflict. That is, most states do not conflict with one another; rivals do and do so repeatedly as serial disputants. They certainly are responsible for much more than their proportional share of discord in world politics. If we are interested in the interstate conflict potential of Asia, then rivalries are the processes to watch. They are not exactly the canaries in the mineshaft; rather, they are the mineshaft.

This book brings together seven treatments of rivalry in Asia. We are certainly not the first to write about Asian rivalries, but we may be among the first to write about Asian rivalry processes in general—as opposed to the many studies of various aspects of specific, individual rivalries.[4] One of our main goals in bringing together these essays is to make a pitch for more explicit study of Asian rivalries as rivalries—and not as simply long-term conflicts or disputes, each of which is entirely different. We do not argue that all Asian conflict is precisely the same. Far from it. But many Asian conflicts are framed by interstate rivalries, and it is the rivalry relationship per se that carries some potential for generalization. Yet that type of generalization can only come about if we recognize that some types of disputes are rivalries and treat them as representatives of a more general category. Greater sensitivity to the utility of explicit rivalry analysis should serve us well in deciphering the nature and implications of Asian conflict.[5]

Analysts of Asian international politics engage in implicit rivalry analysis all the time. Making such analysis more explicit involves recognizing that some (but not all) interstate relationships qualify as rivalries and that rivalries are characterized by processes that bear some potential for generalization, as opposed to dealing with each pair of antagonists as a unique set of adversaries. In other words, the premise is that we should not be dependent solely on area expertise in decoding what hostile states are up to. If we improve our understanding of how rivalries work in general, then the possibility of marrying area expertise with rivalry theory should enhance our ability to understand and cope with dangerous situations.

Our second motivation for bringing together these essays is to address a particular question about international politics in general and Asian rivalries in particular. The most typical treatment of international relations is to conceive it as a tennis match between two states. Beijing did X to Washington and Washington responded with Y. This imagery reflects a conceptualization involving two mythical, unitary decision-makers volleying back and forth. Sometimes, the conceptualization reflects a shorthand way of focusing on who is doing what to whom, but all too often people (journalists, analysts, decision-makers, and the proverbial man/woman-in-the-street) actually perceive international relations between two states operating along these lines.[6] We know better. We know that interstate relations are often at least two-level games in which decision-makers operate in competitive domestic and international environments.[7] Action X by a state may represent a signal to another state, it may be oriented toward domestic political consumption, or both at the same time. The problem is that elites compete for control of governments and governmental policies while at the same time they devise strategies for competing with other states.[8]

Which type of competition is more important in understanding interstate actions? Do we need to integrate both levels to make sense of international relations? Or, does this "need" vary by place, time, or issue area? Are some regions less susceptible to two-level games than others? Have two-level games become more likely than they were in the past due to democratization or the increased availability of information? Are all types of international politics equally susceptible to two-level gaming? For example, it may be one thing to threaten trade protectionism with a domestic audience uppermost in the threatener's mind. It may be entirely a different matter to engage in a nuclear crisis in which salient domestic group preferences may or may not fade into the background because of the seriousness of the situation.[9] Moreover, is it possible or desirable to integrate both levels?

The main foci of rivalry analyses can be divided into four categories. One, how and why do rivalries begin? Two, what maintains them at various levels—or, alternatively, what causes them to escalate and de-escalate in hostility?[10] Three, how and why do they end? Fourth, what are the implications and effects of engaging in rivalry? Origins, maintenance, termination, and consequences span the rivalry topical spectrum. This book focuses primarily on the second category. What causes rivalries to fluctuate in their perceived levels of threat and conflict? Our interest in two-level games is one place to start. Do two-level games in Asia contribute to rivalry fluctuations in intensity and hostility? Or, are there other factors that seem more important to rivalry escalation and de-escalation?

Why Asia?

Not quite two decades ago, Aaron Friedberg published an essay asking whether a new, enlarged Asian regional subsystem was ripe for rivalry.[11] He concluded that it was. Europe's half millennium run as the primary generator of war was closing, but Europe's past could well be Asia's future. Why? To explain and elaborate his conclusion, Freidberg advances a theory of war and peace that revolves around whether factors that promote war (peace) are stronger than factors that mitigate against war (peace). Table 1.1 provides a summary of these factors and contrasts Europe with Asia.

Both Europe and Asia have been and continue to be multipolar. Historically, multipolarity in Europe increased the chances for miscalculation, misperception, and failures to balance quickly enough. After 1945, European multipolarity was subordinated to the cold war's bipolarity, and only with the demise of the cold war has multipolarity returned. Asia has been multipolar for centuries, and the new Asian subsystem will be decidedly multipolar in structure with the United States, China, Russia, Japan, and India as the leading states.

If multipolarity is inherently dangerous or unstable, what factors work against systemic structure to dampen the probability of war? Freidberg isolates three main categories of factors operating at different levels of analysis. State/national attributes include regime type, economic inequality and prosperity, nationalism, and attachment to territory. Europe is highly democratic, inequality is relatively low and prosperity is relatively high, nationalism seems to be declining in most parts of the region, and territorial disputes are few. In contrast, Asia has a strong mix of democracies and authoritarian political systems that operate at different levels of intensity.[12] That is, some political systems are more democratic than others while the degree of authoritarianism also varies. A number of Asian economies are experiencing rapid economic growth, but only a few can be described as affluent, and inequality remains especially problematic in those economies expanding most quickly. There is no evidence of declining nationalism in Asia. On the contrary, the opposite appears to be the case. There are also a large number of outstanding territorial disputes with which to be reckoned.

The state/nation attributes that work against conflict in Europe are largely missing in Asia or, worse, are apt to be facilitators of war in Asia. Something similar applies to the nature of interstate linkages in the two regions. Europe is relatively homogenous in culture, thickly embedded in a large number of intergovernmental and nongovernmental organizations, and characterized by a remarkable flow of people and goods. More heterogeneous Asia may be moving very slowly toward increased economic interdependence, but it has

TABLE 1.1. Friedberg's Comparison of Europe and Asia After the Cold War

Factors	*Europe*	*Asia*
Polarity	· Multipolar	· Multipolar
States	· Spread and consolidation of democracy · Increased equality and material well-being · Decline in nationalism in most parts of the region · Absence of territorial disputes	· Mixture of democratic and authoritarian regimes · Rapid economic growth; large pockets of high inequality · Increase in nationalism · Multiple territorial disputes
Linkages	· Increased economic interdependence and transnational flow of people, goods, capital, and technology · Thick web of transnational institutions · Cultural homogeneity	· Economic interdependence increasing in parts of Asia but still limited with strong resistance to economic subordination by Japan or China · Underinstitutionalized · Cultural heterogeneity
Costs/ Benefits	· Destructiveness of weaponry → costs of warfare up · Limited appeal of territorial conquest → benefits of warfare down	· Destructive weaponry unevenly distributed with dangerous transition period toward proliferation · Less decline in perceived benefits of war

SOURCE: Based on the discussion in Aaron L. Friedberg, "Ripe for Rivalry: Prospects for Peace in Multipolar Asia," International Security 18 (1993/94): 5–33.

a very long way to go. Compared to Europe, the region is underinstitutionalized at the transnational level. If economic interdependence, international organizations, and cultural homogeneity work as reducers of conflict propensities, Europe is in good shape and Asia is not.

Finally, European warfare became increasingly lethal during the past five hundred years. With the advent of nuclear weapons, the costs of warfare have become exceedingly high. The perceived benefits of territorial conquest, by contrast, seem to have declined for states that are no longer agrarian. Nuclear weapons can certainly be found in Asia as well, but they are both unevenly distributed and proliferating. In a transition period toward increasingly high costs of warfare, there are a number of dangers ranging from the temptations of preemptive strikes against small nuclear capabilities to daisy chains of arms races as rivals attempt to get ahead or stay even with their adversaries. Asian states are also becoming less agrarian, but territorial conquest is only one of several motivations for war. Unification desires (think Korea or Taiwan), punishment for perceived transgressions (China versus India and Vietnam), and classic boundary disputes still persist.

Thus, both Europe and Asia are multipolar in the twenty-first century, but a host of mitigating factors work in the European region against conflict escalation. In Asia, the same factors appear to be more conflict facilitators than suppressants. It may be that the processes highlighted by Friedberg will eventually work toward reducing conflict propensities in Asia, but all of the factors evolve rather slowly. For the immediate future, there is at least no reason to anticipate Asian international relations functioning as European international relations currently do. Curiously, Freidberg never evokes the term rivalry beyond the title of his article, but his conclusion, in answer to his own question, that Asia is ripe for rivalry is quite clear.

We find his argument and interregional comparison quite appealing in some respects. Despite its age, it is still highly pertinent. But it does have two flaws. One is that there is an assumption that, given the same mix of variables, regions will work the same way. Yet the historical geopolitics of Asia have been much different than those of Europe. In Europe of the last five hundred years, states were highly competitive and frequently at war. A Dehioan mixture of sea powers allied with more distant land powers managed to keep the region from becoming unipolar when Spain, France, or Germany made hegemonic bids.[13] In contrast, highly competitive states frequently at war have not been the norm in Asia. A respectable portion of Asia, on the contrary, has been accustomed to Chinese hegemony for long stretches of time.[14] If history matters, the very different histories of Europe and Asia might lead us to be cautious in assuming that peace and conflict processes in Asia are likely to replicate closely those of Europe.

The second problem is that the conclusion that Asia was ripe for rivalry seems to imply that with the demise of the cold war, Asian rivalries were likely to emerge in the multipolar future. The problem, though, is that Asia has long experienced rivalries. It may be ripe for new and renewed rivalries. It cannot be ripe for types of interstate relationships that are already there and have been there for some time.

Thompson and Dreyer list thirty-two Asian rivalries in their inventory of rivalries mainly since 1815.[15] Thirteen ended before 1950. These older ones are of two types if we put the Japan-U.S. rivalry aside for a moment. One type involves resistance to European penetration of various regional systems. The history of this type, of course, could easily be pushed back before 1816. But this type of rivalry has become obsolete as European imperialism has run its course. The other type involves contention among various Asian states for preeminence within their region. Neither category fits the Japan-U.S. rivalry

TABLE 1.2. Asian Rivalries Separated by Timing

Asian Rivalries, Nineteenth to Mid-Twentieth Centuries		*Asian Rivalries, Mid-Twentieth to Twenty-first Centuries*	
East Asia		**East Asia**	
Britain-China	1839–1900	China-Japan II	1996–ongoing
Britain-Japan	1932–1945	China-Soviet Union II	1958–1989
China-France	1856–1900	China-Taiwan	1949–ongoing
China-Germany	1897–1900	China-U.S. II	1949–1972
China-Japan I	1873–1945	China-U.S. II	1996–ongoing
China-Russia I	P1816–1949[a]	North Korea-South Korea	1948–ongoing
Japan-Russia	1874–1945		
Japan-U.S.	1900–1945		
Southeast Asia		**Southeast Asia**	
Burma-Thailand	P1816–1826	Cambodia-South Vietnam	1956–1975
France-Vietnam	1858–1884	Cambodia-Vietnam	1976–1983
Thailand-Vietnam I	P1816–1884	China-Vietnam	1973–1991
		Indonesia-Malaysia	1962–1966
		Indonesia-Netherlands	1951–1962
		Malaysia-Singapore	1965–ongoing
		Thailand-Vietnam II	1954–1988
		North Vietnam-South Vietnam	1954–1975
Central Asia		**Central Asia**	
Afghanistan-Iran	P1816–1937	Afghanistan-Iran	1996–2001
		Afghanistan-Pakistan	1947–ongoing
		Kazakhstan-Uzbekistan	1991–ongoing
South Asia		**South Asia**	
Britain-Burma	P1816–1826	China-India	1948–ongoing
		India-Pakistan	1947–ongoing

[a] A "P" prefix indicates that the rivalry began prior to 1816.

SOURCE: Based on information reported in William R. Thompson and David R. Dryer, *Handbook of Strategic Rivals* (Washington, DC: Congressional Quarterly Press, 2011).

all that well because their rivalry is better described as one of mutual imperialism and contention in the Pacific and various parts of Asia. As a categorical type, it shares some similarity with two rivalries not shown in Table 1.2, the Anglo-Russian and U.S.-Soviet rivalries, both of which had strong Asian linkages.[16] Yet none of the three was exclusively Asian in terms of their scope.

The nineteen rivalries in the right hand side of Table 1.2, of which nine are ongoing, can be differentiated as well. Most can be categorized as either reflecting contention over regional preeminence or the more common rivalry of two adjacent states over some local desiderata. China-Japan, China-USSR, China-U.S., China-Vietnam, Kazakhstan-Uzbekistan, and China-India reflect the former type.[17] Most of the rest reflect the adjacent states quarreling usually over territory that is contiguous to both. The three divided states (the two Koreas, the two Vietnams, and the two Chinas) are better viewed as a separate category. In this type, there is a fundamental disagreement about which state deserves to represent or rule the two states that were once one state and might be one state again.[18]

Do Rivalries Really Matter in Asia?

Have rivalries mattered in Asia? One index is to take a look at the wars fought in Asia in the past two centuries. The Asian wars found on the Correlates of War list, arrayed in Table 1.3, number twenty-eight.[19] The list could be longer, but Correlates of War procedures discriminate against including most Asian states as full members of a Eurocentric international system prior to the twentieth century. Still, twenty-eight wars in the past century and a quarter is an impressive figure. Equally impressive is that twenty-five of the twenty-eight wars (89 percent) involved confrontations between rivals. Rivalry does not tell us everything we might want to know about these conflicts, but this one factor at least provides an important clue as to what was at stake in most of the disputes. Rivals tend to fight over status (position) and territory (space), among other things including ideological differences. That still does not tell us exactly why the wars were fought, but emphasizing rivalry does tell us that these states are "recidivists" in international politics. They have a history of competing intensely and presumably keep at it because they are unable to resolve definitively their outstanding issues. Once they do resolve them, they tend to cease being rivals—unless they invent some new issues to quarrel over.[20] Yet the development of new issues to dispute are not as unusual as one might think because another hallmark of rivalries is that the antagonists develop intense feelings of suspicion and distrust about their adversaries. Rivalries are embedded in psychological baggage, warranted or otherwise, that is often extremely difficult to shed. The longer they are rivals, presumably, the greater is the buildup of the psychological baggage, not unlike scar tissue. As in the case of scar tissue, the adversaries become increasingly inflexible in dealing with their opponents. Distrust of any conciliatory move or signal becomes reflexive.

Still another way of answering the question of whether rivalries matter in Asia is to ask which conflicts are most likely to break out into physical conflict

TABLE 1.3. Asian Wars, 1816–2007

War	*Timing*	*Main Rivals in Confrontation*
Sino-French War	1884–1885	China-France
First Sino-Japanese War	1894–1895	China-Japan
Boxer Rebellion	1900	China-Britain, France, Russia, Germany
Sino-Russian War	1900	China-Russia
Russo-Japanese	1904–1905	Japan-Russia
World War I	1914–1918	
Manchurian War	1929	Japan-Soviet Union
Second Sino-Japanese	1931–1933	China-Japan
Third Sino-Japanese	1937–1941	China-Japan
Changkufeng War	1938	Japan-Soviet Union
Nomonhan	1939	Japan-Soviet Union
World War II	1939–1945	China-Japan, Britain-Japan, Japan-U.S., Japan-Soviet Union
Franco-Thai War	1940–1941	
First Kashmir	1947–1949	India-Pakistan
Korean	1950–1953	North-South Korea, China-U.S.
Off-shore Islands Wars	1954–1955	China-Taiwan, China-U.S.
Taiwan Straits	1958	China-Taiwan, China-U.S.
War in Assam	1962	China-India
Vietnam War Phase 2	1965–1975	North Vietnam-South Vietnam
Second Kashmir	1965	India-Pakistan
Second Laotian War Phase 2	1968–1973	North Vietnam-South Vietnam
War of the Communist Coalition	1970–1971	North Vietnam-South Vietnam
War for Bangladesh	1971	India-Pakistan
Vietnamese-Cambodian Border War	1977–1979	Cambodia-Vietnam
Sino-Vietnamese Punitive War	1979	China-Vietnam
Sino-Vietnamese Border War	1987	China-Vietnam
Kargil	1999	India-Pakistan
Invasion of Afghanistan	2001	

SOURCE: The first two columns are based on information in Meredith Sarkees and Frank W. Wayman, *Resort to War* (Washington, DC: Congressional Quarterly Press, 2010), 76–77.

in the future. One would be hard pressed to find more salient candidates for future conflict than the Indo-Pakistani dispute over Kashmir, skirmishing on the land and sea borders of the two Koreas, or Chinese frustrations over bringing Taiwan to heel. We cannot rule out future Sino-Japanese clashes in the East China Sea, Sino-Vietnamese confrontations in the South China Sea, or Sino-Indian frictions in the Indian Ocean (or along their long land border). All of these statements are quite easy to make because examples of precisely such clashes are quite recent or ongoing. If we add the looming potential of a more explicit competition for regional leadership between two ascending states with very large populations (China and India), a similar looming competition for regional economic leadership between China and Japan, a declining former superpower struggling to get back into the Eurasian game (Russia) with or without the assistance of China, and the external surviving superpower (the United States) attempting to stay preeminent in the Eurasian game, along with the likely increasing competition between an ascending China and the United States in and outside Asia, can there be any question that rivalries matter in Asia? It should be just as clear that Asian rivalries have mattered and will continue to matter to people residing outside of Asia.

Two-level Rivalries in Asia

It is not enough to merely say that Asia has had rivalries, continues to have rivalries, and that they matter. We need to go further and probe how they function. There are a host of questions that might be asked. How do rivalries begin? How do they terminate? How are they maintained for years without shedding blood? Why do they suddenly erupt into outbursts of combat? These are all worthwhile questions. However, we chose instead to focus on two-level questions. How do internal and external politics interact, if they do, in bringing about outcomes in Asian rivalries?

We asked a small group of specialists on Asian rivalries to examine three related questions: (1) What is the mix of internal (domestic politics) and external (interstate politics) stimuli in the dynamics of their rivalries? (2) In what types of circumstances do domestic politics become the predominant influence on rivalry dynamics? and (3) When domestic politics become predominant, is their effect more likely to lead to the escalation or de-escalation of rivalry hostility? Asking these questions in an absolute sense is unlikely to prove profitable, especially for rivalries that have persisted for a number of years. Instead, we asked each analyst to isolate two relatively similar types of episodes—such as elections or the selection of authoritarian leaders, negotiations over winding down an ongoing interstate rivalry, border disputes/clashes, or interstate crises—in which one case involved a considerable amount of influence from domestic politics and the other case did not. In this context, we posed two questions as the main analytical foci of the papers:

a. Why did domestic politics seem to play a strong role in the one case but not the other? and
b. Did the "intrusion" of domestic politics in the one case, especially in comparison to the other case, lead to rivalry escalation or de-escalation?[21]

The answers to these questions are unlikely to resolve all of the questions we might have about the interaction of two-level political games and rivalries, but they constitute a beginning attempt to unravel how these processes work to maintain or increase/decrease the intensity of interstate antagonisms. Moreover, we need to be alert to the possibility that two-level games are not all that predominant in Asian rivalries.[22] Rivalries do not seem to work the same in all regions. For instance, in the Middle East, rivalries seem to be especially susceptible to two-level games. This characteristic might best be attributed to the porosity of Arab states in which populations have been attuned to both national and regional leaders and issues. A Gamal Abd al Nasser in the 1960s could be one of the leading politicians in half a dozen Arab states. Alternatively, how Palestinians are treated in the West Bank or Gaza is not an issue confined to the state of Israel or even the states immediately adjacent to Israel. In 2011, onlookers watched a politicized suicide in Tunisia lead to the toppling of two North African states, at least one internationalized civil war, and political reverberations throughout the Middle East and North Africa.

Moreover, a number of Middle Eastern states possess domestic groups with some interest in taking over the state from the minority group in power. The minority group in power must also weigh alternative courses of action in terms of how it might affect its ability to stay in power. Then, too, there is the problem of external patrons desiring one course of action and domestic constituencies desiring another. How does one stay in power without forgoing external patronage and domestic support? Thus, for several reasons, Middle Eastern international politics tend to have strong two-level attributes. When Middle Eastern politicians speak or act, it is not always clear which audience(s)—internal or external—are being addressed.

Should we anticipate Asian politics working the same way? There have been Asian politicians with substantial political influence in other countries. Mao readily comes to mind. External patrons with preferences at odds with domestic group preferences certainly can be found in Asian politics. Yet one way in which Asian rivalries might prove to be different than, say, Middle Eastern rivalries, is the prevalence of single-party regimes in a number of key states. Single-party regimes do not necessarily function as monoliths. There are factions organized around major players contending for policy influence and leadership succession. There are differential constituencies within the party to placate based on regional weight or function (for instance, the military or economic planners). It may be, though, that it is possible to constrain these influences when it comes time to engage in foreign policy activity.

The presence of single-party regimes in Asia does not mean that we should anticipate the complete absence of two-level games in Asian rivalries. For that matter, all states in Asia are not ruled by single-party regimes, but enough are that we might expect to find that these processes play themselves out differently in different parts of Asia. Figure 1.1 provides a summary sketch of recent and contemporary rivalries in Asia. It is very difficult to overlook the centrality of China to Asian rivalries. China, of course, has had a single-party regime since at least 1949. It is not just China, of course; North Korea, Vietnam, Taiwan until the 1980s, and, briefly, Cambodia have had or have single-party regimes as well. Other Asian states have at times been formally multiparty regimes but function as if they were single-party regimes. To the extent that single-party regimes are a significant clue to the presence or absence of two-level rivalry games, we might expect to find some distinctiveness in Asian politics.

Nonetheless, some Arab states have also been single-party regimes without eschewing two-level politics. It may not be single-party regimes per se but how strong the single-party regime's control of state and society that is critical. Alternatively, it could be that foreign policy behavior is somehow too important to tolerate multiple games in regimes that are capable of controlling decision-making. One of the arguments raised against Allison's contrast of unitary actor versus games dominated by competing governmental agencies and policy entrepreneurs is that questions of national security are too important to tolerate too many intragovernmental, policy influences.[23] To the extent that we look at national security questions through our rivalry lens, we may be focusing on precisely the behavior that is least susceptible to two-level gaming. Of course, this speculation remains simply a hypothesis. It is just as easy to contend that the importance of national security questions is likely to encourage simultaneous external and domestic influences on policy and, therefore, the need for decision-makers to seek to address multiple audiences when they act.

But there is also the question of which rivalries to look at. Should we sample or attempt coverage of all rivalries that have ever characterized modern Asia? If we sample, what group of rivalries would be most representative? Actually, we really have no choice but to sample in some fashion. The thirty-two rivalries listed in Table 1.2 are too many (and too far apart in time) to deal with in one volume. Even the nineteen most contemporary ones are too

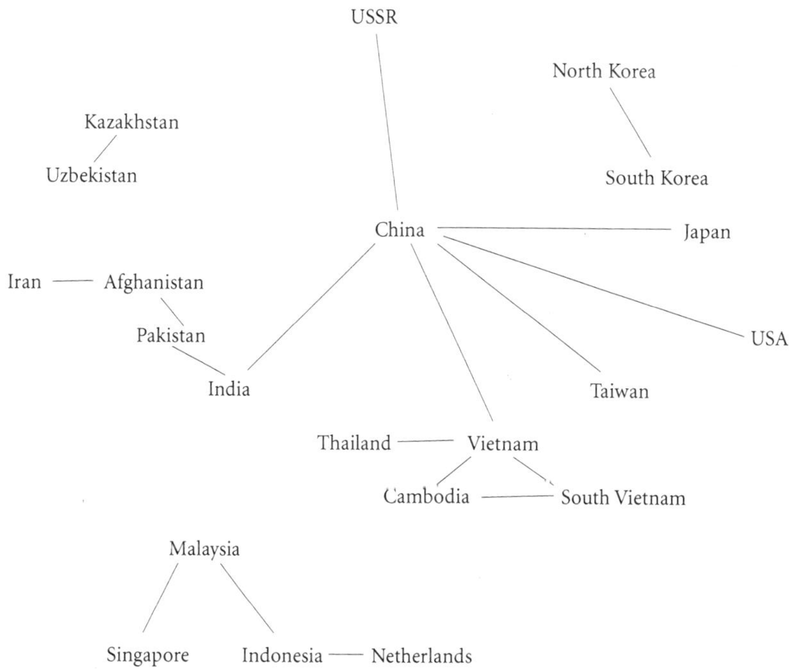

FIGURE 1.1. Recent and Contemporary Rivalries in Asia

many and too disparate in significance to encourage comprehensive coverage. Figure 1.1 sketches the nineteen rivalries, some of which are still ongoing and some of which have been terminated (see Table 1.2). It does not require much manipulation of the figure to underline the "star"-like nature of China in the field of Asian rivalries. It is the one state with the most rivalry experience. It is also the one state with rivalry connections to South Asia, Southeast Asia, and East Asia. In that respect, rivalries are part of the armature bringing Asia writ large together as a single region. Of course, from a conflict perspective, China is also a state with considerable war experience. It has fought wars with India, Vietnam, Japan, and the United States, and it came close to fighting with the Soviet Union in 1969. Clearly, China should figure strongly in our sample. Other clusters are evident in Figure 1.1. There are two Southeast Asian clusters. One cluster (Malaysia, Singapore, Indonesia, and the Netherlands), with the exception of the continuing Malaysian-Singapore rivalry, was a phenomenon that was over by the mid-1960s. The Thailand, Vietnam, Cambodia, South Vietnam rivalry complex has also been over for some two decades.

Iran-Afghanistan proved to be quite short-lived (and may be contingent on the return of Taliban rule in Afghanistan) while the Afghanistan-Pakistan rivalry is more enduring but characterized in a complicated way by the long interruption of the Soviet war in Afghanistan in which Pakistan was (and remains) closely involved as one of the actors in an internationalized civil war. The Kazakhstan-Uzbekistan rivalry for position in Central Asia has not been a high-profile conflict. Thus, little is known about how it has proceeded.

Our decision was to focus on the central cluster focused on China, plus the two Koreas and the Indo-Pakistani dyads. In this respect, we privilege contemporary concerns and discriminate against rivalries that have terminated (at least in Southeast Asia). We also discriminate against some of the more peripheral rivalries in Central Asia. That leaves us with the following cases (moving clockwise in Figure 1.1): China-USSR/Russia, the two Koreas, China-U.S., China-Taiwan, China-Vietnam, China-India, and India-Pakistan.[24] This strong emphasis on authoritarian China may work against finding two-level games, but we also have less authoritarian states represented (India, Taiwan, the United States, South Korea) so that our "experiment" should not be overtly rigged from the outset. Moreover, we can also claim that we have not biased the analytical playing field from the outset in order to find evidence of two-level games.[25]

Caveats aside, what should we expect to find? How will we know two-level games are or are not at work? At least five sets of processes can be delineated as prominent types of domestic political influences on interstate interactions. They may not exhaust the possibilities, but they are likely to encompass the most likely types of internal influences that we may encounter.

Types of Domestic Political Influences on Rivalry Trajectories

Rivalries entail interstate relationships characterized by hostility, threat perception, and mistrust. Interpreting the behavior of one's rivals, or deciphering what rivalries are all about, is fraught with difficulties of determining intentions. Several types of domestic political processes can intervene to make interpretation all the more difficult. One process could be called *factional foreign policies.* This process refers to the tendency for competing domestic groups to develop alternative foreign policies that differentiate themselves from domestic rivals and/or reflecting the perceived interests of the group.

Group X sees external enemy Y as the foremost threat while group Y disagrees and emphasizes the greater threat emanating from external enemy Z. Alternatively, group X may benefit materially from increased government activity abroad while group Y may see its own interests as benefitting most by maintaining as pacific an external environment as possible. Both X and Y compete for control of their state's foreign policies. If they alternate in domestic political power, then rivalry identification may oscillate accordingly. If neither has full control of state policy, then their internal competition and its outcome in terms of governmental behavior may seem simply confusing. An excellent example of this form of factional foreign policy was India's involvement in Sri Lanka's domestic political turmoil during the 1980s.[26]

An alternative process is *rivalry outbidding*.[27] In this process, domestic political competitors more or less agree on the identity of the primary external enemies of the state, but they compete in terms of which politician can outdo his/her internal competition by developing tougher policies to deal with the external enemies. Elections or general selections of governmental decision-makers tend to stimulate this type of behavior. The candidate that can appear most capable of coping with external threats may garner more support for his/her candidacy. Attempts to de-escalate rivalries are another type of prime timing for rivalry outbidding. If a government moves toward de-escalation, then internal rivals can question the wisdom of such a move and emphasize the incompetency of the regime in power to handle the associated risks. To do so successfully, the external rival must be portrayed in highly threatening terms—despite ongoing efforts to de-escalate tensions. Few examples in Asia can possibly compete with this process in Pakistani domestic politics when it comes to the question of the disputed state of Jammu and Kashmir in Indo-Pakistani relations.

A third relevant process is *diversion*. A number of analysts have written on "diversionary theory" without really fully specifying what sorts of behavior are encompassed. The basic idea is that decision-makers will use an external threat (or sometimes an internal threat such as an ethnic group that may or may not have links to an external foe) to distract attention from domestic problems. A rally-round-the-flag syndrome is expected to kick in and expand the support for the government's policies in a time of external attack. One problem is that decision-makers rarely admit engaging in this type of behavior, which means that analysts must infer it from observed activity. As a consequence, it is often difficult to assess the accuracy of the inference. That said, one of the most compelling examples that can be cited involves Pakistan's attempts to divert attention from the domestic crisis in East Pakistan in 1971 that contributed to a major war with India.

The fourth possible process can be labeled *governmental politics*. Instead of a rational and unitary decision-maker making careful cost-benefit calculations to decide foreign policy, foreign policy outcomes are a function of internal struggles among governmental agencies and major players in policy tug of wars over who gets to participate in, and to shape, governmental policy. Different governmental agencies may have different organizational interests (as in foreign ministries versus defense ministries) to pursue, which could affect the nature of the outcome, depending on which organizations are most successful in acquiring pieces of the policy pie. Similarly, different decision-makers and policy players below the chief executive level can play highly influential roles in shaping specific foreign policy and behavior.[28] For example, during the 1995–96 Taiwan Straits crisis, the PLA adopted a particularly aggressive stance toward Taiwan. However, a civil-military coalition settled on a display of military might in the straits.[29]

A fifth process of interest is *threat inflation*. In this process, governmental decision-makers choose to exaggerate the threat posed by some external enemy in order to gain domestic support for initiatives related usually to military spending and expanded foreign policy activity, but sometimes in other spheres such as human rights or, generally, more centralized governmental powers. This fifth process closely resembles the third one on diversionary activities in both spirit and behavior. Perhaps the most obvious case here involves North Korea's propensity to exaggerate the hostility of regional actors toward itself. Threat inflation is hardly a North Korean monopoly.

These five processes are meant only to be suggestive. They certainly do not constitute a theory of how and where we might expect to find two-level games in operation. No doubt, there are other ways in which domestic and international interdependencies can manifest themselves. We merely asked our authors to look for these processes or others like them in their comparisons of cases with more and less connections to domestic politics.

The Cases

China-Taiwan

Andrew Scobell suggests that at first blush the People's Republic of China (PRC)-Taiwan rivalry appears inexplicable because the balance of power across the Taiwan Strait is so lopsided in favor of the PRC. However, he argues that the existence of Taiwan goes to the very heart of the domestic legitimacy of the Chinese Communist Party (CCP) to rule the PRC. The CCP sees the existence of an autonomous Taiwan as such a challenge because it undermines its propagandistic version of its own history. This historical account suggests that the CCP won a decisive victory against the Kuomintang in 1949 in the Chinese civil war.

Scobell contends that the China-Taiwan rivalry persists because the most potent weapon that the island state possesses against the PRC is its democratic regime. President Chiang Ching-Kuo, Chiang Kai-shek's son and political successor, had initiated the democratization process that had culminated in the first free presidential election in 1996. Since then the PRC has focused much attention on the quadrennial presidential elections. According to Scobell, it has viewed the candidacy of Chen Shui-bian of the opposition Democratic Progressive Party (DPP) with particular concern because of his pro-independence orientation.

Given the significance that the PRC attaches to the elections, Scobell chooses to focus on two divergent electoral outcomes, the first in 1996 and the second in 2004. The first escalated into a crisis, but the second, while generating some cross-straits tension, did not. He adduces three possible factors to explain the difference in outcomes. These three factors relate to the posture of the rival's superpower patron vis-à-vis the rival and the PRC, the posture of the rival vis-à-vis the PRC and the international community and the "balance of rivalry" between the PRC and Taiwan.

The first episode stemmed from the American decision to grant a visa to President Lee in 1995. The grant of this visa, Scobell argues, signified to both Beijing and Taipei that Taiwan possessed a national identity of its own. What particularly provoked the ire of the PRC, however, was Lee's June 1995 speech at his alma mater, Cornell University, where he recounted the accomplishments of the "Republic of China on Taiwan." Seeing this as a direct affront to its claims to Taiwan, the PRC reacted harshly and resorted to missile tests in the vicinity of the Taiwan Strait in July 1995.

Subsequently, in mid-1995 it again resorted to similar tactics of intimidation during the lead up to the presidential election and referenda of March 1996. Matters worsened when in his inaugural presidential address Lee suggested that Taiwan could be the new cradle of Chinese civilization, thereby asserting a distinctive identity for Taiwan. The PRC reacted quite predictably, calling Lee a "separatist" and sharply condemning his stance.

The second episode involved the 2004 presidential election and referenda. President Chen Shui-bian in a quest to push on the question of Taiwan's sovereignty had contended that the hundreds of missiles that the PLA deploys against it constituted a threat to the country's sovereignty. Accordingly, he called for a referendum on two issues dealing with matters of sovereignty at the time of the election. Despite overwhelming public approval of both issues, the results were declared invalid because of a KMT boycott.

Since the United States under President George W. Bush had carefully distanced itself earlier from endorsing any notion of Taiwan sovereignty, Beijing's reaction to the referenda and Chen's reelection was relatively subdued. Scobell argues that its restraint in this case stemmed largely from its belief that the "balance of rivalry" was less daunting and dangerous than it had been eight years ago.

From his examination of these two cases, Scobell holds that the primary stimulus in the cross-strait rivalry stems from exogenous sources. To that end, he contends that it is the posture of the primary patron of Beijing's rival and the posture of its rival vis-à-vis the primary patron that prompts the PRC to adopt particular stances to developments in the rivalry.

China-United States

In his chapter on the U.S.-China rivalry, Lyle Goldstein argues that while domestic factors are prominent they are not decisive in determining whether cooperation or conflict will ensue. To that end he focuses on two important episodes in U.S.-China relations since 1989: the Taiwan Straits crisis in 1996–96, and the USNS *Impeccable* crisis of 2009. He justifies the choice of that year on the grounds that it was of pivotal significance in the bilateral relationship. It was the year that marked the end of the cold war, the Tiananmen massacre, and the onset of democratization in Taiwan.

The first crisis, as noted previously, had its roots in the U.S. government's decision to grant a visa to the then president of Taiwan, Lee Tung-Hui, to enable him to attend a ceremony at Cornell University, his alma mater. Goldstein argues that President Clinton had chosen to grant a visa to the Taiwanese head of state largely because of sustained pressure from both the Taiwan lobby in Congress and various human rights groups. In the event, the decision piqued the regime in Beijing sufficiently to launch a series of missiles along the Taiwan Straits. To demonstrate U.S. resolve to protect Taiwan from this form of intimidation Secretary of Defense William Perry called in a carrier group to the straits, bringing the crisis to a close.

Though U.S. domestic politics had led to the granting of the visa, Goldstein argues that the virulence of the reaction from Beijing cannot be easily or clearly attributed to the forces of domestic politics. Indeed he contends that the evidence on this subject remains murky.

The second episode also dealt with an issue that the PRC considers vital to its national security interests, namely, the control of the periphery of its territorial waters. In this case Chinese naval vessels had harassed the USNS *Impeccable*, an unarmed surveillance vessel that had been operating seventy-five miles south of Hainan Island in the South China Sea. President Obama sent in the USS *Chung-Hoon*, a guided missile destroyer, to escort the *Impeccable*. The PRC chose not to escalate matters, and the crisis abated.

This crisis drew limited attention in both the PRC and the United States. Goldstein contends that the difference in domestic reactions between the two cases can be attributed to a complex set of factors. In the PRC, the Taiwan issue is extremely emotive and can provoke strong public reactions. Similarly, particular interest groups in the United States can also stoke the Taiwan issue. In the other case, the U.S. public was preoccupied with two wars in Afghanistan and Iraq and was unlikely to focus on a naval skirmish in the South China Sea. In China, the reactions were sharper at various levels but did not rise to the level of the Taiwan Straits crisis. In this case, the incident though impinging on Chinese national security interests simply lacked the same significance as the status of Taiwan.

Based on his analysis of these two cases, Goldstein contends that in the interests of crisis avoidance, it would behoove U.S. policymakers to be attentive to the risks of provoking jingoistic sentiments in China and also to build ties with the Chinese military to be alert to their sensitivities and concerns.

India-Pakistan

Paul Kapur argues that the roots of the Indo-Pakistani rivalry can be traced to the disputed status of the state of Jammu and Kashmir. The rivalry ensued shortly after their emergence as independent states following the collapse of the British

Indian empire in 1947. The Kashmir dispute is central to the rivalry because it undergirds the self-images of the two rivals: India a constitutionally secular republic based on the principles of civic nationalism; Pakistan as a state based on religious and ethnic nationalism. Both sides lay claim to this predominantly Muslim region to demonstrate the validity of their competing national visions.

These commitments, he contends, have remained constant over time. What explains the shifts in periods of relative peace and conflict, he contends, are related to external factors. Domestic political preferences, though not unimportant, he believes provided permissive conditions for tension and violence in South Asia. However, the "efficient cause" for periods of relative stability and violence can be attributed to international strategic variables.

To that end, he holds that Pakistan's disastrous defeat in the third Indo-Pakistani conflict in 1971 that led to the creation of Bangladesh contributed to a period of long peace in South Asia all the way until 1989. Pakistan during this time did not give up on its commitment to wrest Kashmir from India. However, it simply lacked the requisite capabilities to do so.

In 1989, the outbreak of an indigenous ethnic insurgency in the Indian-controlled portion of Jammu and Kashmir and Pakistan's subsequent acquisition of a nuclear weapons capability enabled it to develop and pursue an asymmetric war strategy against India. Pakistan chose to support the rebels through training and financial and logistical assistance, secure in the knowledge that their nuclear weapons capabilities affectively neutralized an Indian conventional attack for fear of escalation to the nuclear level. As a consequence, Pakistan has been able to continue this asymmetric war strategy against India with virtual impunity.

Even though India has paid a high price, it has obdurately refused to concede ground in Kashmir. Pakistan, for its part, has yet to abandon this strategy even though in recent years some of the terrorist entities it had nurtured to fight in Kashmir are now turning their guns against the Pakistani state. Kapur argues that unless Pakistan recognizes the danger it faces and chooses to rein in the forces it had unleashed and thereby obtains some commensurate strategic reassurance from India, the possibility of tension and war in South Asia will persist in the region.

China-India

Manjeet Pardesi argues that India and China have been locked in a strategic rivalry since their emergence as modern nation-states in the late 1940s. Their rivalry has stemmed from overlapping "spheres of influence" in South, Central, and South East Asia. This rivalry has escalated and de-escalated over time. To understand the dynamics of escalation and de-escalation, Pardesi examines two periods in this fraught relationship. They both involve Chinese crackdowns in Tibet in 1959 and in 1987–89.

The first episode resulted in an escalation of the rivalry and its culmination in the disastrous Sino-Indian border war of 1962. The second, however, did not result in an escalatory spiral and actually led to the breaking of the impasse in bilateral relations that had ensued as a consequence of the 1962 border war. He contends that the perception of threat from the rival was the key factor that influenced the escalation or lack thereof in the rivalry.

He also argues that domestic politics played no role in the decision to escalate the rivalry in either country in 1959. However, subsequently domestic politics in India significantly contributed to an escalation of the rivalry leading to the 1962 border war. In 1987–89 the crisis de-escalated as both sides exercised restraint albeit because of differing external factors. For India the principal factor for restraint was the end of Soviet military and diplomatic support at the termination of the cold war. For the PRC perceptions of an improved security environment enabled it to de-escalate the rivalry even while dealing with other threats in East Asia.

Pardesi concludes his analysis stating that domestic politics played little or no role in the immediate escalation or de-escalation of the rivalry. In both cases in the two countries' foreign and security policy issues were concentrated in the hands of the highest leadership. In this context, regime type appears to have made little difference to the divergent outcomes as domestic political entities such as the legislature, governmental bureaucracies, political parties, the mass media, and the military did not play any independent role in affecting the dynamics of the rivalry. His most compelling conclusion is that perception of a deterioration in the threat environment leads to an escalation of the rivalry.

China-Russia

Lowell Dittmer argues that the Sino-Russian rivalry has deep historical roots. The sources of this rivalry can be traced to an implicit contest for geopolitical status and has involved conflicting territorial ambitions. Beyond these concerns there are mutual suspicions rooted in cultural stereotypes of each other. To Russia, China has represented backwardness, despotism, and the threat of demographic inundation. China, for its part, has seen Russia as the constant source of barbarian depredations.

Despite this competitive and hostile relationship, there have been two periods of brief cooperation in the 1950s and then again post-1989. Dittmer argues that the initial rapprochement was strictly elite-driven. However, he contends that it was based mostly on calculations of national interest rather than ideological passion. Also, the highly asymmetric features of the relationship contributed to its deterioration. China, the net beneficiary, came to expect more, and the Soviet side grew suspicious about the seeming lack of gratitude and reciprocity. In the end, however, the relationship turned hostile, not on the basis of material factors but instead on the pivotal issue of the future course of socialist development. Paradoxically, the shared ideological belief system became the basis of conflict and not cooperation.

After three decades of a relationship that saw ideological polemics, an arms race, diplomatic encirclement and counterencirclement maneuvers, and border incidents, a second period of cooperation emerged. This time cooperation was based on more modest premises. Cross-border peace has been sustained since 1970. The mutual suspicion of overweening American power and trade, though not without problems, has also helped cement the relationship. Furthermore, the relationship also developed a multilateral dimension based on a common desire to counterbalance U.S. global interests in a host of areas both regional and functional. Nevertheless long-standing mutual suspicions have continued to hobble the relationship.

What is one to make of the current period of wary cooperation? Will it endure over time, or is it likely to again descend into mutual recriminations and conflict? Dittmer argues that the first phase ended because of fundamental ideological differences that proved to be unbridgeable. In the current phase, however, he argues that Russia has rejected Marxism-Leninism and China has learnt to deal with the ideology along pragmatic lines. That said, he contends, the two sides still nurse legitimate grievances, and they are more concrete than before. Consequently, the relationship for the foreseeable future can best be characterized as being one of good neighbors and no more.

North Korea-South Korea

At the outset, Samuel Kim identifies four key features of the North-South Korea rivalry. First, he contends that it is a rivalry between two divided incomplete nation-states. Second, he argues that it is more than a mere dyadic rivalry as it is at the vortex of multiple strategic rivalries. Third, he underscores the fact that it is a highly militarized relationship. Fourth and finally, it is also one of the most persistent and long-running rivalries.

According to Kim this dyadic relationship has witnessed eight significant shocks since its inception, internal, external, and mixed. These shocks have had varying consequences for the course of the rivalry, occasionally diminishing tensions while on other occasions exacerbating them.

However, he holds that the most salient feature of this rivalry is the substantial U.S. military presence on the Korean peninsula. The penumbra of the U.S. military presence has affected significant elements of the inter-Korean rivalry and has influenced questions of strategic doctrine, has impacted on an arms race, shaped force structures and military deployments, and impacted upon conflict behavior.

After a discussion of the impact of the various endogenous and exogenous shocks as well as those that had both endogenous and exogenous components, Kim turns to the question of how this enduring rivalry might terminate. This rivalry, he suggests, might be brought to a close if the principal parties, the two Koreas and the United States, pursue a strategy of common security. Such an approach would entail all sides to focus on the legitimate security concerns of one another. Such a shift, Kim argues, would enable the parties involved to break away from the deadly and vicious logic of interactive security dilemmas and the dynamics of self-fulfilling prophecies.

China-Vietnam

Brantly Womack argues that the Sino-Vietnamese relationship has swung from intimate support to hostility to normalcy within a span of sixty years. He also contends that the closed political systems of the two states limit the significance of domestic political variables in the rivalry. Instead he suggests that asymmetry in capabilities is the key feature of this particular rivalry.

For the PRC, Vietnam is simply not a significant concern. For Vietnam, however, its northern neighbor, China, looms large in its foreign and security policy interests even though the relationship has assumed a level of normalcy since 1991. Womack shows how the PRC initially supported Vietnam during the waning days of French colonialism and subsequently the U.S. involvement in Indo-China. He then argues that the end of the Vietnam War led to the termination of Chinese military and economic assistance. Vietnam, in turn, mistreated its ethnic Chinese minority and relations steadily deteriorated.

Matters came to a head when Vietnam invaded Cambodia to overthrow the genocidal Pol Pot regime. This invasion and occupation, in turn, triggered a Chinese attack on Vietnam. In the wake of this war, relations remained strained until the early 1990s. According to Womack, two events led to a shift in Chinese policy toward Vietnam. The PRC faced international isolation in the aftermath of the Tiananmen massacre of June 1989, and the United States dropped its support for the CGDK in 1990. Feeling increasingly isolated, the PRC chose to improve its relations with its neighbors, including Vietnam. However, Womack maintains that there is little evidence to suggest that the thaw could be traced to the forces of domestic or bureaucratic politics in either state.

He concludes his discussion with a reiteration of the asymmetric features of the Sino-Vietnamese relationship. Specifically he argues that the asymmetry has three distinct dimensions. First, it structures the material situation within which the relationship plays out. Second, it is relational. Namely, the disparities in capacity create differences of interest, perspective, and perception that contribute to characteristic patterns of interaction. Third and finally, he underscores that the asymmetry is resilient. During peaceful periods, extant differences call for diplomatic management, and during periods of tension, the PRC has learned that it cannot impose its will on Vietnam.

Evaluating the Case Study Outcomes

Two main goals motivated this collection of case studies. One goal was to make a case for being more explicit about the rivalry nature of many dyadic conflicts in Asia. Despite the many pairs of conflicting states throughout Asia, the number of studies of dyadic conflict in explicit rivalry form remain few. Our position is that the tendency to avoid explicit studies of conflict patterns in the form of rivalry dynamics sacrifices opportunities to enhance our understanding of what states are trying to do to each other. Rivals are recidivists. They tend to retain their suspicions, threat perceptions, and hostility toward one another until they are no longer in a position to do so or until something changes that causes them to reevaluate their stance. Until one of these changes occur, they are likely to persist in clashing, at least intermittently. Therefore, we need to know not only what they have done to each other last week but also the history of their conflict because what they do in any given week is likely to have been shaped by what they have done to each other in the past. Rivalries are about historical and psychological dynamics. Embracing the concept of rivalry explicitly should help underscore how these conflicts that are embedded in space and time are different from less significant, nonrivalry conflicts. Treating the case materials as explicit rivalries also facilitates their comparison, not as distinctive geopolitical cases in various parts of the world but as processes belonging to a generic category—interstate rivalry.

To that end, our seven case studies make some contribution. Obviously, they are not the last word on the rivalries they address. We will need many more explicit studies of Asian rivalry before we can assess the value added of the rivalry approach to understanding war and peace in Asia. But it stands to reason that if most conflict, and especially the most dangerous conflicts, are bound up in rivalry structures, then it should make sense to separate the wheat from the chaff and focus on rivalry dynamics per se—as opposed to limiting ourselves to case-by-case analyses.

The outcome of the second goal of this volume, probing the role of two-level games in maintaining rivalry dynamics, is less clear-cut. On the face of it, the cases studies do not portray two-level games as all that paramount in Asian rivalries. Does that mean that we should simply banish such conceptualization to non-Asian theaters where it might have greater utility? Our answer is no. We can still derive some theoretical lessons from our experiment. It makes more sense to us, however, to do so in a separate, concluding chapter. Our views on two-level games in general and in Asian rivalries in particular may be easier to follow after examining the interpretations put forward in the seven rivalry studies. In general, though, our expectations are that the prospects for two-level games in Asian rivalries are limited.

2 China and Taiwan: Balance of Rivalry with Weapons of Mass Democratization

Andrew Scobell

Introduction: Why a Cross-Strait Rivalry?

Raise the subject of Taiwan with anyone from the People's Republic of China (PRC)—whether the person is a government official or an ordinary citizen—and one will likely get a vehement and passionate articulation of China's sovereign claim to the island. But Taiwan is not just an emotional hot-button issue in China; rather, it is considered the PRC's most sensitive security issue.

Indeed, Beijing views Taipei as a major rival or at least as posing a serious security threat. Certainly there are other political entities that China sees as rivals—the United States and Japan come swiftly to mind. It is easy to understand at a glance why Beijing would perceive Washington and Tokyo as rivals—in terms of the magnitude of the economic and military clout of each as well as the geographic and demographic size of the United States and Japan. In contrast, to the casual observer, Taiwan would not seem likely to be perceived by China as a rival. The balance of power across the Taiwan Strait is extremely lopsided in favor of China. While the island is an economic dynamo and global trading power of considerable significance and possesses a credible defense capability, all these are dwarfed by the gargantuan capabilities of its cross-strait neighbor. Given this glaring asymmetry in the balance of power between China and Taiwan, why would Beijing characterize its relationship with Taipei as a rivalry?

The answer is that Taiwan is the one issue that goes to the heart of the domestic and international legitimacy of Chinese Communist Party (CCP) to rule China. The CCP claims to be the only group that was capable of unifying China and making it strong enough to stand up to the bullying of Western powers and Imperial Japan. Communist propaganda claims that the CCP inspired and engineered a 1945 Chinese victory over Japan in World War II (known in China as the "Anti-Japanese War" with a start date of 1937). Communist propaganda also asserts that the CCP emerged as victors in the Chinese civil war in 1949 by soundly defeating the Kuomintang (KMT, also known as the Nationalist Party, or Guomindang).

The existence of Taiwan as an autonomous political entity that is de facto independent of the PRC calls into question these claims. Taiwan was officially annexed by Japan in 1895, and although the Japanese occupation ended in 1945, the PRC has never actually governed or even controlled the island. The CCP victory in China's civil war was not total—and its adversary, the KMT, withdrew to Taiwan to regroup and proclaim the continued existence of the Republic of China (ROC). The ROC was formally established on the mainland in 1912 following the collapse of the Qing Dynasty and then transplanted to Taiwan in 1949. The ROC has insisted it is the rightful heir to the first republic and its first president, Sun Yat-sen. This heroic figure is considered to be the father of modern China by all Chinese, including both the KMT and CCP. For decades after 1949, Beijing waged a diplomatic struggle to replace Taipei as the regime representing China in international organizations and vied to persuade countries to switch recognition from the ROC to the PRC.

Thus, since 1949, Taipei has, in Beijing's eyes, constituted a rival Chinese regime—one that has long claimed to represent the people on both sides of the Taiwan Strait. Since 1971, when the PRC achieved rapprochement with the United States and Beijing supplanted Taipei in China's seat on the United Nations Security Council, the PRC has seemed destined to defeat its rival diplomatically; since 1979, when Beijing adopted a policy of systemic economic reform and opening to the outside world, the PRC has seemed destined to defeat its rival economically; since 1990, when Beijing began to ramp up defense modernization with double-digit annual growth in defense spending, the PRC has seemed destined to emerge victorious against its rival militarily. And yet, in the face of these daunting adverse developments, Taiwan has declined to capitulate or even concede. Taipei continued to survive diplomatically by being pragmatic and resourceful; Taipei thrived economically becoming a major force in the global trading system and a hub of high technology research and development (while relocating its manufacturing base to the mainland); while Taipei struggled to keep up militarily, in the final analysis it has relied heavily on its superpower patron, the United States, for both weaponry and security assurances.

Rivalry? What Rivalry?

While Taiwan has yet to capitulate formally to China, based on the foregoing discussion of trends an observer might understandably conclude that the rivalry is now essentially over. It seems that Beijing has won or at least that Taipei has lost. In other words, the game is up—and China ought to be able to declare victory and get beyond Taiwan. In some ways Beijing is starting to move beyond a focus on Taipei: China's People's Liberation Army (PLA), for example, has started to explore a host of other scenarios, roles, and missions.[1] And yet, fundamentally, Beijing cannot get completely beyond Taipei.[2]

So why does the China-Taiwan rivalry persist? This is because the island's most potent weapons of recent decades in its rivalry with the mainland appeared not in the diplomatic, economic, or military spheres but in the political arena: democratization. The significance of these political armaments cannot be understated; hence, I have dubbed them "Weapons of Mass Democratization."[3]

Initiated by President Chiang Ching-kuo, Chiang Kai-shek's son and political successor,[4] the process of political reform and liberalization eventually led to democratization and the first-ever popular vote for national office in Chinese history: the presidential election on Taiwan in 1996 won by the incumbent, KMT candidate Lee Teng-hui. Lee was vilified by the PRC as a separatist and accused of being a traitor. Thereafter, quadrennial presidential elections on the island became focal points for Beijing's anxiety about its Taipei rival. Of particular alarm was the candidacy of opposition Democratic Progressive Party (DPP) candidate Chen Shui-bian. Beijing watched with trepidation as Chen emerged victorious in 2000 because he was widely considered a pro-independence candidate from a nativist Taiwan party. Everything Chen did was viewed with deep suspicion and presumed to be part of a larger nefarious scheme to move Taiwan further and further down the path of independence. Beijing was also very concerned with Chen's reelection bid in 2004 and what Beijing viewed as a concomitant populist effort to take further steps toward independence.

Game Changer: Diverging National Identities

The democratic outcomes on Taiwan are manifestations of the evolution of a distinct cultural and political identity for the inhabitants of the island. The result of the appearance of a Taiwan identity as distinct from a mainland Chinese one was a game changer. While the cross-strait rivalry was clearly not new—Beijing and Taipei had been rival regimes since 1949, what had changed by 1995 was the nature of the rivalry. The rivalry had shifted from a contest for control of Chinese territory to a competition for control of China's identity. Here, national identity is defined as "the relationship between nation and state that obtain when the people of that nation identify with the state."[5] In this case there are two states: the PRC headquartered in Beijing, and the ROC headquartered in Taipei. The foregoing definition explicitly identifies the key relationship as being between the people and the state. Implicit is the importance of the nature of this link, specifically the type of political system. Political transformations such as democratization would therefore meaningfully alter the very relationship between people and state and significantly impact national identity.

The change of identity on Taiwan appeared to be sudden. While certainly dramatic, the change was actually evolutionary taking place gradually in three phases during a period of decades. Lowell Dittmer and Samuel Kim suggest that national identity can have two dimensions. One dimension is the "substantive content with which people identify"; the other is the "act of identification."[6] The former had evolved as a result of Taiwan's political, social, and economic division from the mainland and the island's separate development. The latter dimension—the explicit expression of this different identity—did not become readily apparent until the advent of democratization and open multiparty elections in the 1990s.

The first phase of cross-strait rivalry lasted from 1949 until the 1980s. In this phase China and Taiwan were formally engaged in a civil war over territory. While there were hostilities, actual military conflict was largely limited to skirmishes, artillery barrages, and symbolic saber rattling. By late 1950, Beijing had given up on a military seizure of Taiwan, and Taipei gradually lost hope of recapturing the Chinese mainland. Still, the rivalry was ostensibly over territory as each claimed to be the sole legitimate government of one China. The second phase, lasting from the 1980s until the mid-1990s, was a transitional period in which both sides agreed that the combat phase of the civil war was over. Beijing no longer spoke of "liberating" Taiwan and instead urged "peaceful unification" and promised the island a "high degree of autonomy." Taipei officially rescinded martial law in 1987 and established a set of mechanisms to manage the growing economic and social cross-strait interactions with the mainland. However, neither side would concede defeat or display a willingness to negotiate a peaceful resolution. During this period both Beijing and Taipei still more or less agreed that issue was one of a divided nation; however, the two sides differed on how to resolve the matter. Nevertheless, as David Kang notes, the CCP and KMT had each held political power on one side of the Taiwan Strait for decades and maintained " . . . similar goals: both parties wanted to rule all of China."[7]

The third phase witnessed the biggest change in the rivalry as the contest switched from territory to identity. The change was due to an identity shift in Taiwan "while China's conception of itself remains roughly the same." The act of identification was most visible in the process of Taiwan's democratization. Taiwanese leaders articulated a new vision of Taiwan that was at odds with the Chinese identity espoused by the PRC's communist rulers. Taipei saw itself as a democratic pioneer in contrast to the foot-dragging dictatorial Beijing regime. Beijing, meanwhile, viewed the change of identity articulated in Taipei as a direct challenge to the PRC's Chinese identity. For Beijing, the change meant that Taiwan was openly espousing and pursuing separatism, putting it in direct conflict with the PRC's national unity project. This challenge was one that the CCP could not ignore. "When two nations have competing national identities," observes David Kang, "the solutions are either imposed though force by one side over the other or require a new conception of identity that allows for compromise."[8]

From the perspective of Beijing, this newly articulated Taipei identity was entirely fabricated by troublemakers such as Lee Teng-hui, Chen Shui-bian, and other 'splittists.' For the vast majority of CCP leaders and Taiwan analysts on the mainland, the possibility that a separate Taiwan identity emerged entirely naturally and would almost certainly have appeared with or without the machinations of Lee or Chen was unfathomable. Of course, these leaders may have accelerated the spread of this identity or manipulated it to serve their own political ends; however, this does not mean that the genesis of a distinct Taiwan identity was not a genuine expression of popular sentiment fueled by a set of common experiences. Moreover, Beijing does not seem to have considered that its own rhetoric and actions may have been construed as hostile and threatening by the people of Taiwan and hence contributed to the growth of an island identity separate from a mainland one. In the final analysis, perhaps a change of identity on Taiwan is considered secondary in importance to the continuity of the PRC's identity as a "divided nation." Indeed, central to the political legitimacy of the CCP remains its long-stated commitment to complete the unification of China.[9] Since the retrocession of Hong Kong and Macao in 1997 and 1999, respectively—loudly trumpeted as momentous events in the annals of Chinese history—Taiwan is the sole remaining separated component of the Chinese nation in Beijing's eyes. Any trend on the island that appears directly to challenge the CCP's schema of Chinese national identity is cause for grave concern.

Balance of Rivalry

This chapter examines two political events in Taiwan from the perspective of Beijing. Both events are islandwide votes: the 1996 presidential election, and the 2004 presidential election and referenda. Popular elections were selected because these would seem to test directly the relationship between the nation and the state—or "national identity"—because the act of voting is perhaps the most concrete measure of the degree to which a people identify with a state. Each event seemed directly to challenge Beijing's unchanging conception of China's national identity and hence produced a strong reaction from the PRC as it felt threatened. Indeed, as Suisheng Zhao observes, contemporary Chinese nationalism is most accurately characterized as "state nationalism," and this nationalism is a central pillar of political legitimacy for the communist party-state. Taiwan has powerful "symbolic value" within the CCP's conception of national identity and defending Chinese nationalism is "at the heart of [the] CCP's legitimacy."[10]

Yet, in the first episode, the lead up to the 1996 election escalated into a significant crisis whereas in the second episode, the lead up to the 2004 election, although it witnessed some cross-strait tensions, produced no serious crisis. What explains the different outcomes? Several variables seem key to understanding how each episode played out:

1. The posture of the rival's superpower patron vis-à-vis the rival and China.
2. The posture of the rival vis-à-vis China and the international community.
3. The "balance of rivalry" between China and Taiwan.

Generally speaking, while Chinese domestic political dynamics are certainly not unimportant, these seem more reactive to external stimuli than to be the impetus for Taiwan policy initiatives. This is not to say that domestic politics do not play a key role in Taiwan policy; rather, the domestic political environment tends to serve as an inhibitor or barrier to progress on Taiwan rather than as a catalyst. There is a discernible tendency toward overall policy inertia where Beijing's Taiwan policy is concerned. Because the island is viewed as highly sensitive and a vital national security issue, most leaders and organizations tend to avoid anything but restatements of official policy positions and adhering to officially approved activities vis-à-vis Taiwan. Indeed there is a fear that what someone says or does may be construed as appearing soft on Taiwan.

In this sense, every leader is a hardliner on the issue of Taiwan because there are no "softliners" where Taiwan is concerned. As Thomas Christensen observes, every Chinese leader, "must appear tough on Taiwan independence . . . to protect their current positions against potential rivals within the party, but also . . . [to defend against] . . . popular criticism . . . [of] the government's inability or unwillingness to stand up to foreigners and to Taipei."[11] The existence of this dynamic heightens the prospect of rival outbidding. As a result, Chinese leaders are extraordinarily sensitive to posture of the United States vis-à-vis Taiwan and China and the posture of Taiwan vis-à-vis China and the international community. It is in the context of these two variables that Beijing assesses its own position relative to Taipei in what I call the *balance of rivalry*.[12] The balance of rivalry can be assessed on a variety of dimensions involving both hard and soft power. While hard power is clearly important and can be disaggregated into economic and military aspects, soft power, which can be divided into diplomatic and identity elements, may be equally or even more important in tipping a balance of rivalry.

While CCP leaders sincerely hope for a positive sum outcome between China and Taiwan, because of the origins and history of cross-strait relations they cannot help but assess the evolution of the overall relationship as well as specific events and episodes from a zero-sum perspective. This translates into a process of constantly trying to assess on balance which side is winning and which side is losing the rivalry.

The Two Episodes

Episode 1: *Crisis Escalation to the* 1996 *Taiwan Election*

In the summer of 1995, the private visit of the president of Taiwan, Lee Teng-hui, to the United States escalated into the most serious crisis in the Taiwan Strait in more than three decades.[13] The crisis is fleshed out in more detail in Lyle Goldstein's chapter in this volume and is extensively analyzed by existing studies (including one by this writer). Therefore, this event is sketched out only briefly here. Deserving of special mention here is that democratization in Taiwan triggered a vigorous process of outbidding between rival political parties on the island. Specifically, the incumbent head of state, Lee Teng-hui, launched a series of initiatives to demonstrate that the ruling KMT was just as tough if not tougher on the PRC than its domestic political rival, the DPP, and quite adept at waging a campaign of cross-strait rivalry in the international arena.

Since 1993, Taiwan had initiated an annual symbolic effort to reenter the United Nations. A handful of UN member countries would sponsor a resolution supporting Taiwan's admission to the organization. The effort was simply a gesture to demonstrate the commitment of Lee's administration to raise the island's international status since all the sponsoring countries knew there was no chance of success—only a dozen or so countries at most would back the resolution, and it was absolutely certain that China would exercise its veto if by some remarkable twist of fate the effort picked up more votes. The effort was important as a way to defend Taiwan's national identity. In 1994, following similar logic, Lee Teng-hui undertook an unofficial tour of Southeast Asian countries in what became known as called "golf diplomacy."

But what really got Beijing's attention was the visa that was granted to Lee by the United States in 1995. For both Beijing and Taipei the visa signified validation by Washington that Taiwan possessed a national identity of its own. China had reportedly received assurances from the United States that the Clinton administration would not grant a visa to Lee. However, Clinton caved to Congressional pressure and issued the visa. Lee came to the United States as a private citizen, not as a foreign head of state. The ostensive purpose was to attend a reunion at his alma mater, Cornell University, where he had received a doctorate in agricultural economics many years earlier. At the reunion in Ithaca, New York, Lee gave a speech in which he spoke in glowing terms about the accomplishments of Taiwan and referred numerous times to the island as "the Republic of China on Taiwan." While he did not meet with any officials of the Clinton administration, Lee was received by three sitting U.S. senators and considerable publicity.

What really seemed to raise the ire of Chinese leaders was the June 1995 speech Lee gave in Ithaca in which he proudly and repeatedly recounted the accomplishments of the "Republic of China on Taiwan." Significantly, Beijing did not react vehemently toward Taipei until after the Cornell speech.[14] The Taiwan leader claimed that the political system on the island had ushered in "the most free and liberal era in *Chinese* history." He expressed the hope that "our achievements on Taiwan . . . [could] help the process of economic liberalization and the cause of democracy in mainland China." In Beijing's eyes, Lee was directly attacking its national identity by claiming that Taiwan was the authentic representation of China's identity. Moreover, by emphasizing Taiwan's democratization, Lee was introducing the concept of "popular sovereignty."[15] Lee's rhetoric and actions triggered a spirited round of rival outbidding in China. Military elites took the lead in demanding a harsh response by Beijing. After forcing a change of policy toward Taipei, soldiers then seized the limelight by talking in vocal and hawkish terms, clearly outdoing their civilian counterparts in displaying their staunch nationalist credentials to the Chinese people. Thus, China reacted with virulent condemnation and missile tests in the vicinity of the Taiwan Strait in July 1995.

China reprised its mid-1995 saber rattling during the lead up to the presidential election and referenda of March 1996, with additional missile tests and military exercises in the vicinity of the Taiwan Strait. Unbowed, two months later, in May 1996, in his presidential inaugural address in Taipei, Lee Teng-hui went even further than his Cornell speech eleven months earlier. Lee drew a parallel between the importance of the northern central plain (*zhongyuan*) in development of a great civilization several millennia earlier and the key role of Taiwan in the contemporary era in revitalizing a moribund national enterprise. Lee made the case that just as the Wei River Valley had served as the cradle of traditional Chinese culture, so the island of Taiwan could serve as the new cradle or 'central plain' (*xin zhongyuan*) of a modern Chinese revival. This vision turned Taiwan from the periphery of Beijing's contemporary Chinese national identity to its very essence.[16]

The declaration of this new Taiwan identity directly challenged the PRC's identity. Arguably, Lee was not advocating independence for Taiwan; rather, he was championing China's national unity. It is possible that Beijing "misperceived" Lee's rhetoric when it condemned him as a "separatist"; it is also possible that that Lee's pro-unification rhetoric was all too well understood. Whatever the truth, the upshot was the same: a direct assault on the national identity espoused by the CCP. If the Taiwanese leader was advocating independence for the island, then this flew in the face of Beijing's national unification project; if instead, Lee was calling for the unity of all Chinese, then he was directly assailing the CCP's version of one China with a different one. If the latter reality was grasped by CCP leaders, then so too was a realization that the balance of rivalry was being decisively tipped in Taiwan's favor. Indeed, this would mean that the PRC had lost control with the terms of national unification shifting from Beijing's to Taipei's terms. Indeed, even if this had been understood by senior communist leaders it would certainly not have been to their advantage to openly admit that the nature of the rivalry over national identity had qualitatively changed. It would be much simpler and less dangerous to assail Lee Teng-hui as a "splittist."[17]

Lee won the March 23, 1996, presidential election with a clear majority of the votes cast. Fifty-four percent of the voters selected the victorious KMT candidate. The remaining ballots were split among several opposition candidates with the DPP candidate garnishing only 21 percent of the votes. While the result was no cause for celebration in Beijing, the result was something that CCP leaders could live with at least grudgingly.

Episode 2: Slouching Toward CSB's* 2004 *Reelection and Referenda

The impending presidential election and referenda in March 2004 raised tensions in the Taiwan Strait, but these tensions never escalated into a crisis.[18] Vital in contributing to the lessening of tensions was the dramatic backpedalling of a publicly stated position by President George W. Bush regarding U.S. support for Taiwan. With President Chen Shui-bian of Taiwan widely viewed both in Washington and Beijing as a troublemaker, the U.S. president moved from making a declaration in April 2001 on live network television that the United States would do "whatever it takes" to defend Taiwan, to announcing in a joint Washington press conference with Chinese Premier Wen Jiabao in December 2003—two and a half years later—that the United States did not support "any unilateral decision by either China or Taiwan to change the status quo." Bush singled out in his remarks, "*comments and actions made by the leader of Taiwan.*"[19]

Hence, Beijing deemed the posture of the rival's superpower patron prostatus quo in the Taiwan Strait. In fact, relations between Washington and

Taipei seem quite strained. As a result, the PRC seemed relatively confident that the United States was not encouraging or orchestrating Chen's reelection campaign or referenda initiatives.

Meanwhile, Beijing monitored events on Taiwan very closely. Already deeply distrustful of Chen Shui-bian, Chinese leaders viewed an August 2002 speech by the Taiwan leader as "confirmation" that his goal was to engineer the island's full independence. Addressing the World Federation of Taiwanese Associations, Chen declared that there was "one country on either side" of the Taiwan Strait.[20] What was especially troubling for Beijing were Chen's efforts to make referenda a permanent part of the island's political infrastructure. As Shelly Rigger notes, "The concept of a referendum—in which the people of Taiwan directly determine their fate—suggests a level of sovereignty that Chinese leaders are reluctant to concede."[21] This initiative, which gained momentum in early and mid-2003, seemed to have less to do with any clear-cut design to move the island closer to de jure independence and more to do with political maneuvering by Chen to improve his electoral prospects in March 2004. Nevertheless, Chen's rival outbidding on Taiwan provoked anger and alarm in China. Three issues were especially popular candidates for referenda: Taiwanese participation in the World Health Organization (opposed by China); the fate of the island's fourth nuclear power station; and the size of the legislature. These specific issues themselves did not distress Beijing; the CCP leadership was more alarmed about the possibility of a referendum being held to ratify a new constitution. CCP leaders viewed constitutional reform—suggested as a referendum topic in September 2003—as particularly worrisome because in their eyes it signified a serious step toward independence. But Beijing's nightmare scenario was undoubtedly the specter of a vote on the very question of independence being put directly to the people of Taiwan.[22]

The possibility of a plebiscite to accompany the presidential election scheduled for March 2004 seemed to have been averted in November 2003 when opposition legislators ensured that the Legislative Yuan passed a law approving referenda but requiring time-consuming preparation. However, there was one caveat by which these onerous steps could be circumvented—in a crisis situation if Taiwan's sovereignty was deemed to be under threat. Chen quickly declared that the hundreds of missiles deployed by the PLA across the strait targeting Taiwan constituted a threat to the island's sovereignty. On this basis, Chen announced that he would set referenda concomitant with the presidential election scheduled for March 2004.

On March 20, 2004, the people of Taiwan were asked to vote on two issues. The first question asked whether Taiwan should "acquire more advanced anti-missile weapons" if China persisted in threatening Taiwan with ballistic missiles. The second question asked whether the island should negotiate with China to produce a "stable and peaceful framework" for interactions across the Taiwan Strait. Both questions were overwhelmingly approved by more than 90 percent of the votes cast. However, thanks to a boycott organized by the KMT and its allies, the referenda results were ruled invalid because neither of the two questions was voted upon by at least 50 percent of the eligible electorate. While it might be tempting to label the outbidding enterprise a failure or fiasco for Chen and the DPP, this conclusion would be a mistake. Chen did win reelection for another four-year term as Taiwan's president and the enabling legislation and precedent for referenda were firmly in place.[23]

Assessing the posture of the United States and Taiwan relative to that of China meant that from Beijing's perspective the "balance of rivalry" was less daunting and dangerous than it had been eight years earlier. While CCP leaders did not trust Chen Shui-bian, they were more confident that the efforts of the Taiwanese leader could be managed and contained. Because the United States appeared to distance itself from Taiwan, the flurry of activity on the island did not elicit another round of outbidding in China. The experience of the 2000 election—which witnessed the first victory of Chen Shui-bian—had enabled Beijing to put developments in a better context and to not overreact the way it had in 1995–96.

Analysis

What about the balance of rivalry? Were there any drastic changes in the cross-strait balance between the two episodes? Let us examine the dimensions of hard and soft power on both sides. So far as economic and military power are concerned, there were not real dramatic changes to alter the balance significantly. In both areas, China continued to retain the decisive edge. Hard-power trends unmistakably reflected China's seemingly inexorable global rise, which appeared destined to further outpace Taiwan's hard power. Moreover, economically China and Taiwan were drawing ever closer together with the island becoming far more dependent on the mainland. In contrast, although China continued to see its economy become increasingly intertwined with Taiwan's, Beijing's trade and investment patterns were much more diversified than those followed by companies from Taipei.[24] Militarily, China's growing power was more evident and ominous. Certainly, since the mid-1960s, when it became a nuclear power, China began to gradually pull away from Taiwan in terms of military power. Although the island did pursue its own nuclear program, the United States pressured Taipei to close it down. Starting in the 1990s, China began to pull ahead more militarily with a concentrated buildup in ballistic missiles deployed across the Taiwan Strait in an effort to intimidate the island. The cross-strait balance in military manpower and submarines—to take two other examples—remained more or less constant between the two episodes. In 1995, the PLA reportedly had 2.93 million men and women in armed forces while the Taiwanese military had an estimated 376,000 personnel. By 2003 numbers on both sides of the strait had fallen, but the overall balance remained relatively unchanged: 2.25 million soldiers in the PLA while Taiwan had downsized its manpower to 290,000. In terms of submarines, the balance also favored China, and this only increased during the same period. In both episodes, Taiwan possessed four submarines while the number of submarines in China's navy reportedly rose from fifty-two in 1995 to sixty-nine in 2003.[25]

What about the balance of soft power? If one examines diplomacy and political development, then a somewhat different picture emerges. In terms of the number of states extending full diplomatic recognition to each side, China clearly dominated Taiwan, and there was no change in the absolute number of states recognizing Taiwan as a country. Twenty-seven capitals contained an ROC embassy in both 1995 and 2003. In comparison, approximately 170 countries held ambassador-level ties with the PRC during these same years. But comparing the number of countries visited by each side's head of state in the year preceding the onset of the crisis suggests greater parity between the two sides, at least in 1994. In this year, PRC President Jiang Zemin visited eight countries while ROC President Lee Teng-hui visited seven states. By contrast, in 2002, the PRC president visited a total of thirteen states—more than three times the number visited by the ROC president (just four states) during the same year.[26] Indeed, the overseas travels of the ROC president in 1994 got considerable media attention, marking a concerted initiative by Lee to raise Taiwan's international profile. This, of course, was followed in 1995 by the high-profile, much-coveted trip to the United States.

Finally, in terms of the politics of identity, Taiwan's challenge to China rose dramatically with the approach of the first popular election for head of state in a Chinese political system. Moreover, Lee Teng-hui insisted on emphasizing the historic nature of the event. This was followed by the first victory of an opposition candidate—Chen Shui-bian—in a presidential election in 2000 and his reelection four years later. The candidate of course also happened to represent a political party strongly identified with independence for Taiwan. The same candidate also engineered the holding of two referenda to be held concurrently with the March 2004 election date. One would expect this to escalate the tensions with China to an even higher level than in 1995–96. Yet the latter situation did not escalate.

As noted earlier, the key dimension explaining the different between the outcomes of the two episodes is the disposition of the United States vis-à-vis Taiwan and China. Beijing was incensed by several surprise actions by the United States in 1995 and 1996, which seemed to indicate an upgrading of the relationship and increasing level of support by Washington, whereas in 2003 and 2004, the disposition of the United States was seen as cool to Taiwan or even pro-China.

Taking It to Two Levels

What was the mix of internal (domestic politics) and external (interstate politics) stimuli in the dynamics of their rivalry? The primary stimuli in the cross-strait rivalry—at least in the period examined in this paper—are exogenous. It is the posture of the primary patron of Beijing's rival and the posture of its rival vis-à-vis the primary patron and the international community that seem to prompt China to react. The endogenous or internal variables seem largely dependent on the exogenous or external variables. Of particular importance to China were the actions of the United States, which proved crucial to how Beijing responded in each episode. While the actions of Taiwan were also important, they proved secondary to U.S. actions in Chinese thinking.

In the first episode, it was the apparent about face of the Clinton administration in issuing Lee Teng-hui a visa to visit the United States that set into motion a sequence of events that escalated into a full-blown crisis. Subsequent rhetoric and actions by the Taiwanese leader—notably his speech at Cornell University and inaugural address—taken together with earlier moves escalated the balance of rivalry in China's eyes. Washington again surprised Beijing in early March 1996 when the Clinton administration dispatched two aircraft carrier battle groups to the western Pacific.

Yet the crisis seemed to subside just as suddenly as it had escalated. As the March election passed, China's saber rattling ended, and the two U.S. naval flotillas swiftly departed the area. The key reason that the crisis dissipated so quickly was because Beijing judged that Washington's posture vis-à-vis Taipei had moderated. When President Jiang Zemin and President Bill Clinton held a summit in New York City in October, the two leaders had a cordial and good-natured dialogue. At least the PRC concluded that the crisis had left the United States chastened and more sensitive to China's views on Taiwan. Implicit in this judgment was that this would translate into U.S. pressure on Taiwan to apply the brakes to its forward motion down the road to de jure independence. While this was a highly subjective assessment by Beijing, one lesson for Washington was the high priority that Beijing attached to the issue of Taipei and that this required the United States to monitor far more closely Chinese rhetoric and actions toward the island.[27] Thus, in the first episode, although an adjustment of Taiwan's own posture was important, it was perhaps not as decisive as U.S. posture in altering China's assessment of the balance of threat.

In the second episode, by late 2003, it was clear that Bush administration was not in favor of Chen Shui-bian's activities and at the very least was not aiding or abetting his efforts. This was reassuring to Beijing and increased the likelihood of a moderate reaction by China. Moreover, in the second episode, Taiwan's external initiatives vis-à-vis the international community were relatively low profile and quite limited. This was especially in contrast to Taipei's flurry and scope of efforts in the first episode—in the years and months leading up to the March 1996 election.

The very different postures of the rival's patron and the rival itself help explain the different Chinese reaction in each episode. In 1995, China's top leaders were caught off guard when the Clinton administration issued Lee a visa. And President Jiang Zemin and Foreign Minister Qian Qichen looked soft on Taiwan and became vulnerable to rival outbidding. As the foreign minister later remarked, "I was assured a visa would not be issued. Imagine what I thought and what was thought of me when the visa was granted." Military leaders led the charge in demanding a forceful response. The result was civilian leaders hardening their stance to get in line with the hawkish soldiers.[28] By contrast, in 2003, China's top leaders, Hu Jintao and Wen Jiabao felt relatively secure because of the public and private stances of the Bush administration vis-à-vis Taiwan were clear and the actions of Taipei's beyond the island were limited. While incomplete leadership transitions in Beijing characterized both episodes, political rivalry emerged only during the first. Once again, while Taiwan's own disposition was not unimportant to China, of at least equal if not greater importance was the disposition of the United States.

As noted earlier, domestic politics was a predominant influence in the sense that it significantly constrained Chinese policy on Taiwan. This tended to put Beijing in a reactive mode, responding to external stimuli rather than being proactive. The one exception to this tendency is that a new paramount leader is permitted some latitude in putting his personal "stamp" on Taiwan policy by launching a new initiative early in his tenure. However, these initiatives tend to be relatively modest and incremental in nature (with the exception of Deng Xiaoping's innovative "peaceful reunification" policy under the "one country, two systems" principle promoted to the early 1980s).

But when internal politics did play a strong role—in response to external triggers—the effect tended to lead to an escalation of rivalry hostilities. In both cases the process of leadership succession was incomplete. In 1995–96, Jiang Zemin was still cementing his position as China's paramount leader; in 2003–2004, Hu Jintao was still establishing himself as China's top ruler. To explain the different outcomes one must look to the second external level and the disposition of Taiwan's superpower patron. In the former case, Washington's perceived sudden warming to Taipei blind-sided Beijing; by contrast, in the latter case Washington's posture was viewed as in near complete accord with that of Beijing. The result was problems in the 1990s for Jiang but not eight years later for Hu. Domestic dynamics played a key role in the first episode because there was intraelite division over the situation. By contrast, there was swift elite solidarity in the second episode. As a result, there was an "intrusion" of domestic politics that led to escalation only in the first episode.

Conclusion

Taiwan figures prominently in terms of China's national identity and a central irritant in U.S.-China relations (see Lyle Goldstein's chapter in this volume). Beijing considers Taiwan a domestic matter for two reasons: first, because this is considered China's internal affair; second, because the island is an issue that Chinese people feel very strongly about and expect the ruling CCP to vigorously defend.

The island remains the only territory claimed by Beijing that maintains its independence from the PRC in the twenty-first century. Governed by an "authentic" Chinese power structure with its own military capabilities, Taiwan possesses an ocean buffer sufficient to provide the island with options that were unavailable to Hong Kong and Macao.[29] Moreover, the island possesses a trump card: a superpower patron offering security assurances. Taiwan also figures in the enhancement of China's stature internationally because the island is considered a constant thorn in its side. In Beijing's thinking, by competing with China for the diplomatic recognition of small states in the Third World and pressing for entry into organizations from the United Nations to the World Health Organization, Taiwan subjects China to repeated embarrassment. These were constant reminders of the challenge Taipei makes to Beijing's yet-to be-fully-realized national identity project. Moreover, if Taiwan seizes the path of de jure independence and the PRC is not seen to do a successful job of thwarting the move, then CCP leaders fear they will endure the full wrath of the Chinese people—widespread unrest or worse.

But it is the posture of the United States vis-à-vis Taiwan that figures most prominently in mainland China's rivalry with island China. Washington's rhetoric and actions directly impact the cross-strait balance of rivalry in both hard- and soft-power dimensions. In terms of the hard power, U.S. arms sales and security assurances work to counterbalance China's ongoing military buildup. And in terms of the soft-power part of the equation, the words and deeds of prominent Americans, along with U.S. diplomatic verbiage and initiatives matter greatly to the PRC. Such moves out of Washington are viewed as lending considerable credence to Taipei's aspirations for national identity and/or directly assailing or at least undermining Beijing's own national identity project.

As the second decade of the twenty-first century begins, cross-strait relations are the best they have been in many years. Yet the underlying rivalry has submerged not disappeared. The presidential election in March 2008 saw victory for the KMT candidate, Ma Ying-jeou, and Chen Shui-bian left office two months later. Relations have temporarily stabilized, but the rivalry is far from resolved. Ma and the KMT have proved both more adept at managing cross-strait relations and more palatable to Beijing than their predecessors, but the rivalry persists. While China may have emerged victorious in the "balance of rivalry" in the diplomatic, economic, and military arenas, this has not translated into overall victory. This is because the fundamental dynamic of rivalry has been qualitatively changed by democratization and the emergence of a distinctly Taiwanese identity. Dueling national identities have produced a potent rivalry: "a . . . clash between a democratic, capitalist, wealthy, and industrialized Taiwan deciding its own fate versus authoritarian, quasi-capitalist, semitraditional China attempting to control the fate of Taiwan."[30] Popular elections have transformed Taiwan from authoritarian afterthought to the cutting edge of Chinese democracy. Since the 1990s, Beijing has confronted a cross-strait rival armed with a potent force: weapons of mass democratization. This soft-power arsenal has proved difficult to balance against.

3 Domestic Politics and the U.S.-China Rivalry

Lyle J. Goldstein

Among the many interstate rivalries that will impact global politics in the twenty-first century, none is more crucial to international security than the U.S.-China relationship. Indeed, America's current leaders have termed this particular bilateral relationship as perhaps the most important one for U.S. foreign policy.[1] As nuclear powers that each also wield major conventional military forces, it is well understood that hostilities between Washington and Beijing could quickly spiral into a catastrophic war in the same league if not exceeding in destruction the two devastating world wars of the twentieth century. While U.S.-China rivalry is relatively new to the international system, the current rivalry, here covering the period 1989 to the present, is supported by structural and ideological tendencies that are likely to place the two governments in a relatively continuous state of competition. In evaluating these tendencies, domestic political factors are prominent, though not decisive, in determining whether cooperation or conflict will prevail.

This chapter represents a preliminary effort to survey the role of domestic politics in the contemporary U.S.-China rivalry. It will address what kinds of domestic actors are influential in formulating policy in Washington and Beijing, what circumstances enable domestic actors to gain greater influence over policy, and also whether domestic politics generally causes escalation or de-escalation of the rivalry dynamics in this crucial relationship. The paper is organized as follows: section one presents a brief survey of investigations into the impact of domestic politics in U.S.-China relations; section two lays out the broader policy context within which domestic factors may operate in U.S.-China policy; sections three and four delve into two case studies that may help to illustrate the dynamics of domestic politics within the contemporary U.S.-China rivalry; and the fifth and final section attempts to come to some preliminary conclusions regarding domestic politics and escalation with the U.S.-China rivalry.

A couple of methodological caveats are in order at the outset of this paper. First, objections will logically arise regarding the assumption of the U.S.-China relationship as a "rivalry." In China, such characterizations are routinely dismissed as "冷战思想" [cold war thinking]. It is certainly worth noting that U.S. and Chinese military forces have not engaged in major combat in more than half a century, since the Korean War. Still, a certain amount of hostility is readily apparent among segments of the national leadership, the relevant bureaucracies, and populations. Moreover, it is also quite clear that both military structures actively plan for the possibility—if not the likelihood—of conflict.

For the sake of methodological clarity, this paper considers the Sino-American rivalry covering the period 1989 to the present. One could define U.S.-China rivalry as dating back to 1949, but it is clear that U.S.-China relations from 1972–89 constituted more aspects of partnership—entailing instances of genuine strategic coordination—than rivalry. Three developments in 1989 precipitated the onset of new rivalry: the Tiananmen massacre created new antagonism in the relationship, especially when the crackdown in Beijing was contrasted to the peaceful transformations that were simultaneously occurring across Eastern Europe. This event once again brought the ideological hostility back into the relationship. A second and related development was the democratization of Taiwan that began in earnest in the late 1980s. A third factor was the reform and subsequent dissolution of the USSR that rather suddenly removed the threat that had supported Sino-American cooperation during 1972–89. Increased tensions were on display during the 1990s, for example concerning the sale of fighters to Taiwan in 1992, the Yin He incident in 1993, or the *Kitty Hawk* incident in 1994, but the full extent of the rivalry, precipitated by the ideological and structural changes outlined above, was not fully understood by both sides until the 1996 crisis, which is discussed in considerable detail below.[2]

A second caveat worth noting is that American scholars will inevitably have a better understanding of how U.S. policy toward China is formulated. This is primarily the result of the fact that political processes in the United States are much more transparent. The analysis in this chapter is therefore not balanced: understanding the role of Chinese domestic politics in making Beijing's policy toward the United States remains, to a large extent, guess work built on thin evidence. A final caveat concerns case selection. In this chapter, the 1995–96 Taiwan crisis and the 2009 USNS *Impeccable* crisis are examined. As these crises each involved the interaction of military forces from both sides, these crises are taken for study as especially important moments when the rivalry has experienced acute pressure, with the possibility of tending toward conflict. It is readily conceded that more or even other case studies could be useful for studies of domestic political factors in the U.S.-China rivalry.[3]

Domestic Politics as Explanatory Variable in U.S.-China Relations

Focusing on domestic politics in U.S.-China interaction is to a large extent going "back to the future." It was not the balance of power or abstract theorizing about the international system that caused Washington to take up a robust role in East Asia at the end of the nineteenth century. After the Boxer Rebellion, the United States maintained substantial forces in China primarily to protect economic interests that were (then as now) eager to tap the wealth of the boundless China market. Ideological factors served as a powerful impetus for the missionary movement. The material or ideological bases for these policies could certainly be described as arising from the American domestic political arena, rather than exclusively from strategic competition with other powers.[4]

Likewise, the cold war furnishes many, rather clear examples of the important role of domestic politics in determining the course of U.S.-China relations. Major divides in the bureaucracy, described by the editors as *governmental politics*, characterized U.S. policy toward China in the early cold war, such that Korean War strategy precipitated one of the most severe civil-military crises between Truman and General MacArthur that the United States had ever witnessed. The strong anticommunist sensibilities of Americans during the early 1950s no doubt played a role in deepening the U.S.-Chinese hostility during this time. In the seminal academic work on the role of domestic politics in U.S.-China relations, Tom Christensen argues persuasively that Chinese leaders stoked hostility in the 1950s in order to facilitate the mobilization that was perceived necessary to push forward radical economic reforms.[5] He demonstrates that similar *diversionary* or *threat inflation* processes also characterized American politics during the early cold war as American leaders attempted to generate domestic support for much more ambitious global foreign policies. The somewhat infamous "China Lobby," a powerful faction in U.S. foreign policy circles that aggressively beat the drum of "Who lost China?" likely played no small part in precipitating America's disastrous intervention in Vietnam, where they intended to draw a firm line against further communist expansion in Asia.[6]

During the tumult of the Cultural Revolution, domestic politics in China became paramount as ideology, factional politics, and diversionary politics mixed in a volatile brew in Beijing. Some Chinese scholars have attempted to suggest that Mao's keen appreciation of the global balance of power resulted in the Sino-Soviet clashes of 1969 and the resultant rapid rapprochement with the United States in the early 1970s.[7] However, these explanations are not very persuasive. Rather, this appears to be a post-hoc justification, emerging from Mao's crude attempts at crafting a Soviet threat for the purposes of both *diversion* and *threat inflation*.[8] Nor were Nixon's impulses in developing the rapprochement with Mao purely strategic. He knew that the rapprochement with Beijing in 1972 would be popular at home among the war-weary American public, and there was additionally the false hope that Beijing could even "deliver" Hanoi, enabling the honorable victory in Vietnam that he sought and indeed required at home. As the cold war came to an end, two clear camps were rather evident in both the United States and China. In Washington, the old "China Lobby" reinvented itself as the protector of Taiwan's status. President Bush's 1992 decision to sell one hundred and fifty F16s to Taiwan looms large as a classic case of domestic politics having a major impact on U.S.-China relations. As James Mann writes, "Bush's action reflected not only a desire to maintain the military balance in the Taiwan Strait, but also a judgment that selling the planes would help him win votes."[9]

At the same time, mushrooming trade created a new and powerful community of business interests that strongly supported stability in U.S.-China relations. Corresponding domestic political actors are also, to some extent, identifiable in the Chinese political scene: with business interests logically forming a strong faction and a rival faction comprising many nationalists and intellectuals that are deeply skeptical of Washington and its "hegemonic impulses."

Domestic and Strategic Factors Impacting the Current U.S.-China Relationship

This section will succinctly describe the broader political landscape in both capitals, elucidating the constellation of both strategic and domestic factors that impact the complex U.S.-China bilateral relationship.

In Beijing, strategic factors influencing U.S.-China relations include those chiefly relating to sovereignty, military, and economic development. There is a broad perception that China has never been so wealthy, powerful, and influential. In this context, leaders in Beijing intend to guard existing gains on sovereignty questions, but also to enlarge the scope for future concrete gains in contested zones (for example, Taiwan and the South China Sea). With respect to military development, there is a clear intention to build up China as a "强国" [strong country] that could be capable of matching the U.S. military in certain scenarios, particularly those that could arise on its immediate periphery. China's January 2010 exoatmospheric (midcourse) missile intercept test was yet more evidence of Beijing's ambitious military development goals. There is also an evident concern that China's buildup could cause excessive anxiety in the Asia-Pacific region, precipitating balancing behavior.[10] Nevertheless, economic factors seem to retain priority in China's strategic calculus. In Beijing, there seems to be an overarching concern that minor points of tension in the U.S.-China relationship not disturb the relationship that has heretofore been extremely conducive to China's rapid economic growth.

As stated above, domestic political factors are somewhat more difficult to isolate in China's rather opaque decision-making process. It is generally assumed that a pro-business lobby exists in Beijing, but with the possible exception of traceable patronage networks of senior party figures that tie in with large Chinese companies, evidence of large-scale business influence on foreign policy decisions is lacking. Indeed, besides rhetorical flourishes related to the 三个代表 [three represents] concept of Jiang Zemin, the CCP continues to be generally isolated from the nation's business elites. Some evidence supports the importance of *factionalism* in making Chinese foreign and security policy. This is the conventional interpretation of the January 2007 antisatellite test, for example, wherein it seems that military goals prevailed over sound foreign policy analysis—with the attendant costs to China's reputation as a "responsible stakeholder" on the global stage. Far and away the most important tendency with respect to domestic political factors in China is the underlying strength of Chinese nationalism in the present context. There seems to be a wide consensus among almost all segments of China's society that China's time has arrived, and it has earned the trappings that follow for great powers and perhaps even superpowers. This potent sense of nationalism was on display most recently in the October 2009 military parade to commemorate the sixtieth anniversary of the PRC's founding, but also in severe reactions by riotous young Chinese against both American and Japanese consulates around the country during 1999 and again in 2005. The potency of this nationalism could form a major "Pandora's box" for the Chinese leadership in that it may not be fully subject to manipulation and could "blow-back" in destabilizing ways.

Domestic factors may have receded to some extent in the formulation of Washington's China policies. For example, the role of China policy in the 2008 presidential elections was all but nonexistent and notably less than in previous contests. This tendency may be attributable to the much higher salience of other issues such as the financial crisis and the wars in Afghanistan and Iraq. Nevertheless, major interest groups continue to proliferate and attempt to gain influence over Washington's China policy. Among these, human rights groups—propelled in part by religious organizations—continue to wield considerable clout. Pro-Tibet movements are active on almost every campus. Now, such groups are also focusing on Chinese activities outside of China's borders, in areas such as Myanmar and Sudan. The row over Google's status in China, which erupted in January 2010, once again illustrates how ideological dynamics may quickly assume major importance in U.S.-China relations. As the debate in Washington over military spending divides among those focused on "the long war" against terrorism and those focused on a potential rising peer competitor, the potential for factional politics and *threat inflation* among the armed forces, intelligence agencies, and foreign policy apparatus is readily apparent.[11] Balancing these tendencies is strong corporate backing, impacting both parties, in support of the U.S.-China trade relationship. Still, there is strong American labor hostility to Beijing that accuses China of mercantilism and generally "stealing American jobs." While it does seem far-fetched to consider that Beijing and Washington could come to blows over trade policy, it does seem conceivable nevertheless that this major irritant could pervade the relationship with suspicion and hostility, which is driven in part by negative public opinion in both countries.

Overall, Washington's policy toward Beijing is driven by the perceived strategic imperatives to maintain economic stability and growth, compete effectively with expanding Chinese influence in all global regions, and maintain a clear edge in military power. China's holdings of American debt suggest that Washington must actively cooperate with Beijing on financial matters. It is widely noted that Beijing also shares this interest, lest its dollar holdings lose too much value. There is ample concern in Washington that it might be losing the "influence game" in parts of the world including Africa and Southeast Asia. Thus, American strategists are seeking to counter Chinese "soft power," with their own soft-power initiatives, such as humanitarian aid in circumstances of natural disasters. The most concrete form of strategic rivalry, however, is naturally concerned with military capabilities. Thus, the outlays for such complex and expensive new systems ranging from the F-22 fighter to the *Virginia*-class submarine seem to rely to a large extent on assessments of future Chinese military capabilities. A related imperative also emerges from the current international system: the requirement to socialize and integrate China into the institutional framework and security norms prevailing among most of the other great powers. The policy formulation of this objective has been the effort to help China evolve as a "responsible stakeholder" in the international system.

Case 1: The 1995–1996 Taiwan Straits Crisis

The 1995–96 Taiwan Straits Crisis is correctly considered the archetypal U.S.-China crisis of the post-cold war world. Before that point, it was not clear that U.S.-China rivalry was a major tendency of the evolving international system. After that point, few doubted the existence of rivalry, because this crisis featured ample bellicose rhetoric between national leaderships, major movements of military forces, and perhaps most troubling, the apparent issuing of a nuclear threat. Below is a short rendering of the facts of the crisis, followed by a brief discussion of potential roles played by domestic political dynamics in the crisis.

The direct precipitating event for the crisis was the visit by Taiwan President Lee Teng-hui to his alma-mater Cornell University. Chinese diplomats had urged the White House to reject the visa request, but votes by both houses of Congress in May weighed in almost unanimously in favor of granting the visas. The visas were approved soon after, and Lee gave the speech at Cornell on May 22, 1995. Beijing responded immediately by canceling several planned visits and then carried out major missile and other military exercises during July and August. In September, President Clinton met with the Dalai Lama, while an arms shipment of early warning aircraft were sent to Taiwan. In October, Jiang Zemin came to the United States, but he received only an unofficial meeting rather than a formal state visit. During this meeting between heads of state, President Clinton told President Jiang that Taiwan visits to the United States would be "unofficial, private, and rare."[12]

In December, the *Nimitz* battle group transited the Taiwan Strait and was the first U.S. Navy group of ships to do so in decades. Though this warning to Beijing was absolutely clear, it was subsequently claimed by the Pentagon that the transit was undertaken because of bad weather.[13] The U.S. side seemed to regard the matter to be closed when another visa was granted to a senior Taiwan official, this time for Vice-President Li Yuan-zu to transit through Los Angeles. However, Beijing apparently did not accept this conclusion to the crisis. Thus, more than one hundred thousand troops were said to have mobilized in Fujian Province (across the strait from Taiwan). On March 7, China commenced another round of missile launchings that fell into the sea less than twenty miles from Taiwan's major ports. After this, U.S. Secretary of Defense William Perry called Chinese actions "reckless and aggressive," at which point he directed that two U.S. Navy carrier battle groups approach the Taiwan vicinity in order to make a show of force. "The result was that the United States deployed its largest armada [to the western Pacific] since the end of the Vietnam War."[14] On March 9, Beijing announced a new set of live-fire exercises in the vicinity of the Penghu Islands, situated in the Taiwan Strait. These exercises continued until March 25. Examining the long-term effects of this crisis, one can conclude that the rupture was not long lasting—in November 1996, Clinton and Jiang meeting in Manila agreed to hold summits in each country during 1997–98 and relations improved considerably. However, there is little doubt that the military establishments in both countries took as their own lesson that conflict between the two states was possible and that preparations needed to follow accordingly.

Unlike most issues in social science where causation is often very difficult to prove, it can be said with confidence that the 1995–96 Taiwan crisis came about because of domestic political dynamics in the United States. Robert

Ross observes, "President Clinton's decision to issue a visa to Lee Teng-hui did not reflect considered analysis of U.S. interests, but rather White House acquiescence to congressional pressure . . . when in May the Senate voted 97–1 and the House of Representatives 360–0 in support of a visa, the President acquiesced."[15] As Clinton's Asia Policy Director at the NSC later recounted, "It was enormous pressure."[16] Confirming this interpretation, Ross observes, "Leaders in Beijing understood that the catalyst for Washington's changing policy was domestic political pressure on the White House."[17] Robert Suettinger's analysis of the crisis implies the importance of domestic political dynamics when he observes that "Clinton was not a foreign policy president . . . [and moreover] Clinton had visited Taiwan several times when he was governor of Arkansas."[18] It is also important to note that the strong American inclination for "confidential" communications to Chinese leaders in order to mollify tensions with statements that the United States "opposes Taiwan independence." Obvious to any observers, including those from China, is the sense that the American public (and therefore the Congress) has major Taiwan sympathies that could have been offended by such openly pro-Beijing assurances. Suettinger notes, "Public support for Taiwan . . . was very high, mostly owing to admiration for its democratization and its high-profile involvement in trade development in many U.S. localities. In Congress, support for Taiwan was even more pronounced, in part because of the effective lobbying activities of the Taiwan government."[19] According to Ross's analysis of the crisis, Clinton's willingness to meet with the Dalai Lama in September revealed Clinton's "continued willingness to consider domestic politics when making China policy."[20] Likewise, it seems quite plausible that Clinton was reluctant to grant Jiang a formal state visit in November 1996 for fear of alienating either human rights activists or Taiwan sympathizers. Though difficult to prove, the idea that Clinton was more inclined toward a robust show of force in an election year also seems plausible.[21] However, Suettinger concludes that domestic politics had a definite role in the onset of the crisis, but not in Washington's subsequent management of it.[22] Ross's analysis squarely blames Congress, and especially the "Taiwan lobbying on behalf of independence diplomacy," noting that this "U.S.-China confrontation, including the U.S. show of force, was unnecessary and avoidable."[23] Likewise, Michael Swaine, also concludes that "the deployment of two carriers to the Taiwan area, [was] taken in part to mollify congressional pressure for more hard-line actions."[24]

As noted above, there is considerably more uncertainty when it comes to explaining the origins of various decisions in Beijing for the obvious reason that there are few if any press conferences, investigative journalism is limited, and the polling of public opinion is also extremely rare. In general, a very different set of political incentives operates in Beijing since there are no elections to speak of. The paucity of information available on the crisis in Chinese sources was recently discussed by Chinese historian Niu Jun, who writes, "Up to now, Chinese academics have shed little light on the decision-making process in 1995–96 mainly because of the lack of basic historical documents owing to how recent this crisis was."[25] Niu does not mention domestic politics explanations in his rendering of Chinese decision-making in 1995–96. Concerning American decision-making, however, his frustration and befuddlement concerning American domestic politics is readily apparent:

> Is preventing the United States and China from engaging in a Taiwan crisis truly so complicated and difficult as imagined by many? In 1995–96, the Americans themselves created the dangerous situation, which they could have avoided in the first place. Then they sought a solution through international crisis management.... The U.S. government should not continue to act in such a strange manner.[26]

Still, it can be imagined that Chinese scholars could be reluctant to discuss domestic factors in Taiwan decision-making, for fear of showing fault lines on an issue of great sensitivity and thus deprecating the cause of unification.

Some American scholarly analyses seem to reveal the workings of bureaucratic politics in Beijing during the 1995–96 Taiwan crisis. Indeed, Andrew Scobell has written on "Chinese Soldiers, Statesmen, and the 1995–1996 Taiwan Strait Crisis." He argues that China's military represents distinct thinking on this and other national security matters. He describes, for example, a mid-June 1995 meeting of the Taiwan Affairs Leading Small Group, where both President Jiang and Foreign Minister Qian Qichen "were confronted by three irate military men insisting it was time for harsher action.... These men definitely charged the atmosphere and ensured a swift change in policy."[27] Though Scobell cautions that PLA leaders knew that escalation to actual combat was very unlikely, he observes that "the Taiwan issue evokes intensely emotional nationalism among [Chinese] soldiers," and also that "the virulent and aggressive public statements by PLA figures are plays to public opinion ... [because] ... the cause of reunification with Taiwan is strongly supported by ordinary Chinese people."[28] Scobell cites polling data—generally rare in China—to support his conclusion since respondents gave the government high ratings for "ensuring a strong national defense" during a poll taken in December 1995. Yet another tendency that Scobell points out is of interest in this particular study, and this is what he describes as an effort by PLA officers to attract notice from the leadership by submitting "written requests for battle assignments."[29] Of course, this raises the troubling possibility that promotion in the Chinese military could, especially in times of crisis, be tied to a willingness or even an enthusiasm to "defend China's honor" against perceived foreign encroachments. It is worth noting that other American scholars are more skeptical regarding the importance of Chinese public sentiment during the 1995–96 crisis. Michael Swaine, for example, concludes, "although some [Chinese] public anger . . . was evident during the 1995–1996 Taiwan Strait Crisis, there is no solid evidence that such sentiments directly influenced the perceptions or specific actions taken by the [PRC] leadership at that time."[30]

Outside of the Chinese military, a few other tendencies in Beijing's crisis decision-making are worth considering as we explore the role of domestic politics in U.S.-China relations. First, it could be significant that Beijing's quest for a formal state visit or major summits formed a broader political context for the crisis. Most analysts agree that President Jiang had a genuine desire to achieve this goal and all the "pomp and ceremony" that would (and did eventually) follow. It is not clear whether this is just a peculiar psychological need of Jiang or whether it reflects a greater desire among Chinese leaders generally to be accepted in the West and especially to be viewed as equal partners with the United States. It is quite plausible that Chinese leaders view appearances with a powerful figure, such as the U.S. president, as boosting their prestige at home. Another tendency visible in this crisis is that Chinese diplomats, similar to their American counterparts, have relied on the practice of "private assurances"—in this case to make sure that leaders in Washington understood that Beijing had no real intention to start a war.[31] This may suggest, in parallel with the U.S. situation, that Chinese diplomats find it significantly easier to compromise when they are not under the careful scrutiny of their nationalist comrades at home. Thus, it is quite possible that this rivalry suffers from having publics on both sides of the Pacific that are significantly more nationalistic and even jingoistic than are the respective governments. A final observation also highlights the dangerous role of Chinese nationalism in this crisis. The choice of words by Prime Minister Li in January 1996, suggesting that China's commitment to the use of force was "directed . . . against the schemes of foreign forces . . . to bring about 'Taiwan independence,'" implied an intention to view the Taiwan issue as a primarily a conflict with the United States. This is not a new position or even a new phrasing, but this characterization at the height of the crisis did seem designed to play to the nationalism of the Chinese public, and indeed to stoke that nationalism. For historical reasons, Chinese nationalism remains as a potent force in Chinese politics, and American leaders must be conscious of its dangers for the international system and for U.S.-China ties in particular.

Case 2: The March 2009 USNS *Impeccable* Crisis

There are some distinct similarities between the two crises, which make this comparison compelling, though the time duration of the 2009 crisis was only a matter of weeks rather than the span of several months that comprised the earlier Taiwan crisis. The two cases are fundamentally similar in that they encompass major strategic issues on China's maritime periphery. Indeed, the South China Sea has long been identified as a second contending scenario with dangerous potential for disrupting international security after the preeminent Taiwan case. The potential for the rivalry to turn violent in both cases is extant. Indeed, another similarity among the crises is the movement of military forces in both circumstances—albeit much smaller in scope in the latter case—but still a sign of the seriousness of the events for both sides.

Though a variety of events have occurred between U.S. and Chinese ships and aircraft recently, the "*Impeccable* incident" refers to the events of early March 2009. On March 8, the USNS *Impeccable*, an unarmed surveillance vessel, was operating seventy-five miles south of Hainan Island in the northern part of the South China Sea. The mission of the *Impeccable* is to track undersea threats (submarines) with its powerful sonar array. Given that China recently constructed a major new nuclear submarine base on Hainan Island, it is logical to assume that the *Impeccable* was seeking information on Chinese submarine activities in this area. On March 8, the vessel was surrounded by five different Chinese vessels, including one military intelligence vessel, one State Oceanographic Agency (SOA) vessel, one fisheries enforcement vessel, and two small fishing boats. When the fishing vessels approached to within fifty feet, the *Impeccable* turned a water hose on one of the boats, which then proceeded to within twenty-five feet. After the *Impeccable* requested safe passage from the area, the two fishing boats maneuvered in front of the *Impec-*

cable and suddenly stopped, forcing the *Impeccable* to make an emergency stop to avoid a collision. At this point, a sailor on one of the fishing boats attempted to use a grappling hook to snare the *Impeccable*'s towed array cable.

It should be realized that the March 8 incident was not isolated and seemed to fit into a larger pattern of hostile interaction between U.S. and Chinese ships. Indeed, a Chinese Navy frigate had apparently crossed the bow of *Impeccable* at a range of just one hundred yards on March 5, while a Y12 aircraft of the SOA conducted multiple low passes over the ship. Similarly, the USNS *Victorious*, a sister ship of the *Impeccable*, suffered similar harassment in the Yellow Sea twenty miles off the Chinese coast on March 4. On March 12, President Obama ordered the USS *Chung-Hoon*, a guided missile destroyer, to escort the *Impeccable* as it continued its mission in the South China Sea. Beijing did not elect to escalate the crisis by countering this deployment. However, the harassment of U.S. vessels did continue as the USNS *Victorious* was approached as close as thirty yards by Chinese vessels in heavy fog and also was forced to make an emergency stop during May 2009.

The crisis did not make a major stir in either Washington or Beijing, it seems. True, the *Wall Street Journal* did run a picture of the Chinese fisherman attempting to snare the *Impeccable*'s sonar on the front page. Indeed, a *Wall Street Journal* editorial piece on March 11 noted, "The Chinese have a knack for welcoming incoming U.S. administration with these sorts of provocations." The editorial writers concluded that the incident "is another reminder that China's ambitions for regional dominance . . . remain unchanged," and they recommended that Obama "dispatch a destroyer or two."[32] As noted above, Obama did indeed order a destroyer to the scene, but he simultaneously tried to diffuse tensions by saying that the U.S. and Chinese militaries needed to have more dialogues to prevent such incidents from occurring.[33]

In China, the reaction to the crisis was also somewhat muted. The Chinese Foreign Ministry spokesman commented, "The U.S. claims are gravely in contravention of the facts and confuse black and white, and they are totally unacceptable to China," suggesting the *Impeccable* had "conducted activities in China's special economic zone in the South China Sea without China's permission."[34] Authors writing in a popular Chinese military magazine stated emphatically, "The Chinese side cannot accept the American side's unreasonable criticism."[35]

However, reaction among most Chinese articles seems to have been quite muted. In the semiofficial journal 舰船知识 [Naval & Merchant Ships] that is quite close to the PLA Navy, one analyst observed, "Under the guidance of Chinese and American diplomats, there is hope that the 'Impeccable incident' can be resolved by peaceful means. Because there are such controversial points embedded within the Law of the Seas, such maritime confrontations can be said to be '家常便饭' [all in a day's work or routine]. When another incident occurs between Chinese and American vessels, we should not be at all astonished."[36] A long and detailed survey of U.S.-China military relations in the magazine 现代军事 [Contemporary military affairs] that appeared in the May 2009 issue ran a picture from the *Impeccable* incident, but otherwise made no mention of the incident, while actually emphasizing certain positive factors in the military relationship, such as U.S. aid for the Sichuan quake victims and Washington's welcoming of Beijing's new antipiracy mission in the Gulf of Aden.[37] Even some traditionally hawkish commentators, such as Qinghua University Professor Yan Xuetong, said that the chance of military hostilities between the United States and China remained at zero.[38] Some Chinese sources made the dubious claim that the incident was simply provoked by angry fishermen.[39] Interestingly, Zhang Wenmu, a Beijing scholar who has strongly advocated for China's naval buildup, cautioned in an article in May that China would be wrong to shift its strategic focus from Taiwan to the South China Sea.[40]

A popular theory circulating among Chinese strategists in the spring of 2009 was the notion that the U.S. Navy had provoked the incident to avoid major cuts in navy programs that were otherwise imminent as demonstrated by the cancellation of the F-22 fighter.[41] Indeed, a typical Chinese analysis, for example, holds, "Secretary of State Clinton's goal is to improve U.S. -China cooperation and especially to develop cooperation concerning the financial crisis, but this policy is in contradiction to the Pentagon's traditionally hegemonic policies. Perhaps, [the U.S. military] is trying to use this incident to influence Obama's foreign policies."[42] Domestic politics, so it seems, makes for good commentary at least, when explaining American policy to Chinese audiences. In general, it seems quite clear that the reaction in China was more intense—based on the higher level of coverage in the Chinese media—due in large part to China's deep reservoir of nationalism and also the proximity of the event. Fighting wars in Iraq and Afghanistan, and welcoming in a new administration, the *Impeccable* incident gained little traction within U.S. domestic politics. Interestingly, during the course of 2010, it seemed that strategic factors were coming to the fore regarding the South China Sea issue as Washington and Beijing seemed to be acting in a strategic competition for influence in South East Asia.[43]

Case Analysis and Conclusions

The comparison between the two cases allows for some basic conclusions with respect to the role of domestic politics in the U.S.-China rivalry. In the former case, the role of domestic politics was very considerable, both in Beijing and especially Washington. Indeed, it is possible that the Taiwan crisis would never have happened, but for the aggressive promotion by the U.S. Congress of a visa for the Taiwan leader. By contrast, there was no major role for domestic politics in the case of the *Impeccable* incident. Thus, a relatively clear finding of this study is that among two major strategic issues on China's periphery, the Taiwan issue may be substantially more volatile because the domestic factor plays a salient role. There are many examples of where domestic political factors appeared to exaggerate the severity of the Taiwan crisis, for example when Clinton met with the Dalai Lama in September 1995, when Clinton refused to give Jiang a state visit in November, and when in December the Taiwan vice president was offered a transit visa. It seems that Clinton was engaged in a type of *rivalry outbidding* with the potent Taiwan and human rights lobbies—perennially anxious not to be seen as "weak on China." Yet another possibility to consider in analyzing U.S. policy with respect to Taiwan is that American leaders perhaps understand reasonably well the operation of this "two-level game" and may exploit its dynamics for strategic purposes. It may enable, for instance, Washington to simultaneously play "good cop" and "bad cop," allowing U.S. leaders to "have their cake and eat it too."[44]

A much simpler explanation holds that, as the Taiwan issue has been at the center of U.S.-China rivalry since 1949, there has been ample time for interest groups to develop and become entrenched and influential. Since Taiwan's democratization and the Tiananmen Square massacre, the cause of Taiwan has effectively fused with the broader human rights agenda, creating a single, powerful lobby opposed to security cooperation with the PRC. In the 1990s, it should also be said that the business lobby supporting extensive U.S.-China cooperation had not fully developed. Thus, the Taiwan-human rights lobby was virtually unchallenged in its attempt to gain hold of Washington's China policy during the Clinton administration. By contrast, these lobbies are not likely to mobilize on issues related to the South China Sea. As the issue of contention primarily concerns uninhabited islets and reefs, there is no natural constituency with representation, nor any tangible human rights question at issue. With the possible exception of the Philippines, moreover, none of the small state disputants have the potential to form effective lobbying forces to impact the American scene.

In considering the impact of domestic political factors in Beijing, three tendencies emerge from this analysis as especially significant. The first seems to be related to either *governmental politics* or *factional foreign policies*. In either characterization the stance of military leaders seems to be a key part of the outcome. Thus, in the Taiwan crisis, the military leadership occurred to clash continuously with the civilian leadership, whether Chinese diplomats or even President Jiang himself. At this point the position of the military leadership on the *Impeccable* incident remains unknown. However, it is possible to say that the incident was not, as some Chinese sources had claimed, simply the initiative of some patriotic fishermen—the military clearly was involved.[45] Second, the military obviously chose not to escalate the crisis further after the United States opted to send a warship—though it is not clear if that was the military's policy preference. In short, Chinese civil-military relations are of paramount importance. However, China currently lacks a functioning national security council that could effectively reconcile military and civilian viewpoints on difficult national security issues, as many scholars have pointed out. Given the seemingly critical place of the military in Chinese decision-making, the United States would do well to continue to build relationships and trust with the PLA in an attempt to diffuse the jingoism and anti-Americanism that seems to be relatively deeply rooted. Finally, the power of Chinese nationalism in the population generally may be suggested in the former case and hinted at in the latter. At a minimum, American leaders should be aware of the possibility that Chinese public opinion could conceivably even matter more than in a democratic state, such that in China "domestic interests always trump foreign policy interests in crisis."[46] Alternatively, one may hope that "Chinese leaders no longer need to use crises to build popular and elite support for the government."[47]

Unfortunately, U.S.-China military confrontations seem to only be increasing in their frequency. Since 2006, there as has been the *Song* submarine encounter with USS *Kittyhawk*, the ASAT test, the USNS *Impeccable* incident, the USNS *Victorious* incident, and the bumping of a towed array deployed by the USS *McCain*. As China's military grows larger and is deployed in more complex missions at greater distances from home, there is an increased likelihood of contact with U.S. forces. At some level, it is reassuring to know that these events above are regarded as mere "incidents," and not as full-blown "crises," indicating that armed conflict remains a remote possibility. Moreover, the incidents have forced the U.S. and Chinese militaries to dialogue regularly, for example in the maritime consultation talks held annually. Nevertheless, there is great danger in both the chaotic interplay of interest groups in Washington and the nationalism that remains potent in Beijing. A clear lesson of the 1995–96 crisis is that leaders relying on their own "personal assurances" were not always able to keep the crisis from escalating. The recent ebbing of the Taiwan issue as relations across the Taiwan Strait have blossomed since 2008 certainly gives cause for a new optimism in U.S.-China relations, especially given this study's conclusion that the South China Sea issue is inherently less volatile within this rivalry. However, it must be recognized in both capitals that much hard work, compromise, and mutual respect will be required if the U.S.-China rivalry is to be stabilized into a "normal" international relationship. The imperative of security in the twenty-first century and beyond requires that this course be diligently and consistently followed. Such a course would undoubtedly require national leaders in both Washington and Beijing to stand bravely against the obvious temptations to blur domestic and foreign policy, a blending that could have grave consequences.

4 Peace and Conflict in the Indo-Pakistani Rivalry: Domestic and Strategic Causes

S. Paul Kapur

INDIA AND PAKISTAN ARE PERHAPS THE QUINTESSENTIAL ASIAN rivals. The two states emerged from a partition of British India that was characterized by large-scale Hindu-Muslim violence and mass population transfers. By the time partition was over, between two hundred thousand and one million people had died and approximately fifteen million had been displaced. Within a few months of achieving independence in 1947, India and Pakistan were locked in their first war. Three more wars, as well as decades of tension and crisis followed, including a low-intensity conflict between Pakistan-backed militants and Indian security forces that has wracked the Indian state of Jammu and Kashmir since the late 1980s.

Despite the highly conflictual nature of Indo-Pakistani relations, violence on the subcontinent has waxed and waned; it has not remained constant since independence. Indeed, after waging three wars between 1947 and 1971, India and Pakistan did not directly fight again until 1999. Although the 1970s and 1980s were not wholly free of tension, they were far less violent than previous decades. The contrast was so marked that one scholar dubbed these years the era of South Asia's "long peace."[1] But then, during the 1990s, Indo-Pakistani relations became crisis-ridden and violent once again. The decade began with a major militarized standoff between Indian and Pakistani forces. In 1998, India and Pakistan tested nuclear weapons. The decade ended with the 1999 Kargil conflict, India and Pakistan's first war in twenty-eight years. Given the antagonists' nuclear status, Kargil threatened to plunge the subcontinent into a catastrophic conflagration. Although Kargil was ultimately resolved without major escalation, more crises and standoffs followed soon thereafter. These confrontations again raised the specter of major war and perhaps even a nuclear exchange on the subcontinent.

One of the most urgent tasks for scholars of South Asian security is to explain this variance in the Indo-Pakistani rivalry. Why did South Asia, after its initial bouts of violence following independence, experience a "long peace," only to slide back into another period of tension and war? Answering this question can help us to uncover the sources of peace and conflict in South Asia, and to identify the conditions under which the region is likely to shift between them. In order to do so, this chapter compares the peaceful period from 1972 through 1989 with the conflictual periods from independence to 1971, and from 1990 to the present. Specifically, it seeks to understand how domestic Indian and Pakistani political factors, and international strategic variables, interacted to create variance between these periods of relative peace and violence.

By "domestic" I mean factors specific to the internal politics of a particular state, rather than to the international strategic environment, or to domestic politics in another state. By "international," I mean factors related to the external strategic environment, or to the domestic politics of another state. Thus Indian behavior resulting from India's own internal political preferences or calculations would be considered "domestic" in motivation, while Indian behavior resulting from an assessment of its military position vis-à-vis Pakistan, or from variables related to Pakistan's domestic political landscape would be considered "international."[2]

The chapter argues that the relevant domestic political factors remained fairly constant between the time periods in question. The Indo-Pakistani rivalry has been driven primarily by the two countries' dispute over the territory of Kashmir. Although India governs about two-thirds of Kashmir and Pakistan approximately one-third, both countries claim the right to control Kashmir completely. In practice, India has sought only to retain its portion of Kashmir, while Pakistan has attempted to wrest Indian Kashmir from New Delhi's control. This dispute is, at root, a function of domestic politics. The territory's Muslim-majority status makes it impossible for either country to cede the region without undermining the narrative that justifies its state-building enterprise—in Pakistan's case the project of creating a home for South Asian Muslims who could not live in a Hindu-dominated India, and in India's case the task of constructing a secular, polyglot democracy that could serve as a home to all of South Asia's ethnic and religious groups. Thus an Indian or Pakistani government that relinquished its claim to Kashmir would threaten the logic of Indian and Pakistani statehood. This has been true since India and Pakistan's founding, and it explains the intractability of the Kashmir dispute through the decades.[3]

What did change over time, and thus explains the shifts between South Asia's periods of relative peace and conflict, were international strategic variables. Pakistan's crushing defeat in the 1971 Bangladesh War made clear that it could no longer directly challenge India over Kashmir. The war thus ushered in an era of tranquil Indo-Pakistani relations following the violent postindependence decades. Then, in the late 1980s, the strategic environment shifted again, with the eruption of an insurgency in Jammu and Kashmir. Pakistan exploited the uprising, supporting the militants with arms, money, and training. Simultaneously, Pakistan's burgeoning nuclear capability gave its leaders confidence that India would not launch a large-scale retaliation in response to its provocations in Kashmir. This made renewed Pakistani efforts to undo Kashmir's territorial status quo, which might otherwise have been prohibitively dangerous, safe enough to pursue. And Pakistan's support for the Kashmir insurgency, in turn, drove spiraling Indo-Pakistani tension from the 1990s forward. Domestic political preferences can thus be seen as having provided the permissive cause for tension and violence in South Asia; they made Kashmir an extremely important issue for both countries and ensured the dispute's continued relevance even during times of improved Indo-Pakistani relations. But the efficient cause of South Asia's shifts between relative stability and violence lay in the realm of international strategic variables; these factors provided the immediate trigger that caused Pakistani retrenchment post-1971, and then they facilitated Pakistan's adoption of a low-intensity conflict strategy in Kashmir during the late 1980s.

Below, I first discuss the founding narratives of the Indian and Pakistani states. I show that, according to the two-nation theory that justified the creation of Pakistan, South Asian Muslims needed their own independent territory. They could not live as a minority in a larger Indian state dominated by Hindus. India's founders, by contrast, were determined that independent India should not have any particular communal identity and, instead, should provide a homeland to all South Asians regardless of religion. In the next section, I show how Kashmir became central to effectuating these narratives—for

Pakistan changing the territorial division of Kashmir, and for India maintaining existing borders in the region. In the following section, I discuss Indo-Pakistani security relations from independence to 1971. I show that Pakistan repeatedly challenged India over Kashmir until the Bangladesh War. As I explain in the next section, the Bangladesh War changed the regional security environment, making clear that continuing Pakistani provocations could result in catastrophic defeat. The Pakistanis did not abandon their domestic political commitment to Kashmir after Bangladesh. They simply realized that they could not, at present, undo the Kashmiri status quo. The result was a "long peace" that lasted until the late 1980s. In the subsequent section, I show that the shift from the long peace to violence in the late 1980s did not coincide with domestic political changes on the Kashmir issue in either country. Pakistani leaders remained committed to changing regional borders while Indian political actors remained determined to maintain them. I show instead that the eruption of a new period of violence coincided with another shift in the regional security environment—specifically the outbreak of an anti-Indian insurgency in Kashmir, and Pakistan's development of a nuclear weapons capability. This emboldened the Pakistanis to launch a strategy of asymmetric warfare against Indian Kashmir and plunged the region into confrontation and violence once again. Finally, in the chapter's conclusion, I briefly discuss the current state of the Indo-Pakistani rivalry and the prospects for an era of renewed regional stability.

Independence and the Founding Narratives

Pakistan was founded on the belief that South Asian Muslims needed their own autonomous home and could not live as part of a Hindu-dominated India. In Muhammad Ali Jinnah's view, the physical geography of the Indian subcontinent did not coincide with its political architecture. Physical India was not a politically unified whole, but rather was divided between religious groups, in particular Hindus and Muslims.[4] Thus, according to Jinnah, "any idea of a United India could never have worked and . . . would have led . . . to terrific disaster."[5] The creation of Pakistan was therefore necessary to ensure that Muslims could live in a manner that was compatible with their own unique culture and was free from discrimination.

Despite its purpose as a homeland for Muslims, Pakistan's political orientation was initially secular. Jinnah had begun his career with the Indian

National Congress and emerged as one of the independence movement's foremost spokesmen for Hindu-Muslim unity. Even after joining the Muslim league, he remained a passionate advocate for communal harmony, maintaining that good relations between Hindus and Muslims would be essential to successful Indian self-government.[6] Throughout his life, Jinnah also was famously irreligious; he drank alcohol, ate pork, and rarely participated in religious observances. Thus although Jinnah sought to create a home for South Asian Muslims, he did not envision Pakistan being Islamic as such. As Ian Talbot argues, "Jinnah's aim and that of the professional elite who controlled the [Muslim] League was to wrest a state in which Muslim economic, political and cultural interest could be safeguarded, but not to create an Islamic state."[7] Indeed, Jinnah appears to have imagined a Pakistan that, in its domestic politics and social policies, was largely free of religious distinction.[8]

Nonetheless, the fact remains that, despite Jinnah's secularism, Pakistan's raison d'être was rooted in religious identity. Even if the country was supposed to be tolerant toward minority groups, it existed primarily for the benefit of a community defined by religion. Moreover, Jinnah died soon after Pakistan's founding, and his relatively secular vision was soon replaced by a more Islamist approach to state building. Islam was used primarily as a tool for unifying the country. Although this emphasis on Islam may have helped to promote national unity, it also exacerbated Pakistan's differences with India.

The need for such a unifying tool stemmed from the circumstances of Pakistan's creation. The two-nation theory that divided the subcontinent in 1947 clearly required, in Muhammed Iqbal's words, "the fullest national autonomy" for Indian Muslims.[9] However, as Husain Haqqani explains, "A separate Muslim nation could have remained part of a federal or confederal India under special power sharing arrangements."[10] Indeed, Jinnah may not initially have sought the establishment of a sovereign state when he lobbied for Muslim autonomy in the waning days of British rule.[11] Also, the notion that Hindus and Muslims each needed their own autonomous homelands was not universally obvious to Indian Muslims prior to partition.[12] Thus proponents of the creation of Pakistan faced difficulties in convincing many ordinary Muslims to support their project.

As a result, the Muslim League offered a justification for Pakistani statehood that was deliberately vague, and held different meanings for different audiences. It was not always clear, for example, whether Pakistan was to be an Islamic state or whether it was to be an otherwise pluralistic homeland for Muslims. The League's vagueness not only encouraged Pakistanis to have unrealistic expectations as to the state's ability to solve their enduring social and political problems, it also created a crisis of identity and of justification for the Pakistani state itself. What was the purpose of Pakistan, and why was its creation necessary? These questions lingered even after the new state had emerged from the chaos of partition.[13]

Thus, after independence, Pakistanis needed a unifying identity around which they could rally and that would provide their new country with a clear purpose. Islam served this function. Pakistan soon made the transition from being not simply a homeland for Muslims, but a state based on an Islamic identity. The army, which emerged as the preeminent institution in the new Pakistani state, in particular used this Islamic identity as a means of ensuring national unity. It also used religion to justify its own leading position; only the army could protect Pakistan against such foes as "Hindu" India. This shift away from a relatively secular Muslim identity and purpose toward a more Islamist approach to state-building heightened the significance of religious differences between Pakistan and India. It also helped to ensure the political primacy of the army, which emerged as a bulwark against the Indian enemy. Both of these effects helped to make the Indo-Pakistani dispute over Kashmir especially salient. Because of its Muslim-majority status, Kashmir became a central issue for a Pakistan increasingly concerned with promoting its Islamic identity. And the army had an organizational interest in ensuring that the conflict over Kashmir remained alive, thereby creating an enduring threat to national security and ensuring its own continuing relevance.[14]

Indian leaders, by contrast, had sought to portray India as a unified home for all South Asians, regardless of religion. Only rarely in India's history had the subcontinent's physical geography actually coincided with its political architecture. The British colonial project attempted permanently to create such a situation, forging a central political authority rooted in a single, unified sovereignty. The Indian National Congress internalized this approach, adopting the British goal of creating, in Aeysha Jalal's words, "a composite nationalism based on an indivisible central authority." This enabled it to neutralize potential movements for autonomy and to bring the quasi-independent princely states within its control. Congress' claim to be the sole legitimate representative institution in an India riven by religion, ethnicity, and caste, necessarily implied a secular orientation for the new Indian state.[15]

The Importance of Kashmir: From Domestic Politics to Security Issue

We have seen that Islam became the unifying theme around which the Pakistani state was constructed and maintained, particularly by the army. The Congress party insisted that the new Indian state would represent all Indians, regardless of religion or ethnicity. How did Kashmir emerge as the central contest between these contrasting approaches to state-building? First, Kashmir's legal status in the wake of partition was highly controversial. At the time of independence, the fate of India's more than five hundred princely states was unclear. These states had enjoyed considerable autonomy during British rule, but now they had to decide whether to join India or Pakistan. Lord Mountbatten, India's last viceroy, laid down basic ground rules to guide their decision. First, the princely states would have to recognize the realities of geography; a state located deep in India could not opt to join Pakistan, and a state wholly within Pakistan could not become part of India. In addition, the states would be guided by the religion of their populations, with predominantly Muslim states joining Pakistan and Hindu-majority states acceding to India.[16]

Kashmir posed a problem on each front. It bordered both India and Pakistan and did not fall squarely within either state. Although its population was predominantly Muslim, Kashmir's ruler was a Hindu. Thus it was not obvious which country Kashmir should join once the Indian subcontinent had been divided. Kashmir's maharaja, Hari Singh, vacillated and delayed making a decision as to whether to accede to India or to Pakistan. However, in October 1947, a tribal rebellion erupted in the Poonch region of Kashmir. Before long, Pathan tribesmen and Pakistani soldiers in mufti captured Muzaffarabad and began advancing toward the Kashmiri capital of Srinagar. Hari Singh appealed to Mountbatten in the hope of securing Indian assistance in repulsing the intruders. Mountbatten and Prime Minister Nehru agreed to send Indian forces to Kashmir. In return, however, they stipulated that Kashmir must accede to India. The Kashmiri people would ratify the accession through a plebiscite, once hostilities in the region had ceased. Hari Singh agreed to India's terms. On October 26, the maharaja signed an instrument of accession, and Indian troops arrived in Srinagar shortly thereafter.[17]

India and Pakistan adopted diametrically opposed views regarding Kashmir's accession to India. According to the Indians, Maharaja Hari Singh's signature of the instrument of accession made Kashmir an integral part of the

Indian Union. Pakistan's subsequent attempts to seize the territory through war and insurgency were simply efforts to steal something that did not belong to them. The Indians have therefore been prepared to pay significant costs, including the large-scale use of military force, to retain control of Jammu and Kashmir and preserve the status quo in the region.[18]

The Pakistanis, by contrast, believed that Muslim-majority Kashmir's accession to Hindu-majority India contradicted the principles underlying the partition of the Indian subcontinent. The Pakistanis further argued that because a maharaja joined Kashmir to India, and the Indians never submitted the issue to a plebiscite, Kashmir's accession was undemocratic. For Pakistan, the Kashmir dispute became the "core issue" in its relationship with India.[19] And wresting Jammu and Kashmir from India, through tactics ranging from support for insurgency to the outright use of military force, became a central national project.[20]

Why was this controversy over Kashmir's accession so important? Why did a disagreement over a mountainous territory with little economic or military potential emerge as the central issue in a bloody, protracted rivalry between India and Pakistan? What made the disagreement over Kashmir's disposition so important was the territory's Muslim-majority status; this infused Kashmir with enormous political significance following accession and in the decades ahead. Kashmir's disposition served as a test of the principles on which the Pakistani and Indian states were founded.

Pakistan, the creation of which was supposedly necessary because Muslims could not live in a Hindu-majority India, could not allow a predominantly Muslim region to become part of the Indian Union. If it was acceptable for Kashmiri Muslims to live in a Hindu India, surely the Muslims of Pakistani Punjab or Bengal could do the same. If this were the case, then the justification for Pakistan's existence would be tenuous at best. Similarly, an Indian state that staked its legitimacy on its transcendence of religion and ethnicity could not allow the fate of Kashmir to be decided on the basis of the territory's Muslim-majority status. If India could be forced to do so in the case of Kashmir, then it might well be coerced into doing the same elsewhere; nothing in principle could prevent other ethnic or religious minorities from claiming their own independence from the Indian Union. In a state as diverse as India, this could potentially result in an unraveling of the country.[21]

Thus neither India nor Pakistan could relinquish Kashmir, and the territory became the symbolic object of contestation between the two countries.

Within India and Pakistan, Kashmir acquired street-level significance. Domestic political opponents would savage any Indian or Pakistani government that significantly compromised on Kashmir, inflating threats and offering up tough foreign policies in order to outbid the current leadership and energize the public against it. In such an environment, no government could long survive.[22] As a result, finding a solution to the Kashmir dispute became virtually impossible, with both Indian and Pakistani leaders clinging adamantly to their national positions. Thus, in South Asia, as in other cases in this volume, domestic political calculations have limited states' international freedom of action, reducing their ability to avoid conflict with their rivals.[23]

The Kashmir dispute, then, was at root an argument over ideas—the ideas that justified the founding and continued existence of the Pakistani and Indian states.[24] These divergent ideas drove India's and Pakistan's domestic political preferences on Kashmir and turned the two countries' disagreement over the territory into a major Indo-Pakistani security issue.[25] As a result, violence over Kashmir marred India and Pakistan's relationship from virtually their first days of independence.

Conflict over Kashmir Prior to the Long Peace

India's and Pakistan's first war over Kashmir erupted after Indian troops arrived in the territory following Hari Singh's appeal to New Delhi. India's strategy in the conflict employed both diplomacy and military action. On January 1, 1948, the Indians complained formally to the United Nations Security Council about Pakistani actions. They hoped that the UN would condemn Pakistan and call for the attackers' withdrawal from Kashmir.[26] Simultaneously, the Indians commenced large-scale combat operations to oust intruding forces. The Indians confined their operations to Kashmir, though they threatened to expand the fighting into Pakistan if the need arose.[27]

About one-third of Kashmir was under the intruders' control when Indian forces arrived in the territory. Despite its diplomatic and military efforts, India did not succeed in changing this basic territorial division. After roughly one year of conflict, India controlled approximately two-thirds of Kashmir and Pakistan one-third of the territory. The war ground to a stalemate, with neither side able to significantly change the situation. The first Kashmir conflict officially ended on January 1, 1949, under the auspices of a United Nations-sponsored cease-fire.[28]

This was not the last war between India and Pakistan over Kashmir. In August 1965 Pakistani soldiers disguised as tribesmen infiltrated the Kashmir Valley and attempted to instigate a popular uprising. This was to be followed by a conventional invasion of Kashmir, during which the Pakistan Army would seize the territory. The infiltrators did not, however, succeed in fomenting a rebellion. Instead, the Kashmiri population turned the intruders over to Indian authorities.[29]

Nonetheless, Pakistan launched the follow-on phase of its war plan, attacking Indian territory in southern Kashmir. Each side enjoyed some initial successes in the ensuing conflict, with the Pakistanis driving toward the Indian city of Akhnur, and India expanding the war into Pakistan proper and advancing on Lahore and Sialkot. These offensives eventually stalled, however, and by mid-September the war had become a stalemate. The two sides accepted a UN ceasefire resolution later in the month and agreed to return to the status-quo ante. Despite its inconclusive end, the war demonstrated that Kashmir remained a major issue of contention well after partition and the territory's accession to India.[30]

South Asia's "long peace," which saw a decades-long cessation of hostilities between India and Pakistan, began shortly after the 1965 conflict, with India's victory in the Bangladesh war. After Pakistan's first national election in October 1970, large-scale rioting erupted in East Pakistan. West Pakistani troops, deployed to quell the uprising, massacred their Bengali countrymen, and millions of refugees began flowing across the border into India in spring 1971. India was unable to absorb the refugee flow and decided to split East and West Pakistan in order to end the crisis. India began supporting mukti bahini insurgents fighting the East Pakistani government in fall 1971. India attacked Pakistan after the Pakistanis conducted air strikes against Indian Air Force bases on December 3. Six Indian army divisions drove rapidly into East Pakistan and quickly took Dhaka. By December 16 Pakistani forces had surrendered, and the next day India declared a unilateral cease-fire.[31]

After the end of the war, Pakistan stopped challenging India over Kashmir. The two sides did not directly confront one another again until the end of the 1990s. What accounted for this shift? As I demonstrate below, domestic political preferences regarding Kashmir did not change. At the domestic political level, India remained determined to retain the existing territorial division of Kashmir, and Pakistan remained committed to undoing it. What did change was Pakistan's realization that it could no longer face India in direct conflict. As a result the Pakistanis turned their attention to matters unrelated to Kashmir and avoided further confrontation with India.

South Asia's Long Peace

Pakistan's defeat in the Bangladesh war was devastating. The Indians had vivisected the country, creating Bangladesh out of the former East Pakistan. In addition, they had captured approximately five thousand square kilometers of territory and ninety thousand prisoners. India's victory also belied the myth of Pakistani martial superiority. Until this point, many Pakistanis believed that Hindu India was incapable of prevailing over Muslim Pakistan in combat. Bangladesh, however, proved that India could in fact decisively defeat Pakistan on the battlefield. This was a shattering realization for Pakistani leaders.[32]

Together, these developments made clear that the strategic environment in South Asia had decisively changed. Pakistan could no longer face India in a direct, large-scale conflict. If it did, Pakistan ran a serious risk of suffering catastrophic defeat. As a result, Pakistan stopped challenging India in the wake of the Bangladesh war. Instead, Pakistani leaders turned their attention to a variety of projects that did not involve Indo-Pakistani confrontation. For example, the Pakistani government began to pursue closer ties with other Muslim states, hosting an Islamic Summit Conference in Lahore in 1974.[33] Pakistan simultaneously reduced its ties to the United States and the West, withdrawing from the South East Asian Treaty Organization and the British Commonwealth of Nations.[34] Pakistan also took steps to revitalize its military, diversifying its arms suppliers to avoid overdependence on the United States, evaluating the army's Bangladesh war performance, and enhancing civilian control over the military.[35]

Pakistan's domestic political preferences regarding Kashmir did not change during this period. Pakistani leaders were still deeply dissatisfied with Kashmir's territorial division and remained committed to altering it. The Pakistanis simply believed that, given strategic realities on the subcontinent, they could not pursue their goals in Kashmir at the present time. They hoped to do so at some later date, if and when the opportunity arose. As Prime Minister Zulfikar Ali Bhutto said, "Presently, I cannot go to war." But "if tomorrow the people of Kashmir start a freedom movement . . . we will be with them. . . . We will fight if we want to fight. . . . This is an eternal position."[36]

Bhutto believed that Pakistan had retained its right to contest the division of Kashmir by virtue of the Simla Agreement, which had ended the Bangladesh war. The agreement stated that India and Pakistan would "settle their differences by peaceful means through bilateral negotiations or by other means mutually agreed upon by them." It also said that the Line of Control dividing Indian from Pakistani Kashmir would be "respected by both sides without prejudice to the recognized position of either side. Neither side shall seek to alter it unilaterally." In addition, the two sides agreed to "refrain from the threat or use of force in violation of this Line."[37]

The Indian government believed that the agreement solidified both the permanence of the territorial status quo in Kashmir and the principle of bilateralism in Indo-Pakistani dispute resolution. The Pakistanis, however, saw the matter quite differently. They believed that nothing in the Simla Agreement obviated their right to bring the Kashmir dispute before the United Nations. They also pointed out that the agreement expressly stipulated that it would not prejudice either side's recognized position on the issue and that both governments would agree on a time in the future to devise a final settlement of Kashmir. In the Pakistanis' view, this meant that the Simla Agreement did not foist upon them a permanent resolution of the Kashmir dispute. Rather, Simla was a temporary arrangement that preserved Pakistan's right to pursue a more congenial solution to Kashmir at a later date—through the United Nations, if they so desired.[38]

Despite this belief, however, the fact remained that Pakistan could presently do nothing to dislodge India from Kashmir and thus stopped challenging India on the issue. The result was South Asia's "long peace;" the region saw no more major Indo-Pakistani crises until the late 1980s and no more wars until the late 1990s. This was the longest period without a war between India and Pakistan since the two countries achieved independence.

In the late 1980s, the Indo-Pakistani relationship became tense once again. Comparing the period from 1972–89 with the period from 1989–98 reveals that militarized disputes were five times as frequent after 1989 as they were prior to that date. One such dispute, in 1990, was sufficiently serious to cause the deployment of hundreds of thousands of Indian and Pakistani troops and to trigger high-level U.S. diplomatic intervention. Then, from 1998 to 2007, the Indo-Pakistani relationship declined even further; militarized crises between the two countries became 14 percent more frequent than they had been between 1989 and 1998.[39] During this period, India and Pakistan fought their first war since 1971 and experienced their largest-ever militarized standoff following a terrorist attack on the Indian parliament. The end of the 1980s thus marked the beginning of a new period of regional tension.

Why did South Asia's long peace come to a close? It did not do so because of a shift in domestic political preferences regarding the main issue of Indo-Pakistani contention. Both sides remained committed to their long-held positions on Kashmir; India was still determined to maintain the existing division of the territory, while Pakistan wished to undo it.[40] The long peace ended, rather, because of a shift in the regional strategic environment. Specifically, two factors changed in the late 1980s that enabled Pakistan to begin challenging India in Kashmir once again: the emergence in Kashmir of an anti-Indian insurgency, and Pakistan's acquisition of a nuclear weapons capability.

A New Period of Tension

Prior to 1989, the inhabitants of Kashmir had refused to capitalize on opportunities to rebel against India. For example, during the 1965 war, Kashmiris had turned Pakistani infiltrators over to Indian authorities rather than join them in fomenting an anti-Indian uprising. During the late 1980s, however, Kashmiris lost patience with Indian rule. Better educated and more politically active than before, they were frustrated by the erosion of the region's political institutions, which left them without an avenue for legitimate political expression. After the Indian government conspired with the Kashmiri National Congress to rig the state's 1987 elections, violent opposition became the only available means of dissent. Strikes, demonstrations, and antigovernment violence began in 1988 and escalated the following year. By 1990, an outright rebellion had erupted, with militants battling Indian security forces daily, and the Indian government dissolving the Kashmiri State Assembly and placing the territory under Governor's Rule.[41]

Pakistan did not cause the Kashmir uprising, which resulted from the Indian malfeasance and mismanagement noted above. However, the Pakistanis actively supported the insurgency from the beginning.[42] Pakistan's Inter-Services Intelligence agency (ISI) noted the Kashmiris' discontent with Indian rule in the late 1980s. The Pakistanis recognized that Kashmiris would at long last be willing to turn violently against India. Capitalizing on this disaffection, the ISI helped Kashmiri rebels to launch the insurgency between 1988 and 1990.[43] They were aided in their task by the end of the anti-Soviet Afghan war, which provided a model of a successful insurgency strategy that Pakistan could emulate in Kashmir; a group of experienced military and intelligence officers who could support such a strategy; and large numbers of mujahideen who were now free to turn their attention from Afghanistan to Kashmir.[44]

The Kashmiri rebellion offered Pakistani leaders the opportunity they had long awaited, enabling them to take concrete steps to wrest Kashmir from India without risking catastrophic defeat. For the Pakistanis could now fight India by proxy, significantly increasing the costs to New Delhi of maintaining its presence in Kashmir without having to face India in a head-to-head contest on the battlefield.[45] Pakistan became deeply involved in the rebellion, providing the militants with arms, training, and financial and logistical support. This assistance became a major component of Pakistani security policy and fundamentally shaped the character of the insurgency.[46]

Fighting India in Kashmir, even by proxy, was not risk-free, however. The possibility remained that India could lose patience with Pakistani provocations and launch a large-scale military response, with potentially devastating consequences. Pakistan's confidence in its ability to energetically pursue a proxy war in Kashmir while avoiding major Indian retaliation resulted from a second strategic development that occurred during the late 1980s—Pakistan's development of a nuclear weapons capability.

Pakistan's nuclear program dated back to the 1950s. Though initially focused on the production of civilian energy, the program took a military turn in the wake of the Bangladesh war and India's 1974 "peaceful nuclear explosion" [PNE].[47] After the PNE, Zulfikar Ali Bhutto began calling for the creation of an "Islamic bomb," since the communists, Christians, and Hindus now had atomic bombs of their own.[48]

The development of a nuclear capability would enhance the Pakistani government's prestige at home and abroad. Most importantly, though, it would protect Pakistan against the possibility of a large-scale Indian attack. This, in turn, would not only enable Pakistan to defend itself against India—it would allow Pakistan to turn its attention to Kashmir once again after Bangladesh and the ensuing long peace. Insulated by nuclear weapons against the danger of a major Indian reprisal, Pakistan could actively support the Kashmiri insurgency and potentially even seize some of the disputed territory outright, all from a position of relative safety.[49]

Pakistani leaders readily admit the importance of nuclear weapons to their Kashmir policy. According to Benazir Bhutto, for example, nuclear weapons became a major factor in Pakistani thinking on Kashmir because "Islamabad saw its capability as a deterrence to any future war with India." A "conventional war could turn nuclear." Thus, even in the face of major Pakistani provocations in Kashmir, India would not respond with a large-scale conventional retaliation. "India could not have launched a conventional war" against a nuclear Pakistan, Bhutto continued. To do so would have been "suicide."[50]

Pakistani strategic analysts offer a similar opinion. According to Shireen Mazari, for example, "each side knows it cannot cross a particular threshold" in a nuclear environment. Thus "limited warfare in Kashmir becomes a viable option."[51] Even scholars who believe that nuclear weapons have generally stabilized the South Asian security environment admit that Pakistan's nuclear capacity allowed it to pursue a more aggressive Kashmir policy. According to Sumit Ganguly, for example, one of the "compelling reasons" that "emboldened the Pakistani military to aid the insurgency in Kashmir" was that "they believed that their incipient nuclear capabilities had effectively neutralized whatever conventional military advantages India possessed."[52]

Significantly, the Pakistanis' nuclear calculations have largely proven correct. Nuclear weapons have not wholly prevented Indian retaliation against Pakistan; the Indians have undertaken large-scale mobilization, and even limited war, in response to Pakistani provocations, despite Pakistan's nuclear capability. The Indians have not, however, been willing to launch a large-scale attack against a nuclear-armed Pakistan. Indeed, Indian decision-makers openly admit that such a response is not an option, given the risk of nuclear escalation that it would entail.[53] Thus the adoption of an asymmetric warfare strategy backed by nuclear weapons enabled Pakistan to challenge India in Kashmir once again and brought South Asia's long peace to a close. It also presented India with a thorny deterrence problem—how to convince Pakistan that the costs of continuing its proxy campaign in Kashmir will outweigh the benefits of doing so. Thus far, the Indians have yet to devise a solution to this puzzle.[54]

Conclusion

South Asia's shift from a period of frequent conflict between 1947 and 1971, to a "long peace" between 1971 and the late 1980s, and back to period of tension and confrontation from the late 1980s to the present, resulted primarily from changes in the international strategic landscape. At the level of domestic politics, both sides stayed wedded to their long-held positions regarding the central issue of Indo-Pakistani contention; India remained determined to retain its portion of Kashmir and maintain the status quo, while Pakistan remained dissatisfied with the division of Kashmir and sought to wrest Jammu and Kashmir from India. Because they remained relatively constant on the relevant strategic issues, domestic political variables cannot explain changes in the intensity of the Indo-Pakistani rivalry. Rather, such changes were a function of the shifting international strategic environment, where the debacle of the Bangladesh War engendered cautious Pakistani behavior during the long peace, and the Kashmir insurgency and a nuclear weapons capability encouraged provocative Pakistani behavior thereafter.

This is not, of course, to argue that domestic politics were irrelevant to the observed changes in Indo-Pakistani security relations. The Indo-Pakistani rivalry itself was rooted in domestic politics; Kashmir became an issue primarily because of its relevance to India's and Pakistan's founding narratives and state-building projects. Fear of domestic political fallout made it difficult for politicians to back away from their established positions on the Indo-Pakistani dispute. Thus domestic politics clearly mattered to security relations between India and Pakistan during the periods in question. However, they played a primarily permissive role, creating the possibility of both conflict and rapprochement, but not directly causing either development. The proximate cause of changes in the regional security environment lay instead in shifts in the strategic realm.

As noted above, regional security relations since the late 1980s have been relatively conflictual. What is the prognosis for the future? Could yet another strategic change result in the de-escalation of the Indo-Pakistani rivalry?

Some modest improvements in Indo-Pakistani security relations have recently occurred. For example, South Asia has not experienced a large-scale militarized confrontation since the 2001 attack on the Indian parliament. After that crisis, the two countries adopted various confidence-building measures, such as a cease-fire along the Line of Control, and the liberalization of trade and transport between Indian and Pakistani Kashmir. They also began negotiations to resolve the Kashmir dispute.[55] Violence in Kashmir has declined.[56]

This does not mean, however, that we are entering a new period of regional tranquility akin to the earlier long peace. Kashmir remains tense, with terrorist incidents continuing to occur on a regular basis, and militant infiltration declining only slightly in the past several years.[57] Terrorist violence has also targeted India proper, most spectacularly with the 2008 Mumbai attacks. In the wake of the attacks, Indo-Pakistani relations deteriorated once again, and India suspended peace talks indefinitely.[58]

More ominously, a frustrated India is searching for a way to force Pakistan to end its support for Islamist militancy. To this end, it is augmenting its conventional military capabilities and devising a new, aggressive military doctrine that will enable it to attack Pakistan quickly in the event of a crisis. Pakistani officials and analysts predict that Pakistan will respond by lowering its nuclear thresholds. If the jihadis launch another major attack, India could hold Pakistan responsible, regardless of whether the government was actually involved. If this occurs, the combination of increased Indian conventional capabilities backed by an aggressive doctrine, and lower Pakistani nuclear thresholds, could be a recipe for disaster.[59] Thus, far from entering another era of long peace, South Asia faces an especially dangerous period on the near horizon.

What would it take for the region to transition from the dangers of the current security environment to a new period of relative tranquility? Neither India nor Pakistan is likely to abandon its long-standing domestic political goals regarding Kashmir. A major shift in the strategic landscape, however, could make continued pursuit of those goals infeasible, thus reducing the likelihood of destabilizing behavior and increasing the prospects for regional peace. Specifically, the Pakistani government could realize that it is now at a strategic crossroads. The asymmetric warfare strategy that it has pursued for decades against India has spun out of control, with the jihadis unwilling to do the bidding of their erstwhile masters and increasingly challenging Islamabad for control of the Pakistani state.[60] As a result, the Pakistani government may finally recognize that it faces mortal danger if it does not cease its support for militancy and truly work to crush the jihadis.

If the Pakistanis genuinely take up this task, then they could fundamentally change the South Asian security environment. First, such efforts could persuade New Delhi to reduce military pressure on Pakistan, thereby allowing the Pakistanis to focus attention on counterinsurgency efforts at home rather than on protecting themselves against foreign threats. This would help to lower Indo-Pakistani tensions in the near term. Second, if the Pakistanis do manage to crush or cripple the jihadis, then they will remove the major source of regional instability. Kashmir will become more quiescent, terrorism against India proper will decline, regional crises will become less frequent, and the two countries will be able to work to significantly improve their relationship. Thus another period of regional peace is possible, but only if a fundamental shift in the existing strategic environment occurs. Ironically, the great danger of today's security situation provides some hope that India and Pakistan can take the steps necessary to make this happen.

5 Instability in Tibet and the Sino-Indian Strategic Rivalry: Do Domestic Politics Matter?

Manjeet S. Pardesi

Introduction

The aim of this chapter is to understand the role, if any, played by domestic political factors in the escalation, de-escalation, or the maintenance of the Sino-Indian strategic rivalry. China and India have been locked in a strategic rivalry since their emergence as modern nation-states in the late 1940s. At stake are issues of position in their overlapping "spheres of influence" in southern Asia (including the Himalayan region and the Tibetan plateau), Southeast Asia, parts of Central Asia, and increasingly the Indian Ocean region, as well as fundamental national security issues that have emerged as a consequence of the contest between these two states for power and influence in these regions.[1] While mutual suspicion has been the constant theme of the Sino-Indian rivalry since its initiation in the 1940s, the period since then has witnessed rivalry escalation as well as de-escalation. Rivalry escalation and de-escalation has been both military (in the form of one war, several militarized disputes, and military confidence-building measures) and diplomatic (including the severance and restoration of full-scale diplomatic ties).

In an attempt to understand the escalation and de-escalation dynamics, this chapter will study the consequences of instability in Tibet in 1959 and 1987–89 and the Chinese military crackdown that followed it on the Sino-Indian rivalry. China's brutal repression of the Tibetan uprising in 1959 led to an escalation of the Sino-Indian rivalry, which almost immediately resulted in India granting refuge to the Dalai Lama who escaped into exile on March

30, 1959. It also resulted in two military clashes between China and India, at Longju (in what today is India's state of Arunachal Pradesh) in August 1959 and at Kongka Pass (in Ladakh in India's state of Jammu and Kashmir) in October 1959.[2] However, the aftermath of China's armed repression of the circle of protests that began in Tibet in September 1987, which ended with the imposition of martial law in Tibet in March 1989, led to a de-escalation of the Sino-Indian rivalry. In the midst of this crisis in Tibet, the then Indian prime minister Rajiv Gandhi made a landmark trip to China in December 1988, the first such visit made by either side in more than three decades, and broke the impasse plaguing their relations since the 1962 Sino-Indian war.

How can we account for the differences in the rivalry dynamics between China and India to two ostensibly similar events? Did domestic politics in either country have a role in influencing these varying outcomes? If not, what are the other factors that influenced these decisions in China and India, and why did domestic politics not have any influence on the rivalry dynamics? These are some of the questions that this chapter will attempt to answer. Before proceeding it should be noted that as seen from Beijing, Tibet is an "internal" issue for China, and therefore the developments in Tibet and its consequences for the Sino-Indian rivalry means that domestic issues do matter (at least for the Chinese side). However, as explained subsequently, the aim of this paper is to understand the impact of different domestic-level variables on the decision to escalate or de-escalate the rivalry as opposed to merely stating that domestic issues matter because Tibet is an internal issue for China.

The next section of this chapter will propose a causal, mechanisms-based account of rivalry dynamics in order to understand the factors leading to the decisions of Chinese and Indian leaders to escalate or de-escalate their rivalry as the case may be. This will be followed by a brief discussion of the role of domestic political variables in foreign policy decision-making in China India (before the end of the cold war). The subsequent section will discuss the salience of Tibet for the Sino-Indian rivalry. Using the causal, mechanisms-based account of rivalry dynamics proposed here, this section will also explain why Indian and Chinese leaders escalated their rivalry in 1959 while de-escalating it 1987–89.

It will be shown that the most important causal variable influencing the Sino-Indian rivalry has been the perception of threat from the rival by key decision-makers. The Sino-Indian rivalry escalated in 1959 as a consequence of a significant deterioration of their mutual threat environment. As such, domestic politics played no role in the decision to escalate the rivalry in either country in 1959. However, domestic politics became an important factor in India *after* the initial decision to escalate the rivalry and played an important role in the dynamics leading to the 1962 border war with China. It will also be shown that when the threat perception remained unchanged, then *ceteris paribus*, the status quo was maintained. However, when the threat perception remained unchanged but other factors such as the military balance, allies, and other threats changed, they caused the rivalry dynamics to change as well. Both India and China de-escalated their rivalry in 1988 even as the threat perception of their key decision-makers vis-à-vis one another remained unchanged during this period. India de-escalated the rivalry in 1988 because of the loss of support from its Soviet ally. At the same time, India was also militarily involved in other crises in South Asia. However, as a consequence of its perception of a favorable military balance vis-à-vis China, India felt confident enough to de-escalate the rivalry. China de-escalated its rivalry with India in 1988 because India's loss of Soviet support at the time of the Sino-Soviet rapprochement had significantly improved China's security environment. At the same time, China was occupied with other threats in East Asia and was also aware of the India's improving military capabilities. In other words, in none of the cases examined did domestic political variables exert any influence in the *initial* decision to escalate or de-escalate the rivalry.

Two-level Rivalry Dynamics

A Causal, Mechanisms-based Account of Rivalry Dynamics

"*Mechanism*-based accounts select salient features of episodes, or significant differences among episodes, and explain them by identifying within those episodes robust mechanisms of relatively general scope."[3] Two main episodes or cases have been selected for analysis in this research. These include the impact of Chinese armed suppression of the Tibetan uprising in 1959 and 1987–89 on the Sino-Indian rivalry. They have been selected because they represent two instances of a similar class of events—Chinese armed intervention—that generate different outcomes. In the first instance, we observe an escalation of the Sino-Indian rivalry, while we witness de-escalation in the second instance. Chinese armed intervention in the same region—Tibet—also helps us control for a number of other factors such as the importance of the region in question for the rivalry under study. Arguably, Chinese armed intervention in another region claimed and controlled by China such as Inner Mongolia or Xinjiang will not have the same salience for India or the Sino-Indian rivalry.

As a first step, this chapter will employ Mill's "method of difference" to eliminate conditions that are present in both the cases under study.[4] According to the logic of elimination in this method, conditions that are common to both cases cannot account for the difference in their outcomes. Hence, these factors can be eliminated from the explanation. However, the conditions that were not present in both the cases can be regarded only as "possibly"[5] causally associated with the outcome under consideration. In other words, these same conditions may not be present in other cases with the same outcome as a consequence of equifinality.

As such, in order to explain the decisions to escalate or de-escalate the rivalry, this study will employ the process-tracing method as the next step after employing Mill's "method of difference." Process-tracing compensates the inability of Mill's method to accommodate equifinality by identifying the causal mechanisms leading to a particular decision. Causal mechanisms can be identified "after the fact"[6] through an examination of primary and secondary sources pertaining to the decision-making process, and by inferring causal mechanisms after logically eliminating competing explanations. Such explanations "lend themselves to 'local theory' in which the explanatory mechanisms and processes operate quite broadly, but combine locally as a function of initial conditions and adjacent processes to produce distinctive trajectories and outcomes."[7]

This chapter will show that the application of Mill's "method of difference" eliminates all domestic political variables from influencing the decision-making process in China in both of these cases. However, in the case of India, the application of Mill's "method of difference" eliminates all the domestic-level variables with the exception of public opinion and media, and the military (the latter being important only in 1987–89). But the application of the process-tracing method demonstrates that even these domestic-level factors did not play any role in influencing the decisions in India in 1959 or in 1987–89. In other words, in both India and China, it was the international-level variables that determined the *initial* rivalry dynamics. However, domestic-level factors became important in India *after* the initial decision to escalate the rivalry was taken in 1959 and played an important role in the events leading to the 1962 Sino-Indian war.

In order to ascertain that domestic politics indeed did not play any important role in the *initial* decision to escalate or de-escalate the rivalry, this study will also analyze the outcome of a "pathway case"[8]—the impact of Chinese armed suppression of the Tibetan uprising of 2008 on the Sino-Indian rivalry. The purpose of a "pathway case" is to "elucidate causal mechanisms"[9] in cases where a hypothesized cause is expected to have a significant influence. As is explained subsequently, post-1989 there have been important changes in Indian and Chinese domestic political systems that increase the probability of domestic political factors influencing foreign policy decisions. Consequently, if it can be demonstrated that domestic political factors did not play any role in 2008 either, then it increases the robustness of the finding. Indeed, it will be shown that the decision to continue with the status quo in the Sino-Indian rivalry in 2008 was not influenced by domestic political factors, even as some uncertainties remain.

Variables and Hypotheses

The Basic Proposition—Perception of Threat The causal, mechanisms-based explanation begins with a change in the mutual threat environment of the constituent rivals. A state's threat environment represents the security dangers that it faces. These security dangers may be external or internal. External security dangers include the possibility of armed aggression by the rival, the capture of disputed territory, or even the introduction of new military-technological capabilities in the rival's arsenal. Internal security dangers include the possibility of secession and armed insurgency. These internal security dangers may be exploited by the rival. When decision-makers perceive that the state's security environment has deteriorated significantly, they are more likely to engage in risky behavior and raise the stakes. This proposition is supported by prospect theory, which argues that individuals are risk-acceptant when they identify themselves in the domain of loss, but are risk-averse when they identify themselves in the domain of gain.[10] This leads us to our first basic proposition—the perception of an increased threat from the rival will lead the decision-makers to escalate the rivalry.

A state's decision to escalate the rivalry in this instance is impervious to domestic political variables. If a national leader does not escalate the rivalry in the face of a deteriorating threat environment, then he/she may be unlikely to maintain domestic political power. Even if there is no domestic pressure to escalate the rivalry, the national leader is likely to escalate it for its perceived negative consequences for the state's national security. However, if the perception of a state's threat environment remains unchanged then the decision to escalate, de-escalate, or maintain the status quo in the rivalry may depend on a number of other factors, both international and domestic.

Other International-Level Variables At the international level, the decision-makers are likely to factor in the balance of military power between the rivals, the presence or absence of allies, and the presence or absence of other threats, rivals, and military commitments. The balance of military power is a function of both the overall capabilities of the states and their ability to exploit situation-specific opportunities. A favorable military balance exists when a given state has the capabilities as well as the opportunity to use it to change the status quo. Considerations of political goals as well as the future balance of power are almost always involved before deciding whether or not to militarily escalate the rivalry.

The presence of an ally that may step in diplomatically or militarily to defend the state or provide it with advanced military technology provides incentives to escalate the conflict. Finally, the presence or absence of other rivals and threats as well as use of force elsewhere are factors that influence whether or not the given rivalry is escalated. The larger the number of external rivals and threats, and the greater the military commitment to use force elsewhere, the fewer the resources a given state will have at its disposal to escalate the given rivalry.

Logically, we have the following propositions: If the perception of a state's threat environment remains unchanged, then *ceteris paribus*, the status quo in the rivalry is maintained. Otherwise, a decision to escalate, de-escalate, or maintain the rivalry depends on the balance of military power, the presence or absence of external allies, and the presence or absence of other external rivals, threats, and military commitments. A favorable shift in the military balance increases the incentives to escalate the rivalry (and conversely an unfavorable military balance increases the incentives to de-escalate the rivalry), all else being equal. The presence of an ally increases the incentives to escalate the rivalry (and conversely the loss of an ally increases the incentives to de-escalate the rivalry), all else being equal. And finally, the presence of other external threats, rivals, and military commitments increase the incentive to de-escalate the rivalry, all else being equal. Conversely, their absence increases the incentives to escalate the rivalry.

Domestic-Level Variable In addition to the executive and his/her cabinet, there are a number of important actors at the domestic level that can possibly influence the decision to escalate, de-escalate, or maintain the status quo in the rivalry. The most important actors include other governmental agencies (such as the legislature, the ministries of foreign affairs and defense), political parties, public opinion and mass media, and the military. There are a number of variables here, and there is a lively literature in international relations analyzing their impact on a state's foreign policy.

Allison's study of the Cuban missile crisis is the standard text in the literature that argues that bureaucratic politics matters and that foreign policy decisions are a product of bargaining between different governmental agencies and major actors while also being influenced by the routines and standard operating procedures of governmental bureaucracies.[11] However, this view has been challenged, and it has been argued that when the issues at stake are important, the top officials can overcome the tug-of-wars among governmental bureaucracies to formulate foreign policy.[12]

There is also a wide literature on the impact of the split between the legislative and the executive on foreign policy decision-making.[13] However, the chief drawback of this literature is that while we understand that the legislative matters, there is little consensus on when and how it matters. Another strand of scholarship argues that different political parties and factions with different ideas on national security have different impacts on foreign policy especially as they rotate in and out of power.[14]

So far as the impact of public opinion and media on foreign policy is concerned, there are two dominant views in the literature, the "pluralist model" that argues that public opinion and media can influence foreign policy in a bottom-up fashion, and the "elite model" that argues that governments influence the public opinion and media on foreign policy issues in a top-down fashion.[15] However, it remains unclear whether public opinion and media inform the policymaking process itself or if they wield an influence during its implementation.

Finally, studies that analyze the role of militaries in foreign and security policymaking have also put forward a wide variety of arguments ranging from the inherent propensity in the military's organizational culture to escalate conflicts,[16] to identifying the conditions under which militaries engage in foreign aggression to divert attention away from domestic turmoil.[17] However, it remains unclear why certain situations lend themselves to interference by the military in policymaking while others do not.

In sum, this impressive literature on the domestic sources of foreign policy notwithstanding, we have a limited understanding of why these factors matter in some situations but not others, let alone their role in the rivalry process. Moreover, the overwhelming amount of this research focuses on one single country, the United States. Arguably, the domestic political factors that are influential in foreign policymaking in the United States (a presidential democracy) are different from those in India (a parliamentary democracy) or China (an authoritarian state dominated by a single party). As such, it is important to empirically determine which domestic level factors matter in the foreign policymaking arena in India and China before analyzing their influence on the Sino-Indian rivalry dynamic. The next section of this chapter will empirically determine if the legislature, governmental bureaucracies, political parties, public opinion and media, and the military have any impact on the process of foreign policy making in India and China before analyzing the escalation and de-escalation dynamics of the Sino-Indian rivalry.

Domestic Politics and Foreign Policy Decision-making Before 1989[18]

China

The three most important organs in the political process of the People's Republic of China (PRC) since its emergence in 1949 have been the Chinese Communist Party (CCP), the central governing apparatus, and the People's Liberation Army (PLA).[19] However, during the era of Mao Zedong, the first chairman of the CCP, Mao himself stood as the "unchallenged leader" at the apex of the Chinese political system.[20] The PRC was formed in 1949 not as a result of a successful communist revolution, but as a result of the CCP's military victories against "its nationalist rivals domestically and the Japanese invaders."[21] Mao's central position in the PRC was a consequence of his dominant role during the so-called revolutionary period within the CCP as well as his (and the CCP's) relationship with the PLA that ensured the victory of the CCP in the Chinese civil war.

The Leninist discipline of the CCP—a consequence of the CCP's orientation toward the Soviet Union—resulted in a hierarchical organization that demanded strict obedience once a decision was made. As a consequence, the CCP is not only a disciplined party machine with established norms, but also had a charismatic leader in Mao whose leadership was legitimized as a consequence of his central role during the revolutionary period. "There is simply no case of Mao not getting his way when he insisted upon it; to the extent the other top leaders exercised their influence it was through their various assigned roles [assigned by Mao] . . . or by using opportunities presented by Mao to push a particular advocacy thereafter."[22] In other words, Mao alone was ultimately responsible for the decisions made by the Chinese state during his lifetime. This was particularly true in terms of retaining authority over national security issues and setting guidelines on foreign policy.[23] Mao alone received foreign policy papers from Zhou Enlai, his premier and foreign minister, for making decisions with only "information copies"[24] being sent to other leading members of the CCP, particularly Liu Shaoqi[25] and Deng Xiaoping.[26]

The central role of the paramount leader in the Chinese political system continued well into the Dengist era. MacFarquhar has argued that "despite Deng's genuine efforts to avoid playing a Mao-like role, it seemed that the Chinese polity still demanded the linchpin of the *maximum leader*."[27] While other top leaders have played an important role in determining policy in China, the paramount leaders have always been able to intervene and hold his own whenever they have chosen to do so. Deng "could make any foreign policy decision on his own, although he tended to avoid dictatorial fiats and to build consensus through consultation."[28]

Since the beginning of the Maoist era, the CCP established complete control over the formal government apparatus. The most important body in the central state apparatus is the State Council, which runs the daily functioning of the government through different ministries and councils. The Central Committee of the CCP and its Secretariat (which include the paramount leader and his close associates) control the selection of the premier, vice premiers, ministers, and heads of the government departments through an elaborate Soviet-style *nomenklatura* system.[29] At the same time, the CCP had also set up parallel party departments for each functional subsystem of the government (including foreign affairs) during the Maoist era to control its activities.[30] The role of the state organs in the CCP is "to implement party politics."[31] This meant that during the Maoist era, the bureaucracies of the state had no independent influence on foreign policymaking. Prominent leaders in the state institutions like Zhou did bring their own personal style to China's foreign affairs. However, as has already been noted, the ultimate authority in foreign affairs and on national security matters rested with Mao himself.

During the Dengist era, especially in the 1980s, there was a conscious effort to separate the organs of the state from the CCP, especially in the realm of economic decision-making. However, this program was suspended and even reversed somewhat after the 1989 Tiananmen Square incident.[32] In spite of this, there has been a "pluralization of actors and interests" in the realm of foreign policymaking in China, and the State Council has become somewhat more involved in foreign affairs. However, with the limited exception of economic diplomacy, the State Council mostly plays the role of policy coordination as opposed to policy formulation.[33] Indeed, decision-making power with regard to key countries, including India, rests with the paramount leader and his close associates. "This has been particularly true during periods of policy adjustment and when implementation details could have affected the posture of China's overall relationship with the major powers."[34]

The CCP tightly controls the media as well as the topics of permissible discussion in China. The media serves as the "mouthpiece" of the CCP and the government, and it stresses uniformity in public opinion. The Chinese media have two faces—open (*gongkai*) and closed (*neibu*)—which serve different purposes.[35] The aim of the closed media, which is carefully restricted to targeted audiences, primarily the party cadre and members with political responsibilities to implement party/governmental policies, is to provide them with adequate information to carry out their duties. The aim of the open media is to inform the public about party (and governmental) policies and to build a consensus for their implementation. China's powerful propaganda and education *xitong* carefully controls the *gongkai* print and broadcast media in the country to shape public behavior.[36] In the Maoist and Dengist eras, the Chinese leadership strictly controlled the creation and dissemination of information in a top-down fashion to shape and reshape public opinion on domestic as well as foreign policy issues.

Given its revolutionary and postrevolutionary history, the PLA has always been a highly politicized organization.[37] However, the CCP maintains strict control over the PLA. The Central Military Commission (CMC) of the CCP controls the PLA and national security affairs. It is an unwritten rule in the political system of the PRC that the paramount leader should be in charge of the CMC.[38] The relationship between the party and the army can be traced back to the revolutionary period when the PLA functioned under the leadership of the CCP. However, during the Maoist period, it became a relationship between "Mao and his generals" as the only civilian who served continuously in the CMC apart from Mao himself until 1975 was Deng.[39] With the control of the CMC, Mao was able to control the highest-level body responsible for making defense policy for the PRC.

Like Mao before him, Deng assumed the leadership of the CMC in 1981 and controlled the formulation of defense policy in China. He also enjoyed high military status as a consequence of the role that he had played during the revolution.[40] However, analogous to Mao he was "unable to restore full civilian control" on the party's CMC.[41] In other words, China's paramount leaders were able to control the PLA and formulate the country's defense policy through their leadership in the CMC even as they were unable to civilianize that body itself.

In sum, the Chinese foreign policy decision-making process during the Maoist and Dengist eras was dominated by the paramount leader and his small team of close associates with the paramount leader essentially having a veto on the policy.[42] The legislature, other state bureaucracies, and military were tightly controlled by the paramount leader and the top leadership and, as such, were unable to independently influence foreign policy. Finally, being a textbook example of the elite model described above, public opinion and the media played no independent role in foreign policymaking during this period either. While the Dengist state was less monolithic and autocratic than the Maoist state, the essential authoritarian nature of the Chinese state and the Leninist organization and discipline of the CCP survived this leadership transition.[43] As the decision-making process in China was restricted to the top leadership led by the paramount leader, Mill's "method of difference" eliminates domestic-level variables from having any independent effect on the Sino-Indian rivalry dynamics, as they remained constant throughout the period under consideration and therefore in the two cases under investigation here.

India

Jawaharlal Nehru, the first prime minister of India and the "founding architect" of its foreign policy, was also the minister of external affairs until his death in 1964.[44] After independence, Nehru dominated the conceptualization and implementation of India's foreign policy. This was not only due to his position in the government but also because he was the only senior leader of the Indian National Congress (INC, the political party that won for India its freedom) with an extensive knowledge of foreign affairs. Nehru's role in India's foreign policymaking was further enhanced because two of India's three most important leaders died soon after independence. Mahatma Gandhi was assassinated in 1948 while Vallabhbhai Patel, Nehru's deputy prime minister and an individual with very different ideas on foreign policy, died in 1950. Nehru's assumption of the foreign affairs portfolio and the concentration of foreign policy decision-making in the Prime Minister's Office (PMO) meant that the institutional framework of foreign policymaking remained underdeveloped during the Nehru years.[45]

According to the Indian Constitution, the president is the nominal commander-in-chief; however, foreign policymaking in India is dominated by the prime minister and members of his/her cabinet in charge of foreign and security policies, which primarily includes the ministers of external affairs, defense, finance, and home affairs.[46] Even as the Parliament is the "cornerstone" of the Indian political system, it only exercises "ex post facto" control over issues related to foreign affairs and national security.[47] The primary influence of the Parliament over defense and foreign affairs is via their budgetary control over the annual funds allocated to the ministries concerned.[48] Control by the Parliament is otherwise exercised through parliamentary debates after the PMO or the cabinet has taken a decision or via various investigative committees (many ad hoc) that are created to monitor the implementation of a decision. In other words, the legislature in India has no influence over the formulation of foreign affairs and national security policies. Cohen sums this up succinctly:

> Parliament has little voice in the routine conduct of foreign policy . . . and need not be consulted prior to or during a crisis. It does not even have a role in the declaration of war, nor is its consent necessary to ratify a treaty. The guiding principle is that the prime minister is the leader of the majority party, and a parliamentary vote would be redundant.[49]

Nehru's overwhelming dominance in the making of Indian foreign policy notwithstanding, he tried to consult opposition leaders on important policy issues despite their weakness and the small representation of their parties in the Parliament.[50] However, after the passing away of Nehru, "India began moving toward the de facto presidentialization of the political system and the further centralization of the foreign policymaking process" as the PMO strengthened its role in this arena.[51] The prime ministers that followed Nehru—Lal Bahadur Shastri (INC), Indira Gandhi (INC), Morarji Desai (Janata Party), and Rajiv Gandhi (INC)—further centralized the foreign policymaking process in the PMO and even stopped consulting opposition leaders. In fact, during Rajiv

Gandhi's tenure as the prime minister (1984–89), the Congress Party enjoyed an overwhelming dominance in the Parliament by controlling almost 80 percent of the seats in the Indian Parliament—the highest ever—and saw no need to consult with the Parliament whatsoever.[52] While independent India has been a multiparty democracy from the very beginning, the Congress Party enjoyed near-hegemonic status at the all-India level until 1989. The domination of the Congress Party ensured that India's foreign and security policy was not affected by opposition parties.[53]

Given the centrality of the PMO and the cabinet, the different foreign and security policy bureaucracies in India—the Ministry of External Affairs, the Ministry of Defense, the Ministry of Home Affairs, and the Ministry of Finance—play no direct role in the formulation of policies. The impact of these bureaucracies on policymaking is only felt via the ministers heading these bureaucracies through their inclusion in the prime minister's cabinet. However, like the Parliament, these bureaucracies do affect the implementation of the policies.[54]

The role of public opinion and the media on the making of Indian foreign policy remains understudied.[55] By and large, the Indian population has not concerned itself with foreign affairs. Until recently, foreign policy issues have not been of electoral concern in the Indian democracy.[56] Even though there are no explicit opinion surveys, the only possible exceptions to this lack of public interest in foreign affairs are in India's relations with its immediate neighbors,[57] and in its nuclear policy.[58] Despite public interest in these issues, it is not clear how it actually impacts foreign and security policy formulation.

In the case of India's relations with China, it has been argued that the Indian public opinion was "repulsed" by the brutality and repression of religion by the PLA in Tibet, and being the leader of a democratic state Nehru had no choice but to grant refuge to the Dalai Lama in 1959.[59] However, in the run-up to Rajiv Gandhi's landmark trip to China in 1988 that de-escalated the Sino-Indian rivalry, it is argued that there was an "orchestrated attempt" by the Indian government to influence public opinion through coverage in the news media.[60] The 1959 case seems like an example of the "plural model" discussed above, while the 1988 case seems to fit the "elite model." Therefore, it remains to be empirically determined if these factors were indeed at work influencing the Sino-Indian rivalry dynamics.

Finally, India is perhaps unique among middle and great powers in that the military plays almost no role in the making of its foreign and security policies in the sense that the military's advice is "detached from political and strategic decisions."[61] Unlike China, "India did not start its independent life with a political army that claimed a share in the nationalist movement and the winning of independence."[62] In fact, the loyalty of the Indian Army to the British colonial government had made India's civilian leaders very suspicious of the military.[63] From the very beginning, the civilian leadership of independent India under the leadership of Nehru took a number of steps to reduce its political role and to guarantee its complete subordination to civilian leaders.[64] Under the colonial regime, the chief of the armed forces had direct access to the political leadership and in the decision-making process. However, after independence, the decision-making apparatus did not make any provisions for the armed forces to provide direct representation in the Defense Committee of the Cabinet, the apex defense policymaking body.[65] Nehru strengthened the idea that "professional competence, not political initiatives was the first requirement of the Indian Army."[66]

Consequently, India has a professional and largely apolitical military. For example, even when India flirted briefly with authoritarianism from 1975–77 under Prime Minister Indira Gandhi's "emergency rule," she did not involve the armed forces.[67] The one possible exception to the subdued role of the military in defense and security policymaking is during General K. Sundarji's term as the chief of army staff (1986–1989). It is believed that "inadequate civilian oversight" in the planning and execution of Operation Brasstacks, a military exercise conducted by the Indian military as an experiment of armed diplomacy vis-à-vis Pakistan, heightened the tensions between India and Pakistan in 1986–87.[68] Since General Sundarji's term coincides with the planning and execution of Operation Chequerboard—a military exercise conducted by the Indian military as an experiment of armed diplomacy vis-à-vis China (1987–88)—and also with the de-escalation of the Sino-Indian rivalry in December 1988, the impact of the Indian military and its leadership on the Sino-Indian rivalry dynamics needs to be empirically determined.

In sum, analogous to the Chinese case, the foreign policy decision-making apparatus in India is controlled by the top leadership, which in the Indian case includes the prime minister at the apex along with his/her cabinet. The application of Mill's "method of difference" eliminates domestic factors like the influence of the legislature, opposition political parties, and governmental bureaucracies from influencing the Sino-Indian rivalry dynamics as their influence remains constant in the two cases under study here. However, the

Indian case does include the possibility of two domestic-level factors-public opinion and mass media (in 1959 and 1987–89), and the military (in 1987–89)-in influencing rivalry dynamics. The mechanisms through which these factors influence their rivalry (if they do) will be determined through process-tracing in the next section.

Instability in Tibet and the Sino-Indian Rivalry

The Importance of Tibet

Tibet is an important factor in Sino-Indian relations. "The Tibet issue is not simply the internal affair of China that the Chinese government insists it is. It has ramifications that touch on international concerns and regional stability; particularly with regard to India."[69] This is not to argue that the Sino-Indian rivalry is Tibet-centric or that Tibet is the most important factor in the Sino-Indian relationship. However, the salience of Tibet lies in the fact that it influences both the positional and the spatial dimensions of the Sino-Indian strategic rivalry.[70]

The Salience of Tibet for China The major thrust behind China's foreign and security policy is China's deep-rooted quest to "regain major-power status."[71] Throughout the twentieth century, Chinese nationalist elite from across the political spectrum, whether republican, nationalist, or communist have sought to reclaim China's status at the apex of the power hierarchy in Asia.[72] Apart from its sheer size and power potential, Chinese claims to primacy in Asia stemmed from a number of real and perceived historical memories,[73] the most important strands of which were the memory of a Sinocentric international order in East Asia, Southeast Asia, as well as parts of Central Asia;[74] China's "national humiliation" at the hands of Western and Japanese imperial powers from roughly the mid-nineteenth century onward (which ended up destroying this Sinocentric international order);[75] and the immense pride in the brilliant achievements of the Chinese civilization over the course of its long and continuous history, including (but not limited to) the invention of gunpowder, paper, printing, and the magnetic compass.[76]

The exploitation of the weakened Qing Empire and the destruction of the Sinocentric international order by Western imperial powers and Japan led the Chinese political leaders and even the masses to perceive the post-1842 period as an era of "national humiliation."[77] According to Gries, national humiliation is neither an objective representation of China's past, nor is it an invention of the Chinese nationalists. Instead, the constant reworking of its meaning is central to what it means to be Chinese today.[78] However, as a consequence of this perception of national humiliation, China is "determined to end all aspects of China's 'humiliation,' to block out all remnants of China's past weakness and degradation, and to prevent its recurrence."[79]

In other words, at the center of the worldview of the Chinese leaders from the early twentieth century has been the quest to reemerge as a great power in Asia and to undo the remnants of all "unequal treaties" and "extraterritorial" concessions made to the imperial powers. The 1903–4 British Indian military expedition into Tibet had granted extraterritorial rights to British India, including the right to place a small military contingent there while placing limits on Chinese military presence in that region. Consequently, the "repossession" of Tibet became linked with reversing China's national humiliation. In the Chinese worldview, the repossession of Tibet, reversing national humiliation, and reclaiming its lost great power status in Asia were all interlinked. Consequently, a year after proclaiming the creation of the PRC, Mao launched the military invasion of Tibet in 1950 and legitimized this military annexation of Tibet after signing the 17–Point Agreement with the Dalai Lama.[80]

A discussion of the ambiguous international status of Tibet through its history is beyond the scope of this study.[81] Suffice it to say here that in spite of the official Chinese claim that Tibet has been an integral part of China since the Yuan Dynasty (1279–1368), it was only the Manchu rulers of the Qing Dynasty (1644–1911) who managed to politically and militarily control Tibet. However, even their direct control of Tibet's political and military affairs lasted for only eight decades at best—from 1720 when the Qing sent a military expedition into Tibet in response to the Zungharian (a Mongol tribe) invasion of Tibet until the White Lotus Rebellion (1796–1804), which marked the beginning of the decline of the Qing. In spite of this, a Qing representative known as the Amban and a small Qing military contingent were stationed in Lhasa from 1720 until the formal collapse of the Qing in 1911.[82] After the collapse of the Qing Dynasty, Tibet formally declared its independence in 1913.[83]

The Salience of Tibet for India The noted Indian strategist K. M. Panikkar made a prescient observation around the time of India's independence in 1947. He pointed out that the Himalayas would not be able to serve as India's protective barriers in the north. He further added:

> The essential point about the Himalayas is not their width of 150 miles, but the [Tibetan] plateau behind it, which in itself is at an elevation of about 15000 feet and is guarded on all four sides by high mountains. In fact, the vast barrier upland behind the Himalayas provides the most significant defense in depth imaginable. . . . The creation of a broader no man's land on both sides of the Himalayas will give to the Indian peninsula sufficient area for the development of her defence potential free from interference.[84]

Panikkar's thoughts on Indian defense assume additional importance for he served as India's ambassador to Nationalist China and then to the PRC from 1948–52. Furthermore, this conception of Indian strategic defense needs to be seen in the context of the geostrategy of the British Raj, which was inherited and modified by the leaders of independent India.[85]

Broadly speaking, the British policy of defending their Indian empire was implicitly based on the belief that any hostile and well-armed subcontinental power posed an existential threat to the British Raj. Furthermore, the British believed that this threat could prove even more serious in the event that this hostile subcontinental power allied with an extraregional power. In order to defend the core of their Indian empire, the British developed a security system of "concentric rings."[86] In the "Inner Ring," which was more or less coterminous with the subcontinent, the British had adopted a policy of political absorption and strategic domination in order to achieve paramountcy. Thus the British annexed Sindh and Punjab in the 1840s and adopted a system of protectorate relationships with the Himalayan states of Nepal, Bhutan, and Sikkim. In the "Outer Ring"—Iran, Afghanistan, Siam (Thailand), and Tibet—the British created a *cordon sanitaire* of "buffer states" along the periphery of the subcontinent to exclude other powers from it, particularly Russia and France, but also China. Independent India inherited this notion of security from the British Raj. It was believed that only this would allow independent India to develop economically and militarily, thus enabling India to project its power in Asia and beyond.[87]

The task for independent India vis-à-vis Tibet became the maintenance of Tibet's status as a buffer state between India and China at best, or the maintenance of Tibetan autonomy with minimal Chinese military presence in that region at the very least. The Indian policy as stated by the then Indian ambassador at Nanjing, K. P. S. Menon,[88] was to "support the independence of Tibet, subject to the suzerainty of China."[89] According to Menon, who was following the policy set by Nehru, independent India had inherited this policy from British India. However, the British had never supported Tibetan independence. According to British policy, Tibet was under the suzerainty of China. "*Suzerainty* implied a low level of Chinese administrative and military presence and a high level of both Tibetan *autonomy* and British Indian influence in Tibet."[90] Moreover, Menon had explained to the Chinese that India had no intentions of subverting China, whether in Tibet or elsewhere, especially since China was facing great difficulties as a consequence of its civil war.[91] Therefore, even as Menon used the term "independence" for Tibet in his autobiography, as noted above, it is possible that he had in fact meant Tibetan "autonomy" as well as Indian influence in that region.

The stage was now set for Sino-Indian positional rivalry that centered around the status of Tibet. For the Chinese, the "repossession" of Tibet was important for the defense of their southwestern frontier and to end their national humiliation before reemerging as a great power. For the Indians, the maintenance of Tibet as a genuine "buffer state" or at least an autonomous region with minimal Chinese military presence was deemed essential to develop economically and militarily in order to project power in Asia and beyond.

The Ambiguous Status of Tibet and the Sino-Indian Positional Rivalry

Fearing hostile Chinese intentions, the Tibetans had approached the British government in March 1947 with a request for a substantial amount of arms and ammunition. With a few exceptions, the British government and the interim government of India approved and supplied these arms to Tibet.[92] Nehru had held the portfolio of the vice president of the interim government of India, and he was also the member in charge of foreign affairs. The supply of arms and ammunition to Tibet could not have taken place without his explicit approval. India supplied a modest amount of arms and ammunition to Tibet throughout the late 1940s, even after its independence (on August 15, 1947), and also dispatched a few Indian officers to train Tibetan soldiers.[93]

It was widely believed in India that moral and diplomatic support coupled with a modest amount of Indian military aid and Tibet's forbidding terrain would enable the Tibetans to maintain their autonomy vis-à-vis China (especially since China was economically devastated as a consequence of its civil war).[94] In July 1947, the British government as well as the interim government of India made formal statements to the Tibetans assuring them that the British rights and obligations under the existing treaties with Tibet would devolve upon the successor government of India with the transfer of power and Indian independence.[95] From the Indian point of view, this covered three specific agreements. The first one was a tripartite agreement between British India, Tibet, and China which was negotiated and signed in Simla in 1913–14. This agreement divided Tibet into "inner" and "outer" regions. Outer Tibet was to retain complete autonomy under a nominal Chinese suzerainty. Furthermore, the Tibetan government of Inner Tibet was allowed complete control in all matters pertaining to religious institutions. The Chinese were not to convert "outer" Tibet into a province of China and were only allowed a limited military presence there. British India was also allowed to station a small number of troops there. In other words, this agreement was about the nature of the relationship between Tibet and China, and it was guaranteed by British India. Not surprisingly, Nationalist China and later the PRC refused to accept it. In addition to this tripartite agreement, British India signed two agreements with Tibet alone in Simla in 1914. The first of these granted Britain extraterritorial trading rights in Tibet, while the second of these marked the boundary between British India and Tibet to the east of Bhutan. This boundary came to be known as the McMahon Line.[96] After independence, India assured the Tibetans that the British Indian policy of recognizing Tibetan autonomy under Chinese suzerainty would continue.

In the months preceding Indian independence, Nehru had authorized the Indian Council of World Affairs to organize an "unofficial" Asian Relations Conference (ARC) in New Delhi. The ARC, which ran from March 23 through April 12, 1947, was the first regional gathering of countries in Asia. It was a gathering of more than two hundred delegates from thirty countries and colonial territories from all over Asia—South Asia, Southeast Asia, (Soviet) Central Asia, West Asia (or the Middle East), and East Asia—and included separate delegations from both Tibet and China.[97] The Chinese were particularly unhappy with New Delhi's decision to host and organize the ARC.

Nationalist China protested against Tibetan participation at the ARC, suspected Indian "ulterior motives" behind extending this invitation to Tibet, and resented India's extension of formal government reception to the 1947 trade delegation from Tibet.[98] Furthermore, they had "no wish to be tied to an organization in which India was predominant. Their tactics at the conference were to keep India's status within bounds."[99] China also complained about India's retention of Hugh Richardson, the British Indian head of the mission at Lhasa, as the head of the mission of independent India there.[100] India responded by saying that the extraordinary circumstances surrounding its independence, partition, and the accession of the princely states had necessitated this. However, it is indeed notable that Richardson was the only British citizen to be retained in an Indian mission abroad after independence.

In September 1949, the Chinese press complained against "Indian and Anglo-American Imperialism" and its designs for annexation of Tibet.[101] This was perhaps in response to the expulsion of the representatives of Nationalist China from Lhasa in July 1949. Claiming that the communists had infiltrated the Chinese mission in Lhasa, the Tibetan authorities used this as a pretext to take advantage of the confusion in China to rid itself of even symbolic Chinese control. However, in the Chinese view, Richardson, the British officer heading independent India's mission was complicit in this Tibetan policy.[102] Not surprisingly, Richardson has denied this charge.[103] While India had made a conscious decision not to seek help from Britain or America for its policies toward Tibet, the Chinese had no way of knowing this.[104] To preempt any possible Indian designs on Tibet with or without Anglo-American help, Mao announced the "liberation" of Tibet on January 1, 1950, and legitimized it by signing the 17–Point Agreement with the representatives of the Dalai Lama in March 1951.

The Ambiguous Status of Tibet and the Sino-Indian Spatial Rivalry India felt sustained Chinese political and military power for the first time along its northern border with the Chinese invasion of Tibet in 1950–51.[105] India was forced to respond to the Chinese occupation of Tibet from a position of military weakness. India's Deputy Prime Minister Patel urged Nehru to rethink India's China policy in the face of China's military conquest of Tibet.[106] Nehru replied by arguing that Pakistan was India's "major possible enemy" and that India could not have "two possible enemies" on either side.[107] India could take on the Chinese challenge only by abandoning its policy of nonalignment, which was not acceptable to Nehru.[108]

Furthermore, on the eve of India's independence, Nehru had articulated an "Asian Monroe Doctrine," that is, the complete disappearance of Western militaries from Asia, for which cooperation with China was deemed essential.[109] In addition to this, an inchoate India-centered pan-Asianism was central to Nehru's approach to Asia. "India will . . . develop as the centre of economic and political activity in the Indian Ocean area, in South-East Asia and right up to the Middle East,"[110] wrote Nehru prior to India's independence.

Nehru envisioned India playing a "leading role in the revival of Asia,"[111] and at the same time, he thought that India-China collaboration was essential for the resurgence of Asia.[112]

Consequently, Nehru replied to Patel saying that "the real protection" that India should seek "is some kind of understanding with China."[113] According to Ganguly, Nehru adopted a policy of "conciliation and appeasement" to respond to the Chinese occupation of Tibet—although "appeasement" in its pre-Munich sense, which meant that states "could accommodate the legitimate demands of their rivals without compromising their own vital interests."[114] Nehru was of the impression that a muted Indian response would limit the nature of Chinese military presence in Tibet and guarantee it considerable internal autonomy. Furthermore, Nehru believed that Tibet's harsh terrain (and the logistical and financial difficulties that it would impose) would in itself limit the nature of Chinese military presence in Tibet. Consequently, it would ensure India's basic interest of minimizing Chinese military presence along its northern frontier. Nehru "sacrificed Tibet for the sake of Sino-Indian friendship. . . . This friendship policy was expected to neutralize the security threat from the PLA stationed in Tibet, as well as enhance Asian solidarity,"[115] while allowing India to maintain its policy of nonalignment.

Subsequently, India and China signed an agreement in 1954 in which India recognized Chinese sovereignty in Tibet. This agreement became famous as the Five Principles of Peaceful Coexistence, or *Panchshila*.[116] Within months after the signing of this agreement, India relinquished its special rights in Tibet—the stationing of a small garrison of troops and extraterritorial trading rights—which it had inherited from the British Raj. However, the agreement, while making reference to the "Tibet Region of China," said nothing about Tibet's autonomy under Chinese rule. India did not extract any explicit concessions from the Chinese, for Nehru believed that this act of good faith on the part of the Indians would remove all of China's suspicions regarding Indian intentions and promote good bilateral relations. However, Nehru did believe that genuine Tibetan autonomy and the continuation of the border agreements between British India and Tibet were implied by the 1954 "gentleman's deal" struck with Zhou Enlai's China.[117]

However, the Chinese soon made it clear that Tibet did not have the authority to enter into treaties with foreign powers, as it had always been a part of China. At the level of broad principles, the acceptance of an agreement signed between Tibet and a foreign power would have highlighted the fiction of China's historical claim over Tibet. China specifically rejected the 1913–14 Simla Agreement signed between British India and Tibet (but only initialed by the Chinese) because it allowed an external party—India—to guarantee the nature of the relationship between Tibet and China (including the boundary between "inner" and "outer" Tibet), while placing specific limits on the nature of Chinese military presence in "outer" Tibet. As noted, China was not a party to the boundary agreement between British India and Tibet. In any case, that boundary agreement only covered the region east of Bhutan. The Tibet-India border in the western regions, particularly between Kashmir and Tibet, and the status of Aksai Chin, was ambiguous.[118] As such, the entire Sino-Indian border came under question in the early 1950s.

However, Nehru was not completely naïve in responding to the Chinese occupation of Tibet in 1951. Soon after the invasion of Tibet, China realized that control over the Aksai Chin region in the western sector was very important for the consolidation of its rule in Tibet.[119] There were only three main routes from China into Tibet—the northern route from Qinghai, the eastern route from Sichuan, and the western route from Xinjiang. Terrain and weather conspired against China in effectively reaching Tibet via the first two routes. The western route, in spite of its many difficulties, was the only route that was open throughout the year, in winter as well as the monsoon. However, this route traversed the Aksai Chin region. "Control of Aksai Chin was thus essential to Chinese control of western Tibet and very important to its control over all of Tibet."[120]

It is highly plausible that Nehru was aware of the importance of Aksai Chin for Chinese control over Tibet as well as China's road-building activities linking Xinjiang and Tibet through this region. The Indian Intelligence Bureau (IB) and army had established a joint check post in the Ladakh region at Panamik/Shyok immediately after the fall of Xinjiang to the PLA in September 1949, and it also established an intelligence post in Leh "to collect information about what was happening on the borders in Sinkiang [Xinjiang]."[121] Furthermore, at the request of the IB, the Indian government established twenty-one more check posts all along the Indo-Tibetan frontier between mid-1950 and early 1951 to safeguard India's northern frontiers and to collect vital intelligence information.[122] Interestingly, the Indian government made the decision about the location of the boundary in the western sector only in 1953.[123] The Ardagh-Johnson line, which included Aksai Chin, was chosen as it was thought to be the extent of the precolonial Dogra kingdom in Kashmir. Garver speculates that Nehru chose the Ardagh-Johnson line as he may have been of the opinion that once China recognized the diplomatic hurdles that this would create in its plans to integrate Tibet (coupled with its equally formidable climate), China would station a limited number of PLA troops there. This would automatically assure Tibet's internal autonomy and promote Indian security.[124]

It is equally plausible that the decision to bolster India's control in Tawang (in the eastern sector) was made after similar calculations. According to Hoffman, "The . . . government in India annexed the town and monastery of Tawang [south of the McMahon Line] in February 1951, possibly in response to China's actions [in Tibet] in 1950."[125] To be sure, Tawang was already a part of British India as per the 1913–14 Simla Agreement. However, independent India had not consolidated its position there until early 1951.[126] From India's perspective, the possession of Tawang was deemed crucial for the defense of northeastern India as the southern Himalayan slopes provided tactical offensive advantages to the Chinese. Indian control of this region was expected to increase the cost of any Chinese military adventurism.[127]

The military advantage of controlling Tawang vis-à-vis India was not lost on the Chinese, and China claimed Tawang and the region that now corresponds with the Indian state of Arunachal Pradesh (of which Tawang is a part). China claimed that Tawang was historically controlled by Tibet and as such was a part of China. China further claimed that since the sixth Dalai Lama was born in Tawang, it should be rightfully returned to Tibet (and hence, China). Furthermore, it is believed that the fertile tract of Tawang can support a third of Tibet's economy.[128] Feeding the Tibetan population and the PLA troops based there is a huge concern for China. In fact, in the early 1950s when the PLA was consolidating China's control over Tibet, food and other essential goods were being imported into Tibet from India.[129]

The 1959 Tibetan Revolt and the Escalation of the Sino-Indian Rivalry

The 17–Point Agreement that legitimized Chinese military annexation of Tibet granted a substantial degree of genuine autonomy to Tibet.[130] As per the agreement it was decided that the CCP would not alter Tibet's existing political system. The CCP also agreed not to interfere in the religious affairs of the Tibetan people; not to alter the status, function, and powers of the Dalai Lama; and to guarantee linguistic rights to the Tibetan people. And finally, the CCP agreed that the various social and economic "reforms" that it was carrying out in the rest of China, would be carried out in Tibet in accordance with the wishes of the Tibetan people (and leaders) and after consultation with them. In the immediate aftermath of its implementation, the CCP respected these commitments.

However, the presence of PLA troops in Tibet began to affect the economy of Tibet. "The burden of provisioning an occupying army of more than 10,000 men inevitably led to food shortages."[131] The CCP also tried to win over the local government by paying them an additional monthly salary. Both of these factors led to massive inflation, "and Tibetans were soon on the brink of starvation."[132]

The other major issue was the reorganization of Tibet. In this regard it should be noted that there is a difference between "ethnographic Tibet" (or Inner Tibet that includes the ethnic Tibetan regions of Kham and Amdo that were incorporated into the Chinese provinces of Qinghai, Sichuan, Yunnan, and Gansu), and "political Tibet" (Outer Tibet) that comprises the region under the Dalai Lama's jurisdiction. According to the Tibetan interpretation of the 17–Point Agreement, the religious freedoms that were promised were also applicable to "ethnographic Tibet." Furthermore, the CCP's social and economic "democratic reforms" were not to be carried out in "ethnographic Tibet." However, for the CCP, Tibet meant "political Tibet."[133]

As a consequence of the reforms that were implemented in "ethnographic Tibet," in the mid-1950s, the Chinese suppressed religious activity in these regions, implemented a draconian land-reform program, forced ethnic Tibetans (including monks) into manual labor and reeducation programs, and brought all economic and social activity in those regions under the control of the Communist Party. When that led to small insurgencies and local revolts, the CCP responded militarily, including the bombing of monasteries where a large number of Tibetans had taken refuge.[134] The intensity of these reforms and the CCP's brutality increased further after the launch of the "Great Leap Forward" in 1958. This led to the flow of a large number of refugees into "political Tibet" and all the Tibetan regions of China became volatile.[135] The political situation in Lhasa and Tibet was already very tense when the rumor that PLA was trying to kidnap the Dalai Lama resulted in a full-blown rebellion against the Chinese in Lhasa in March 1959.[136]

India's Decision to Escalate the Rivalry As a consequence of China's "reforms" and the military crackdown that followed it, any semblance of

Tibetan autonomy as promised by the 17–Point Agreement and actually implemented in the early 1950s "was destroyed" by late 1958 and early 1959.[137] Moreover, until the late 1950s, the defense of the Tibetan-Indian frontier was the responsibility of the small Tibetan army (even after 1951), with the PLA guarding only the key strategic and communication nodes. However, the PLA presence in Tibet increased dramatically as a consequence of the Lhasa revolt, and the PLA troops were also deployed in large numbers along the Tibetan-Indian frontiers to pursue Tibetan rebels fleeing to India.[138] With the disappearance of Tibetan autonomy and the massive increase in the number of PLA troops in Tibet, India's threat environment deteriorated significantly.

The exact reason why Nehru granted asylum to the Dalai Lama is more difficult to gauge in the absence of declassification of the relevant reports by the Indian government. However, the motivation can be inferred through careful reasoning and the elimination of rival explanations. To begin with, public opinion seems to have played no role in the decision to grant asylum to the Dalai Lama. The Dalai Lama crossed over into India only after it was confirmed by the Tibetans that Nehru was prepared to grant asylum to him.[139] There was no demand in the media or even the Indian Parliament to extend asylum to the Dalai Lama before he crossed over. The Dalai Lama's formal request to the Indian government for political asylum in India came via the United States.[140] From the available evidence it seems like the decision was made by executive fiat, and the news of the Dalai Lama's escape into India was simply broadcast on the All India Radio.[141] That Indian public opinion, including the nonelite public opinion, became extremely anti-Chinese (especially after the 1959 rebellion in Lhasa) at what they saw as China's brutal destruction of Tibet's India-inspired culture only seemed to legitimize Nehru's decision.

In his correspondence with the British prime ministers Anthony Eden and Harold Macmillan in the 1950s, Nehru had informed them that since China had itself granted asylum to a Nepali communist leader, it was unlikely to perceive India's extension of asylum to the Dalai Lama as an unfriendly act, as granting asylum was a part of accepted international behavior.[142] However, this argument is less than convincing and seems like a mere diplomatic ruse at a closer examination. Surely, a world statesman like Nehru understood the importance of the Dalai Lama for the Tibetan cause was in no way comparable to a Nepalese communist. Unlike the Nepalese communist, the Dalai Lama was a symbol of Tibet with implications for China's "unity," including sovereignty and territorial integrity. In his personal assessment, Nehru could not have missed this point.

Furthermore, when it seemed like the Dalai Lama would continue staying back in India in 1956–57, when he went there to participate in the 2,500th anniversary of the birth of the Buddha, Nehru informed Zhou Enlai who in turn flew to India in November 1956 and January 1957 to persuade the Dalai Lama to return. Nehru used these occasions to talk to Zhou about Tibetan autonomy and believed that he had obtained such a commitment from him. Nehru also tried to persuade the Dalai Lama that the Tibetan cause would be better served if he returned to Lhasa.[143] Since the situation in Tibet in 1956–57 had not deteriorated like it would in a little over two years' time as a consequence of China's "reforms," it can be inferred that Nehru felt comfortable in asking the Dalai Lama to leave. At the same time it must also be noted that Nehru's talks with Zhou also indicate that he seemed comfortable playing the role of an interlocutor between Tibet and China to promote the former's autonomy (and India's defense)—a role reminiscent of the British Raj's efforts to act as an interlocutor between Tibet and China.

Therefore, it can be reasonably deduced that when the situation in Tibet deteriorated significantly after the 1959 revolt, Nehru saw no option but to use the Dalai Lama as a bargaining chip in any future negotiations with China. It seems reasonable to assume that Nehru granted asylum to the Dalai Lama to ensconce himself as an interlocutor between Tibet and China in order to secure India's defense interests in any future agreement between them. In other words, once Nehru believed that the situation in Tibet had changed for the worse, he had no choice but to up the ante by granting refuge to the Dalai Lama, who crossed the Indo-Tibetan border on March 30, 1959.

China's Decision to Escalate the Rivalry On the Chinese side, senior leaders including Mao, Zhou, and Deng believed that the Indian government and Nehru in particular were involved in the 1959 revolt in Lhasa.[144] Perhaps the Chinese leadership believed so because the Indian consul-general in Lhasa had "met with the Tibetan demonstrators at the start of the uprising."[145] However, according to the available evidence, Nehru and India did not play any role in causing the 1959 revolt in Lhasa.[146] According to Zhou, India's involvement was revealed by the fact that the "commanding center of the rebellion" had been established "in Kalimpong on Indian territory."[147] Zhou further believed that Nehru's ultimate goal was to establish a buffer zone in Tibet and to force the PLA to withdraw from Tibet.[148]

The Chinese were further suspicious because they believed that the Indians and the Americans were collaborating with the Tibetans to undermine China's authority in that region. From the mid-1950s onward, the U.S. Central Intelligence Agency began aiding Tibetan resistance against the Chinese.[149] U.S. airplanes were being used for parachute drops of guns, ammunition, and U.S.-trained Tibetan guerilla fighters into Tibet via Indian air space.[150] While India was not directly involved with CIA-led activities in Tibet at this time; New Delhi certainly turned a blind eye to American activities.[151]

The Chinese side grew more alarmed when the Dalai Lama's statement issued from Tezpur in India on April 18, 1959, nearly called for Tibetan independence after complaining that the 17–Point Agreement had been signed under duress by the Tibetans. He further added that he was in India out of his own free will.[152] In response, while addressing the Politburo on April 25, 1959, Mao said that China would begin a "counteroffensive against India's anti-China activities," and he further added that China "would carry this struggle through to the end."[153]

In other words, the Chinese escalated the rivalry because they were of the opinion that India had caused the deterioration in the Chinese threat environment by instigating the events in Tibet as the Indians wished to create a buffer zone there. This was perceived all the more threatening because India was receiving help from the Americans (at least in Chinese perceptions). Sino-Indian relations deteriorated as both sides had decided to up the ante. On May 4, 1959, Zhou announced that the Chinese troops "had reached the borders" with India to "seal" and "trap" the Tibetan rebels.[154]

However, since the border between India and China was not defined, it was bound to create more problems. Nehru had to respond to China's increased military presence along India's northern frontier and to defend what was perceived to be Indian territory. This further escalated the tensions between the two countries when their troops clashed twice along their ill-defined borders—in Longju in the eastern sector in August 1959 when one Indian soldier was killed and another was seriously injured, and at Kongka Pass in the western sector in October 1959, when ten soldiers from the Indian side and one from the Chinese side were killed while several others were seriously injured.[155]

Sino-Indian Relations After the 1959 Tibetan Uprising

The Indian and Chinese decision to escalate their rivalry in 1959 was a function of their mutual threat perception vis-à-vis one another and was not influenced by domestic politics as such. Their relations continued to deteriorate after 1959. Furthermore, the exigencies of domestic politics became significant after 1959, especially on the Indian side. Nehru consistently began to inform the Indian Parliament about the state of Sino-Indian relations only after Zhou's September 8, 1959, letter to him in which Zhou openly claimed that the entire Sino-Indian border was unmarked and also laid claim to forty thousand square miles of territory under Indian control.[156] India imposed a host of economic sanctions on Tibet in response to the brutal Chinese repression there.[157] However, Beijing interpreted this as Indian duplicity and an act of meddling in China's internal affairs. In the following period, talks between India and China to resolve their border dispute did not produce any results. Indian elite and public opinion had become extremely anti-Chinese, and in an attempt to bolster Indian claims in Aksai Chin, the Indian government formulated what came to be called the "forward policy" in Ladakh.[158] Between July 1961 and September 1962, India sent a small number of troops to the disputed area around Ladakh.[159] According to Ganguly, "The forward policy amounted to a strategy of compellence—namely, an effort to force an adversary to undo the consequences of a hostile act."[160] However, the Indian military was ill prepared to actually implement such a strategy for the troops in and around Ladakh were lightly armed with insufficient firepower and poor supply and logistics lines.

The Sino-Indian border war began on October 20, 1962, when PLA forces simultaneously attacked Indian positions in both the eastern and the western sectors.[161] The Chinese decision to wage war was a product of two factors.[162] First, the Chinese leadership misperceived India's policy toward Tibet. While India had accepted Chinese sovereignty in Tibet, New Delhi was interested in ensuring internal autonomy for Tibet. However, the Chinese believed that India was interested in restoring the pre-1949 status of Tibet. Second, the Chinese wanted to punish Indian "aggression" against Chinese territory. In other words, the Chinese wanted to respond to India's forward policy. In both the eastern sector and Ladakh, the Chinese troops reached the positions that Beijing had claimed. China declared a unilateral ceasefire on November 21, 1962, and withdrew its forces to their prewar positions in the eastern sector. However, they came to occupy their stated position in Aksai Chin in Ladakh. Furthermore, the Chinese warned the Indians that any Indian attempts to dislodge the Chinese troops from the western sector would be met with a swift Chinese attack.[163]

In the aftermath of the war, India's threat environment vis-à-vis China permanently changed with the militarization of Tibet. The Sino-Indian border war had come as a huge shock to the Indian political and strategic communities. "The issue of military reverses at the hands of China went beyond military preparedness to India's conceptual approach to international affairs."[164] The war with China proved that India needed military help from external powers to meet the Chinese military challenge. India sought and received military assistance from the United States and the UK, but that support proved short-lived and was suspended after the 1965 Indo-Pakistani war. India's security environment further deteriorated after China conducted its first nuclear test on October 16, 1964, in Lop Nur.[165] In its wake, India sought a nuclear guarantee from the great powers, but this effort proved to be fruitless.[166] In its aftermath, Prime Minister Indira Gandhi authorized India's Subterranean Nuclear Explosions Project, which culminated in India's first nuclear test in 1974.[167]

Although the Western powers proved unreliable suppliers of advanced military technology, India was able to forge a strong defense-industrial partnership with the Soviet Union. The Soviet Union offered India advanced technology under financial terms favorable to New Delhi. It offered India technology through licensed production, agreed to payments under barter arrangements principally through commodities, provided New Delhi with cheap long-term credit agreements to pay for these systems, and also entered into rupee-based trade arrangements, manipulating the rupee-ruble exchange rate to achieve favorable trade balances for India.[168] India forged a strategic relationship with the former Soviet Union to balance China as well as to procure advanced military hardware. This culminated in the 1971 Treaty of Peace, Friendship, and Cooperation between India and the former Soviet Union. Signed on the eve of the 1971 Bangladesh war, the 1971 treaty with the Soviet Union was India's answer to the emerging entente between the United States, Pakistan, and China.[169]

In the meanwhile, China had dramatically improved its relations with India's subcontinental rival, Pakistan. In May 1962, even before the Sino-Indian border war, China and Pakistan agreed to demarcate their boundaries.[170] In fact, while the Sino-Indian border war was underway, China and Pakistan were negotiating the exact location of their boundaries. The agreement was announced in May 1963. China received 1,050 square miles from Pakistan in exchange for 750 square miles of its own territory.[171] India was particularly irked that Pakistan had ceded away parts of a region that was a disputed territory between India and Pakistan. China also threatened to open a second front against India during the 1965 and 1971 Indo-Pakistani wars. After India's 1974 nuclear test, Pakistan sought China's help with its nuclear and missile programs that took off in earnest in the early 1980s.[172] "China's cooperative relationship with Pakistan is arguably *the most* stable and durable element in China's foreign relations."[173]

After the 1962 war, India and China had withdrawn their ambassadors, but diplomatic relations were never fully severed. Full diplomatic links with China were restored in 1976 under Prime Minister Indira Gandhi's initiative in an attempt to lessen political tensions with Beijing after India absorbed Sikkim.[174] This was followed by a change of government in New Delhi after Indira Gandhi was ousted in the 1977 general elections. Atal Bihari Vajpayee, the foreign minister of the new Janata Party coalition government, visited China in 1979 in an attempt to improve ties. Vajpayee was the senior-most Indian dignitary to visit China since Vice President Sarvepalli Radhakrishnan's visit to Beijing in 1958. However, during Vajpayee's visit, China attacked Vietnam, which was India's communist friend in Southeast Asia. Furthermore, the Chinese leader Deng Xiaoping spoke of teaching Vietnam a "lesson" just as China had done to India in 1962. As a consequence, Vajpayee cut short his visit and returned to India.

A number of factors in the 1980s further complicated Sino-Indian ties. In 1984, the seizure of key positions by Indian soldiers in the Siachen Glacier—a disputed region between India and Pakistan—worried Chinese strategists.[175] In 1978, China and Pakistan had announced the opening of the Karakoram Highway linking the two countries across their Himalayan borderlands. This was the main supply route connecting these two countries. Furthermore, by providing China access to the Gilgit region in Pakistan's Northern Areas, it also gave China the access to monitor any Indian attempt to cut the lines of communication between Xinjiang and Tibet through the Aksai Chin region.[176] However, the Indian position in Siachen now gave India the ability to isolate Pakistan from mainland China "within a few hours, with little or no warning."[177]

Two years later, in December 1986, India granted full statehood to Arunachal Pradesh (the region in the eastern sector that was claimed by China). Although this was simply a "logical evolution of [Indian] administrative process," the Chinese saw this as a "possible legal erosion to their claim."[178] Sino-Indian forces clashed briefly in 1986 in the Sumdorong Chu Valley in Arunachal Pradesh after the Indians claimed that the PLA had built a helipad at a place called Wandung in the valley. The mobilization of forces by both sides over the next year or so sparked "fears of a second China-India war."[179]

In 1986–87, under the leadership of the maverick Indian General K. Sundarji, India launched an exercise in armed diplomacy that combined air and land-based operations along the disputed border with China along the eastern sector. Code-named Operation Chequerboard, its mission was to get a sense of China's response as well as that of the United States and the former Soviet Union. This mock exercise that simulated a limited war in the McMahon Line area had heightened tensions along the Sino-Indian border as close to four hundred thousand troops had amassed from both the sides along this border at its peak.[180] However, the exercise was quickly terminated under mounting international pressure.[181] But by then, the Indian air force had estimated that its kill ratio in a conflict with China in this region was ten to one (in India's favor).[182] The overall results of this exercise convinced the Indian government "of its capability to successfully decide any regional confrontation" with China.[183] It was against this politico-military background in Sino-Indian relations when the riots and revolts erupted in Tibet in late 1987.

The 1987–1989 *Tibetan Revolts and the De-escalation of the Sino-Indian Rivalry*

A number of peaceful demonstrations that began in Lhasa from late 1987 onward were suppressed by force by the CCP.[184] There is little or no evidence that the protests that erupted in Lhasa in late 1987 after decades of calm were manipulated by Tibetan leaders in exile in India or elsewhere. In fact, it seems like the Tibetan protestors were angered by the official media attacks by the CCP on the Dalai Lama in September 1987.[185] While addressing the U.S. Congress in September 1987, the Dalai Lama's Five-Point Plan for Tibet called for the transformation of Tibet into a "zone of peace."[186] In response to this proposal, the Chinese launched a vicious attack in their official media against the Dalai Lama for "internationalization of the Tibetan issue" and for trying to seek independence.[187]

More importantly, the Chinese government believed that the Dalai Lama's speech in Washington was an outcome of Indian foreign policy decisions.[188] After all, apart from Tibet, India would have been the only other country to benefit from the removal of PLA troops from Tibet as it transformed into a "zone of peace." While there is some evidence to indicate that India was aware that the Dalai Lama's trip to Washington would be different from his other trips outside India, it is not clear if the Indians were aware of what the Dalai Lama was about to propose.[189] Moreover, there is no evidence at all to indicate that it was the Indians who designed this proposal.

Later, in June 1988, the Dalai Lama put forward a "new proposal" in Strasbourg, France, where he built upon his "zone of peace" proposal. The Dalai Lama gave up the cause of Tibet's independence in this proposal in exchange for genuine political autonomy for Tibet and with a restricted number of PLA military installations in Tibet. However, he added that Tibet's foreign policy would be determined by China under this arrangement.[190] This caused a lot of resentment in Tibet who felt betrayed that the Tibetan cause of independence was being given up.

The confusion with the Dalai Lama's proposals in the United States and Europe notwithstanding, the protest that began in Tibet in late 1987 was in direct response to them. The Tibetan protestors felt that their cause was finally gathering international momentum. However, the Dalai Lama received no political or military support from the West. Furthermore, the Chinese made it abundantly clear that it would not accept Tibet's "independence, semi-independence, or even independence in a disguised form."[191] Consequently, they brutally repressed all protests in Tibet. Finally, when the protests seemed to be getting out of hand, the CCP responded by declaring martial law in Tibet in March 1989.

Indian Decision to De-escalate the Rivalry First of all, it must be noted that unlike the 1959 Tibetan revolt that ended any remnants of Tibetan autonomy, the wave of protests that began in Tibet in 1987 did not alter India's threat environment. India's threat environment had been altered a few decades ago as a consequence of the massive PLA presence in Tibet since 1959 (for Tibet had enjoyed a genuine degree of autonomy before that). Given that there had been the militarization of Tibet after 1959 (and especially after 1962), India's threat environment remained more or less unchanged since then, even after 1987. Secondly, the protests, while numerous, were mostly small in scale. Therefore, India did not feel that its security environment vis-à-vis China was deteriorating in 1987.

In spite of this, soon after the eruption of riots in Tibet, India declared that it would not exploit the situation in Tibet. Furthermore, India restrained the activities of Tibetan exiles within its border. And finally, unlike 1959, when India welcomed thousands of refugees from Tibet, the Indian army took precautions in 1987 in order to prevent the arrival of any refugees.[192] Finally, Rajiv

Gandhi made a landmark trip to China in December 1988, the first such visit by an Indian prime minister since 1954, to break the impasse between these Asian giants.

What factors prompted India to de-escalate the rivalry? While India's threat environment remained unchanged during this period, the balance of military capabilities seemed to favor India as indicated by India's gains in Siachen and from the results of Operation Chequerboard as discussed above. However, the decision to use force is not dictated by military capabilities alone, but by the political objectives. While India clearly had robust military capabilities by the late 1980s (especially when compared to 1962) and could successfully withstand a Chinese military attack, India had no clear political and military objectives as far as the offensive use of force against China was concerned. The late 1980s further saw the emergence of India as a regional power with military interventions in Sri Lanka and the Maldives.[193] At the same time, Operation Brasstacks had caused a serious war-scare with Pakistan. As such, India's military resources were seriously stretched, and it made sense to de-escalate the Sino-Indian rivalry, especially since it did not offer a military solution.

Moreover, as an organization, the military or its leaders seem not to have exercised any influence either. In 1986, General Sundarji had announced to Prime Minister Gandhi's Political Affairs Committee that India could take on both China and Pakistan. However, Natwar Singh, the minister of state for external affairs, intervened and convinced the prime minister that war with China was not a realistic option.[194] It was clear to India's political decision-makers that India could not unilaterally use its armed forces to settle the boundary issue with China or to guarantee Tibetan autonomy.[195] However, India's strong military capabilities meant that India extended a warm hand to China from what it perceived to be a position of military strength.

Furthermore, an important reason why India decided to de-escalate its rivalry with China seems to be a consequence of the loss of unqualified Soviet support that it had received in its relations with China. As will be discussed later, this was also the period of Sino-Soviet rapprochement. The loss of Soviet support became apparent during the 1986 Sumdorong Chu incident mentioned above when the Soviet press made absolutely no statement about the incident.[196] Later, when the Soviet leader Mikhail Gorbachev traveled to India in 1986, he refused to side with India in its conflict with China.[197] Finally, during his visit to Delhi a month before Rajiv Gandhi's trip to China, Gorbachev stressed the common interests of the three states.[198] This was the clearest sign that India was losing the strong diplomatic and military support that it had received from the Soviets since 1971 in New Delhi's competition with Beijing.

Public opinion in India does not seem to have played any role in influencing India's decision to warm up to Beijing. After all, it has been demonstrated that the government (and the Congress Party) had tried to influence public opinion through the media to convince the Indian masses that it was a wise strategy to normalize relations with Beijing. It was stressed in the media coverage that even as the border issue would not be resolved any time soon, the visit would help set the guiding principles to form the basis of a future settlement.[199] Indeed, Gandhi's visit led to the creation of the Joint Working Group (JWG) to work on a resolution of their border dispute. Clearly, the decision to de-escalate had already been made, and the media was used in a fashion as is typical in the elite model.

China's Decision to De-escalate the Rivalry While China initially suspected an Indian hand behind the Dalai Lama's proposals that were spelt out in the United States and Europe, India's distancing itself from the issue as well as curbing the activities of its Tibetan exiles in addition to sealing its borders with Tibet almost as soon as the riots broke out in Tibet convinced the Chinese leaders that India was not seeking to exploit the situation. Consequently, China's threat perception vis-à-vis India did not increase with the outbreak of the riots in Tibet in 1987.

The Chinese strategists were certainly aware of India's military gains in Siachen and their impact on the Sino-Indian conflict. However, there is no reason to believe that the Chinese leadership felt that the overall military balance was shifting in India's favor. Speaking to a Janata Party Minister in 1981, Deng had said that India was not a threat by itself "even as you [India] have many more troops on your side of the border than we [China] have on ours."[200] The real threat from India came from the fact that it had been siding with the Soviet Union, China's primary enemy.[201] Indeed, Chinese leaders noted with great satisfaction that the Soviets had not declared the Chinese side responsible for the Sumdorong Chu incident.[202] Soviet force reductions along the Sino-Soviet and Sino-Mongolian frontiers, the acceptance by the Soviets of the main channel of the Amur and Ussuri rivers as the demarcation line for the Sino-Soviet boundary, and the Soviet withdrawal from Afghanistan in the late 1980s led to a major thaw in Sino-Soviet relations. "Deng Xiaoping now hoped that Sino-Soviet rapprochement could accelerate improvements in Sino-Indian relations."[203]

Finally, China was also concerned with other security threats in the late 1980s. China had engaged in some naval clashes with the Vietnamese over the Spratly Islands in 1988.[204] Furthermore, the democratization of Taiwan from 1987 onward was a serious concern for the Chinese. Taiwan democratized under a tacit security guarantee by the United States in an attempt to make itself a more attractive partner of the United States (and the Western world).[205] Given its security preoccupations in East Asia during the period of Sino-Soviet rapprochement and India's growing military capabilities meant that it was a prudent strategy for China to de-escalate its rivalry with India, especially since India was not exploiting the unrest in Tibet.

Conclusion

The aim of this study has been to understand if domestic politics has had any effect on the rivalry dynamics of the Sino-Indian dyad. A two-stepped strategy, starting with Mill's "method of difference" followed by process-tracing to determine the underlying mechanisms of the dynamics of this rivalry was proposed. This chapter applied this two-stepped strategy to study the consequences of instability in Tibet in 1959 and 1987–89 and the Chinese military crackdown that followed it on the Sino-Indian rivalry. It was observed that domestic-level factors played no role in either country in influencing the escalation or de-escalation of this rivalry. However, domestic politics does seem to have played an important role on the Indian side after the *initial* decision to escalate the rivalry was taken in 1959.

Both sides escalated the rivalry in 1959 as a consequence of heightened threat perception vis-à-vis the other. By contrast, the Indian side de-escalated the rivalry in the late 1980s because its threat perception vis-à-vis China remained unchanged at a time when it lost a significant ally, the Soviet Union. However, given its recent military gains, the Indian side de-escalated the rivalry from a position of military confidence. India's military commitments in other parts of South Asia only reinforced this tendency. At the same time, the Chinese side de-escalated its rivalry with India in the late 1980s because the loss of India's Soviet ally was an indirect gain for the Chinese. Sino-Soviet rapprochement and China's security commitments in East Asia only reinforced this tendency.

In other words, domestic political factors like the legislature, governmental bureaucracies, political parties, public opinion and mass media, and the military did not play any independent role in affecting the dynamics of this rivalry. This is because the foreign policy decision-making process was concentrated in the hands of the top leadership in these countries during the period under consideration. In the Chinese case, the decision-making group included the paramount leader and his closest aides, while in the Indian case it included the prime minister and the members of his/her cabinet.

However, the Indian and Chinese political systems have changed substantially since then. In particular, India has entered an era of multiparty coalition governments as the Congress Party has lost its hegemony in the Indian political system after 1989. India's foreign policymaking process has become somewhat more complex in recent years even as it faces a number of challenges.[206] Similarly, with the beginning of economic reforms in China and the end of the cold war, communist ideology has lost its salience in the Chinese political sphere, and nationalism has become an important factor, especially in foreign affairs. At the same time, the Chinese elite politics has become far more institutionalized in the post-Deng era as the main leader has lost his cultlike status. The addition of several new actors in foreign policymaking has also made the process in China more complicated even as it remains opaque to a large extent, especially on decisions related to national security.[207] As such, it is important to understand whether domestic-level factors matter in the period since 1989.

An attempt will now be made to briefly analyze the consequence of the 2008 uprising in Tibet and the armed crackdown that followed it on the Sino-Indian rivalry. Interestingly, the status quo in the rivalry was maintained in this 2008 "pathway case" by both of the sides in this rivalry. In the wake of the protests in Tibet that began in March 2008 (around the time of the 49th anniversary of the 1959 Lhasa revolt) and the military crackdown that followed it, there was widespread concern in India. Similar to 1959 and the late 1980s, the Congress Party was leading the government in India in 2008. However, this time around the Congress Party was leading a coalition government comprising several parties, including the Left parties with their pro-China sympathies. The Indian media and all Indian political parties (barring the Left parties) condemned China's policies in Tibet in unequivocal terms.[208] However, the Indian minister of external affairs responded by saying that there was no change in Indian policies regarding Tibet.[209] In fact it is widely believed that

India went out of its way to restrict the activities of the Dalai Lama and the Tibetan exiles in India during the crisis.[210]

So why did India respond by maintaining the status quo in the rivalry and even curbing the activities of the Tibetan community living in exile in India? To begin with, India's perception of its security vis-à-vis China remained unchanged even with the outbreak of protests in Tibet, as that region has been heavily militarized for several decades now. Moreover, India still maintains a robust military balance vis-à-vis China along their common border.[211] At the time of the Tibet crisis, India had no significant external security commitments. However, India was then in the process of establishing a close strategic partnership with the United States, the cornerstone of which was the Indo-U.S. Civil Nuclear Agreement. This agreement—which required the approval from the Chinese at the Nuclear Suppliers Group (NSG)—may have played an important role in India's decision to not exploit the situation in Tibet. In the end, even as the Chinese tried to play the role of a spoiler for India at the NSG, the agreement went through.[212] However, even without such an agreement, India would have refrained from doing so as New Delhi does not have a military strategy—as India remains the weaker economic and military power in the Sino-Indian dyad—to exploit the Tibetan situation to settle the Sino-Indian border dispute on terms favorable to New Delhi or to guarantee the internal autonomy of Tibet.

The only other plausible explanation is that it was the Congress Party's alliance with India's pro-China Left parties that explain India's choices. However, this argument is less than convincing, for when the Left parties tried to scuttle the implementation of the Civil Nuclear Agreement with the United States, the Congress Party called its bluff. As a consequence, the Left stopped supporting the Congress-led government, though it managed to survive its full term. This further demonstrates that foreign policymaking remains concentrated in the hands of the prime minister and his close aides even in the era of coalition governments.[213]

As such, it seems like that it was the need to get Chinese approval at the NSG on the Indo-U.S. Civil Nuclear Agreement, the cornerstone of the Indo-U.S. strategic partnership, and the fact that India does not have viable politico-military options vis-à-vis Tibet that explains India's response. However, a few weeks after the NSG granted its approval for this agreement, the Indian external affairs minister stated that "China was pursuing its interests more aggressively than in the past," and that India needed to develop novel ways of dealing with the strategic and geopolitical challenges posed by China.[214] Since then, India tried to boost its own military position along the Sino-Indian border by opening new bases/airfields, stationing sophisticated aircraft, and by sending more troops along the Sino-Indian border.[215] However, there is no evidence to indicate that India seeks to exploit the unrest in Tibet by building up its military along the Sino-Indian border. If anything, India's military build-up along the Sino-Indian border is a response to Chinese military modernization and China's massive investment in physical infrastructure along their common frontiers. As such, it seems almost certain that domestic politics did not play a role in influencing India's response to the crisis in Tibet in 2008.

Why did China maintain the status quo in the Sino-Indian rivalry in 2008? While the official Chinese media did blame the India-resident Dalai Lama for the riots,[216] India's swift actions in accordance with Beijing's wishes must have convinced Beijing that India was not seeking to exploit the situation. As such, China's threat perception vis-à-vis India was not heightened during this crisis. Furthermore, as has already been noted, there had been no significant changes in the military balance along their common border. Moreover, China was not developing any new strategic partnerships with the potential to influence its security policy toward India. Therefore, it can be inferred that in the absence of heightened threat perceptions vis-à-vis India in the aftermath of the 2008 protests in Tibet, Beijing did not see the need to change the status quo in its relationship with India.

There is another plausible explanation—a highly contingent one—that further bolsters this tendency toward status quo. In the run up to the Beijing Olympic Games, which were widely perceived to be the symbolic stage of China's emergence as a great power, Beijing wanted to avoid confrontation with any external power. As such, it does not seem likely that the decision to maintain the status quo with India was affected by Chinese nationalism, the semi-institutionalized nature of its central leadership, or any other domestic-level factor. However, as mentioned above, soon after the completion of Beijing Olympics, China raised the ante by trying to play a spoiler for India at the NSG. In fact, Chinese strategists are extremely concerned about the growing Indo-U.S. partnerships and its consequences for China's geostrategy.[217] China seems to have raised the ante in its relations with India; however, this seems to be the result of the changing developments at the global level and not as a consequence of developments in Tibet.

In sum, this study has demonstrated that in the two cases studied here—the consequences of instability in Tibet in 1959 and 1987–89 and the Chinese military crackdown that followed it on the Sino-Indian rivalry—domestic political variables played no role. The most important causal variables affecting the Sino-Indian rivalry are international-level variables. This does not mean that domestic-level factors are unimportant. After all, domestic politics in India did affect the Sino-Indian dynamics in the events leading to their 1962 war. However, domestic-level variables became important only *after* the *initial* decision to escalate the rivalry—based on threat perception vis-à-vis the rival—was taken. The perception of threat from the rival is the most important international variable determining escalation dynamics, although other international-level variables such as the presence or absence of allies, the changing military balance, and other external threats, rivals, and military commitments also matter. This general framework seems to fit the "pathway case" of 2008 as well. However, given the overall lack of empirical information providing insights into the actual decision-making process in the "pathway case," these conclusions remain tentative for the moment for that case.

6 The Sino-Russian Strategic Partnership: The End of Rivalry?

Lowell Dittmer

THE RELATIONSHIP BETWEEN THESE TWO VAST EMPIRES ASTRIDE the Eurasian heartland has been a political roller coaster. The premodern relationship was for the most part distant but increasingly predatory. This was seemingly overcome in the first half of the twentieth century by the Soviet adoption of a revolutionary, national liberationist foreign policy, only to lapse once again into fierce ideological and limited physical violence during the second half of the century. The relationship currently finds itself in full flower of postrevolutionary, postideological cooperation. Yet despite the current elaborately institutionalized diplomacy of "constructive and strategic partnership," the historical default relationship between these two vast empires is one of suspicion and intermittent strife, relieved by only two relatively brief periods of cooperation: the 1950s and post-1989. Yet the overwhelming emphasis in the analytical literature has been on the disputatiously "hot" phases, leaving us very little factual basis for understanding the nature and dynamics of the peaceable continental *cohabitation* that has now resumed.

The aim of this chapter, in accord with the theoretical framework set forth in the introduction and pursued throughout the volume, is a relatively systematic analysis of this relationship in the context of a "two-level game" framework. The two games are, of course, domestic politics on one level and the international power constellation on the other. Chronologically, after briefly reviewing the acrimonious historical background of the relationship, we focus on the two periods of relatively harmonious cooperation (1949–59 and 1990–2000), concluding with a review of the postmillennial period. In each case we ask: What were the domestic and international events that precipitated and then maintained this particular dynamic? What changes then brought it to an end? What are the most serious threats to the current "partnership," and what are likely to be the political-economic consequences if efforts at cooperation ultimately lapse—as they so often have in the past?

The Historical Legacy

Until the rise of the Mongol Yuan dynasty, the Chinese empire was largely oblivious of the still less developed Slavic principalities only recently brought to a semblance of unity under Kievan Rus' (ca. 880–1250). In 1223–40, Batu Khan, grandson of Genghis (Temuchin) and leader of the Golden Horde assigned to the northern realms, invaded the Russian principalities, sacking and burning Moscow, Kiev, and twelve other cities, sparing only Smolensk and Novgorod once they agreed to pay tribute. The Golden Horde subsequently built a capital, Sarai, on the lower Volga, where they continued to collect taxes and otherwise exercise dominion for nearly three centuries, far outlasting the reign of the Mongol Yuan dynasty in China. The impact of what became known as the "Tatar/Mongol yoke" has been mythologized as one of barbaric suffering, the source of Oriental despotism (as practiced by Ivan the Terrible), the death penalty, long-term imprisonment and torture, even Russia's failure to become involved in the European Renaissance, Reformation, and subsequent Industrial Revolution.[1] However retrospectively distasteful, there was considerable fraternization between occupier and occupied, as indicated by the fact that some 15 percent of the families of the Boyars, or Russian nobility (for example, Boris Godunov), claim Mongol ancestry. Yet the overall impact of the experience was to foster a Russian national identity as tenaciously (if borderline) Europeans, perpetually threatened on the eastern frontiers by Oriental "barbarism" (as Doestoevskii put it, "In Europe we are too Asiatic, whereas in Asia we are too European")—a self-image ironically mirror-imaging the Chinese perception of their northern neighbors as menacing barbarians (against whom the Great Wall was erected). Russia, though its imperial thrust was largely to the east and the south, remained culturally oriented westward; China's self-image was, by contrast, that of a self-sufficient "central kingdom," exacting tribute from abroad with no perceived need for international peer groups.

Russia's modernization experience was signaled in a sense by overcoming the Mongol-Tatar occupation. After pushing back the Teutonic Knights and the Swedes, the initial Russian direction of imperial expansion was to the east, sweeping aside the last remnants of Mongol rule in the sixteenth and seventeenth centuries in a drive to the Siberian Pacific even before turning south. Initial contacts with the Qing were deferential, but at the first signs of Chinese weakness the Russians seized their chances. In 1854–59, while China was engulfed by the Taiping Rebellion (1851–64), General N. N. Murawjew and twenty thousand troops occupied the delta and north shore of the Amur/Heilong R. and the maritime provinces without firing a shot. During the second Opium War, Russian forces made further inroads. These gains were consolidated in the treaties of Kuldja (1851), Aigun (1858), and Tarbagatai (1864); though later denounced for being "unequal," they awarded Russia a vast swath of some 665,000 square miles of land in the region of the Amur and Ussuri rivers in northern Manchuria to the Pacific Ocean. During the Yakub Beg Rebellion in Xinjiang, Russian troops occupied part of the Yili region, formalized in the Treaty of Livadia (later modified in China's favor in the Treaty of St. Petersburg). In 1898 Russia relegated Lu-shun (Port Arthur) and Dalian to treaty port status and demanded a leasehold on the Liaodong peninsula to construct a port there. Russian claims on Manchuria and Liaodog, however, fell athwart those of Japan, precipitating defeat in the Russo-Japanese War (1904–5). Count Witte's skillful negotiations at Portsmouth, however, forestalled punitive sanctions, and Moscow took advantage of the 1911 Xinhai revolution to establish a protectorate over Outer Mongolia.

The Bolshevik Revolution was intended to signal a no less revolutionary transformation of relations with China, as the new Soviet regime renounced its share of the Boxer reparations as well as many other imperial privileges in the seemingly magnanimous but ultimately equivocal Karakhan Declaration (1919) and established diplomatic relations with the short-lived Peking Republic (1924).[2] Playing all its options in a still ambiguous situation, Moscow also helped to organize and advise the Chinese Communist Party (CCP) in 1921, while assisting in the reorganization of the Nationalist Party (Kuomintang, or KMT), along Leninist lines two years later.[3] Even after the bloody 1927 split and ensuing civil war between KMT and CCP, Moscow divided its commitments, advocating a second united front, signing a nonaggression pact in 1937 as well as a "treaty of friendship and alliance" with the Nanking regime in 1945 (in which Moscow, promising not to support the CCP, introduced stipulations for Mongolian "independence").[4] At the same time Comintern advisors continued to support the beleaguered CCP. While it is true that Comintern advice during the late 1920s and early 1930s contributed to the near annihilation of the CCP by the KMT and that Mao's subsequent adoption of guerrilla warfare waged by peasant armies proved far more successful than the prior Comintern policy of urban insurrections, the adoption of "united front" tactics at Moscow's insistence in 1936 may have rescued the embattled CCP at a crucial juncture (true, the Japanese invasion also provided a timely diversion). In any case, the CCP made better use of its opportunities during the Sino-Japanese war than the nationalists and reemerged to defeat republican armies (with timely Soviet help, especially in Manchuria) and march into Beijing in October 1949, driving remnant KMT forces into exile in Taiwan. Victory was promptly followed by negotiating a thirty–year "treaty of friendship, alliance and mutual assistance" with Moscow in 1950, superseding the August 1945 treaty with Nanking (and relinquishing many of the concessions Moscow had gained from the KMT). But although this alliance would endure formally until abrogated by the Chinese side upon its expiration in 1980, it became a hollow shell after scarcely a decade, giving way to bitter reciprocal polemics culminating in border violence before finally being laid to rest in exhaustive "normalization" negotiations in the course of the 1980s. Despite the collapse of the Soviet Union into fifteen different independent republics in 1991 (to the CCP's consternation), the two have managed to maintain conciliatory momentum, negotiating and demarcating a border agreement, opening demilitarized borders to growing commerce, all sealed by a "comprehensive strategic partnership" in the late 1990s and a twenty–year friendship treaty (but not an alliance, both sides insist) in 2001.

The point is that despite the currently cordial "constructive and strategic partnership," the historical default relationship between these two vast empires is one of suspicion and intermittent mutual predation, relieved by only two relatively brief periods of cooperation between Russians and Chinese: the 1950s and post-1989. Yet the overwhelming emphasis in the analytical literature is just the reverse, focusing on the Sino-Soviet dispute and leaving us very little factual basis for understanding the nature and dynamics of viable cooperation. Thus our focus here will be on these two periods of cooperation. What factors explain the top-down de-escalation of tensions, and are they the same or similar? What role have domestic factors played in these phases? Are these mere "axes of convenience" due primarily to the need to refurbish domestic resource bases and/or to confront the United States, or is the Sino-Russian "partnership" as it exists today more deeply rooted? Finally, what are the most serious threats to the relationship, and what are likely to be the political-economic consequences if they escalate or ultimately prevail? This chapter consists of two parts, the first focused on the initial Sino-Soviet Alliance period, and the second on the post-1989 partnership.

The Sino-Soviet Alliance, 1950–1980

In his first departure from native soil, Mao spent two months in Moscow in January-February 1950, just two months after final victory in the civil war, to negotiate the Sino-Soviet Treaty of Friendship and Alliance, which comprised a US$300 million low-interest loan and a thirty–year military alliance. Although the alliance fell into desuetude after scarcely a decade in terms of either bilateral assistance or international strategic coordination, it continued to inhibit any opening to the West for another ten years. In retrospect, for Mao to have so closely aligned his country's foreign policy with that of its northern neighbor was to prove strategically unwise and regrettable.

Why did he do so? What complex of domestic and international power-political factors drove this decision? In terms of the correlation of international force, it is important to remember that he was not constrained to do so in the way the Eastern European satellite republics (East Germany, Poland, et al.) were by the presence of Soviet troops on their soil, who had liberated them from the Nazi occupation only to impose socialist regimes friendly to the USSR. The Chinese revolution, though certainly conducted with Soviet advice and material support, had an autochthonous leadership, was based on domestic political interests and innovative war strategies, and finally succeeded despite its departure from the Soviet revolutionary "model" in significant respects (for example, the elevation of the "rural proletariat" or peasantry to a major role, the manipulation of anti-Japanese nationalism in "white" areas, the reliance on guerrilla warfare). And China did have viable alternatives in the international arena. True, the United States had, despite disagreements, supported the CCP's domestic opponents in the civil war to the bitter end. But before the invasion of South Korea, Washington was prepared to write off residual KMT forces in Taiwan and accept CCP victory in the civil war. There were other indications of U.S. interest in cultivating a relationship with the victorious CCP forces (such as Ambassador Leighton Stewart's attempts at conciliation through Huang Hua), in hopes of turning the PRC against the USSR and splitting the bloc. To which there were seemingly favorable CCP responses, particularly in late 1948. Though these may have been sincere, they were no doubt premised on the assumption that there was no necessary contradiction between maintaining a strong Sino-Soviet relationship and reconciliation with Washington (after all, the United States and USSR has been anti-Axis allies only three years ago). But as the Soviet-American relationship cooled after 1947 as a result of rigged elections in Poland, the communist coup in Czechoslovakia, the Berlin blockade, and the countervailing organization of the Marshall Plan and North Atlantic Treaty Organization, the PRC was forced to choose between "two camps" (as Zhdanov put it). In the context of international polarization, although Stalin did not force him to choose, Mao boldly declared in June 1949 that China would "lean to one side." To both Moscow and Washington, the Chinese decision to intervene in the Korean War after McArthur's Inchon landing threatened to unify the Korean peninsula under American auspices confirmed this choice in blood.

In terms of the international power calculus, China's choice was thus to balance rather than to bandwagon, a functional option in terms of balance of power theory in the sense of restoring equilibrium to the international system. Yet as a revolutionary power China had little interest in preserving an international equilibrium. In terms of China's national interest this choice was ill advised. Participation in the Korean War protected its northeastern flank, where the Japanese invasion had begun, but China lost at least half a million men in the conflict (including Mao's oldest son), thereby also sacrificing its chance to take Taiwan. The American 7th Fleet quickly imposed a blockade that would inhibit China's economic development for the next three decades and force its dependency on the Soviet bloc. In terms of balance of power theory it is often considered strategically preferable to align with a geopolitically distant power against a proximate one.

In terms of domestic politics, too, the alliance was also of dubious value. The alliance was clearly elite-driven, and more specifically the decision was one in which Mao and Stalin personally had ultimate discretion. But although both systems were Leninist and highly monocratic, judging from their sole face-to-face meeting in the winter of 1949–50 in Moscow, neither Stalin nor Mao seemed to have much personal affinity for the other (though Stalin did do Mao a personal favor by revealing to him at this meeting that Gao Gang, party chief of the Northeast Bureau in Manchuria and a member of the

Politburo, was communicating private information about CCP politics to the CPSU leadership, preparing the way for his future purge).[5] China had been devastated by the anti-Japanese and revolutionary civil wars, with conservative estimates of ten million military and civilian war deaths, but according to best estimates the Soviet Union had suffered still higher casualties from the Nazi invasion (following Stalin's Great Terror).[6] The United States, alone among the great powers, emerged from the war relatively unscathed and in an internationally unprecedented position of political and economic dominance. Whereas the Soviet aid package that accompanied the thirty–year security alliance was very generous in view of the ruinous postwar condition of the Soviet economy, it was dwarfed by postwar American aid to, say, Greece, Germany, or South Korea, no doubt contributing to later CCP criticisms of the niggardly terms of the alliance. From a developmental perspective the Chinese leadership would no doubt have been better advised to flout the Soviet embrace and "completely Westernize" (*quanpan xifanghua*, as Chen Duxiu, the CCP's founding leader, had once advocated).

If neither international nor domestic factors can account for the alliance, what can? The most recent and authoritative research on the origins of the alliance agrees in attributing the decision to a profoundly skewed ideological perspective.[7] Was ideology an "international" or a "domestic" factor? In this case Marxist-Leninist ideology was a partial international factor, limited in effect to those countries (the "communist bloc") that had embraced it. To both the Soviet Union and the People's Republic of China, it was an essential part of their categorical identity. At this time both identified themselves as "communist" party-states who shared the vision of world revolution and political economic salvation through a transformative reorganization of the human condition, and this shared vision gave both far more optimistic expectations of future developmental prospects than would prove to be realistic. Facing an overwhelming national reconstruction imperative with scarce resources, both Communist Party leaderships were united in their approaches to domestic nation-building and modernization as well as their aspirations to spread Marxist-Leninist salvation to the rest of the world (especially the decolonizing "new nations" in Africa and Asia). To China, the alliance meant not only aid and cooperation but also a comprehensive blueprint to reorganize the Chinese nation-state; to the Soviet Union it contributed to the biggest expansion of communist influence in the history of that doctrine, consolidating its geopolitical hold on the Eurasian "world-island" and making world revolutionary prospects more feasible than ever before. Pyongyang's initiation of the Korean War in June 1950, and the subsequent U.S. invocation of sanctions and blockade of the PRC strengthened the alliance by raising the profile of the common threat and for the time being foreclosing the possibility of a triangular alternative.

The relationship was described as one between "big elder brother" and "little brother," between "father" and "son," between "lips and teeth." As Mao put it on one occasion, "The Communist Party of the Soviet Union . . . is the most advanced, the most experienced, and the most theoretically cultivated party in the world. This Party has been our model in the past, is our model at present, and will be our model in the future." He acknowledged as late as 1962 that the Chinese simply did not know how to build socialism on their own. From 1950 through 1966 the Soviets helped the Chinese to construct a total of 256 industrial projects (by Chinese count), two-thirds of the 320 "complete sets of industrial plant and equipment" that China purchased from the bloc during this period. These projects, described in China's first Five-Year Plan as "the core of our industrial construction plans," included the largest iron and steel complex in China, the largest ball-bearing plant (Luoyang, Henan), one of the largest coal mines, the largest linen mill (Harbin Flax, Helongjiang), the largest paper mill, and so on.[8] These projects included aid in all phases of the construction process. In all, Soviet aid projects plus those directly supporting them absorbed more than half of all construction investment in the First Five-Year Plan, and a high proportion of Chinese heavy industrial production for the next two decades came from these plants. China acquired whole branches of industry that never existed there before: aviation, automobile and tractor manufacture, radio, and many branches of chemical production. Indeed, some 70 percent of the industrial machinery operating in Chinese factories as late as the early 1980s was still of Soviet or East European provenance. Among these was China's first atomic reactor and cyclotron (completed April 1957), which would form the basis for all subsequent Chinese research in nuclear physics. The Soviet contribution to Chinese industrialization was not gratis, as Khrushchev himself conceded; it was based on mutual benefit: nearly all of the industrial plant and equipment was purchased based on low-interest loans, and the sales were beneficial to Soviet industry as well.[9]

Even more significant than Soviet material assistance is what has been called "the most comprehensive technology transfer in modern history." It was also more generous, based on grants rather than loans. The Soviets sent about ten thousand experts of various types to China to advise in socialist reconstruction. They also sent thousands of books, blueprints, and technical documents and hosted Chinese students and scholars at Soviet educational institutions and industrial enterprises. Not only the basic party-state structure but also the entire Chinese educational and research institutional framework were patterned after the Soviet model, and they have retained this basic structure to the present, notwithstanding the post-1978 reforms. Young communist cadres also studied in the Soviet Union, later rising to elite positions, from Liu Shaoqi and Zhu De in the first generation of leadership to Yang Shangkun and Ye Jianying in the second and Jiang Zemin and Li Peng in the third. Russian became the most popular foreign language taught in the schools. Thus the impact of this experience on Chinese economic construction, particular heavy industrialization, was deep and lasting. Whereas previous Chinese industry was located mostly along the eastern seaboard, during the period of cooperation this shifted to northern and central locations, based on a logic of being close to natural resources and distant from sources of threat (then conceived to stem from U.S. air and naval power in the Pacific). This shift in locational preference was to continue in the 1960s under the "Third Front" strategy and (despite the return in the reform period to east coast industrialization with the "opening to the outside world") even revived in 1999 in the form of the attempt to "develop the west" [*xibu da kaifa*].

This period of cooperation and unity however culminated in growing interpartisan disagreements by the end of the first decade and in an open, sporadically violent schism by the end of the second. Why did the relationship, apparently so solid, disintegrate? Relevant new archival materials are still emerging, but tentative retrospective findings concur on the following points. First, the dispute was not mainly based on marginal frictional factors such as the imbalance of trade, the arrogance of visiting Soviet experts, or other aspects of bilateral cooperation in the relationship, but on the very pivotal issues of the future direction of socialist development for both countries. The shared categorical identity that brought them together meant that since both are committed to socialism both should take the same future developmental path: if the USSR turned left, then China must also turn left, and vice versa). This issue also complicated the question of the "correct" strategy to lead the international communist movement, for this was not only a diplomatic but also a world revolutionary developmental issue and hence an ideological one. This accounts for the irony that sharing the same belief system both facilitated and then greatly complicated bilateral cooperation. A second paradox is that the chief grievant in the split was also its principal beneficiary: China. It turned out to be easier to give than to receive. Third, within the CCP leadership Mao was personally the main driving force, not only in so decisively siding with the Soviet Union at the outset but in the subsequent critique of the Soviet "road." In both cases he used ideology to rationalize his decision (in the latter case after having adapted Marxism-Leninism to Chinese national conditions. Framing the dispute in this increasingly personalized ideological framework (viz., "Mao Zedong Thought"), he then used it to articulate and give broader international significance to intramural disputes with many of his own colleagues during China's Great Proletarian Cultural Revolution—indeed, the same epithets to first appear in the Sino-Soviet polemics of the early 1960s ('capitalist-roaders," etc.) were to be recycled against Mao's domestic rivals during the Cultural Revolution. And the identification of Mao's factional opponents with Soviet sponsorship in turn further exacerbated the domestic cleavage.

Sino-Russian Partnership, 1989–2000

After nearly three decades of ideological polemics, arms race, diplomatic encirclement and counterencirclement maneuvers, border incidents and other manifestations of an enmity that Mao predicted would last "one hundred years," the post-Mao leadership began a cautious climb down. They found the Soviet leadership, from the outset somewhat perplexed by the schism, to be cautiously receptive.[10] After Mao's death in August 1976 the ideological polemic against "social revisionism" gradually disappeared, though fear of the "polar bear" still provided the cement for Sino-American diplomatic normalization in 1971–79, facilitating collaboration against perceived Soviet-inspired initiatives in Afghanistan and Cambodia.[11] In 1981 China formally declined Moscow's offer to renew the expiring Sino-Soviet alliance but suggested "normalization" talks (formal diplomatic ties had never broken, but socialist nations have a three-tiered relation, and party-to-party ties had been suspended during the Cultural Revolution), and Moscow accepted. Beginning in 1982, after concluding the third Sino-American communiqué to resolve outstanding issues regarding Taiwan, the PRC and the USSR convoked a series of talks, alternating semiannually between the two capitals in the spring and fall of each year, involving approximately the same team of officials on either side. Progress was initially glacial due to Soviet intransigence over the "three fundamental obstacles" that Beijing stipulated as a precondition for improved relations: heavy fortification of the Sino-Soviet border and Outer Mongolia, Soviet troops in Afghanistan, and support of the Vietnamese threat to China's southeastern flank. Talks nevertheless continued on schedule, betokening a high degree of stubborn patience on each side, helping to contain the dispute during the series of post-Brezhnev and the post-Mao succession crises.

When Gorbachev decided to cut Soviet foreign policy losses in the late 1980s, he also decided, while terminating high-risk ventures in the Third World, to try to revive the Sino-Soviet friendship, thereby alleviating a very expensive defense burden and opening the way to greater involvement in the economically dynamic Pacific Rim. In speeches at Vladivostok (July 1986) and Krasnoyarsk (September 1988), he proposed a freeze on deployment of nuclear weapons in the Asia-Pacific region, conditional Soviet withdrawal from the Cam Ranh Bay naval facility in Vietnam, and unilateral reduction of the Soviet military by five hundred thousand troops within two years, nearly half (two hundred thousand) of which would come from the region east of the Urals. This Soviet "new thinking" [*novo myshlenie*], according to which Brezhnev's vaunted strategic parity with the United States had achieved few substantial gains at immense cost, eventually satisfied all three Chinese "obstacles." The international constellation was favorable in that the Reagan administration at once made clear in its Star Wars initiative its ability to outspend the Soviet Union, it simultaneously launched Strategic Arms Reduction Talks offering a way out of the arms race, leading eventually to simultaneous détente between Washington and both communist giants—generating a less-threatening climate also conducive to détente between them. Domestically, inasmuch as both countries' economies were running aground on the limits of "extensive development" under command planning—the Soviet Union after years of stagnation under Brezhnev, and China after radical Maoism had reached its dead end in the Cultural Revolution—fresh leadership teams in both capitols turned to "socialist reform," an attempt at revitalization referred to respectively as *perestroika*/glasnost and *gaige kaifang*. There was again a sense among policy intellectuals that both countries, with symmetrically structured and ideologically oriented economies, could learn from one another. While during the Maoist period Soviet criticism of China was taken up by Soviet liberals as an Aesopian way of criticizing analogous tendencies in the Soviet Union, now it was the liberals who rallied to China's support. Because China had been first in the bloc to experiment with reform, most of the initial learning was on the Soviet side—but China also paid close attention to Soviet experiments, and in fact the liberalization that led to the 1986 protest movement (and to the demotion of Hu Yaobang) was inspired not only by Deng Xiaoping's Delphic encouragement but by Gorbachev's earlier call for Soviet political reform. Whereas such "learning" was, to be sure, selective and would eventually lead in divergent directions, the fact that both countries were engaged in analogous socioeconomic experiments and interested in each other's experience helped to revitalize ideology as a common language facilitating their détente. Based then on both international and domestic policy convergence, it had become possible by the end of the 1980s, after seven years of negotiations, to hold a summit to seal the "normalization" of party-to-party relations.

This summit, held in early May 1989 amid student demonstrations at Tiananmen Square that necessitated moving all ceremonies indoors, quite unexpectedly marked both climax and terminus to this process of reconvergence around a socialist reform agenda. The visiting Soviet delegation was more sympathetic to the Chinese demonstrators than their hosts but understood the CCP leadership's embarrassment and diplomatically avoided taking sides publicly. The sanguinary Chinese solution to spontaneous student protests, implemented within a fortnight of Gorbachev's departure, led to international sanctions and to a quiet Soviet resolve to avoid any analogous "solution," whether domestically or among Warsaw Pact Organization signatories.[12] But without resort to outside force, the European socialist regimes (which were unsympathetic both to the demonstrators and to the conciliatory concessions Gorbachev recommended) could not stand, and by the end of 1991 all but China, North Korea, Laos, Vietnam, and Cuba had succumbed to a wave of anticommunist protest movements. Throughout 1989–91 the Chinese leadership, still defending both Marxism-Leninism-Mao Zedong Thought and the crackdown, deplored this as "peaceful evolution," an insidious capitalist conspiracy to undermine socialism with "sugar-coated bullets," but more immediately blamed on Gorbachev's passive leadership, "deviating from the path of socialism." The Propaganda Department compiled seven hundred thousand characters of "black" materials, and Deng Liqun submitted a six hundred thousand–character draft resolution to the Politburo before the 6th Plenum in early March 1990 (which had been personally reviewed by Wang Zhen), proposing a systematic public demolition of Soviet revisionism. But Deng Xiaoping held the line at "internal" criticism: "First of all we should mobilize the entire Party to do our own work well," he said. "I do not favor issuing documents like the 'first to ninth commentaries on the CPSU'" (published in the early 1960s). He also advised Jiang Zemin against trying to play a major role in the remnant international communist movement. Three factors conceivably influenced his decision. First, the Soviets dispatched several emissaries to Beijing asking them to avoid polemics, which would hurt bilateral relations. In late December, Gorbachev sent his envoy, Valentin Falin, with a personal missive from Gorbachev to Jiang Zemin, but this fence-mending visit apparently came to naught (Jiang Zemin indefinitely postponed his reciprocal visit to Moscow), so Vice Foreign Minister Igor Rogachev was dispatched to Beijing (January 9–11, 1990), and he succeeded in fixing a date for a visit by Li Peng in April 1990. Second, Gorbachev himself made two statements during the February 1990 CPSU CC Plenum that had a redeeming impact: he reaffirmed his commitment to socialism; moreover, despite having approved legislation renouncing the party's "leading role," he declined calls by the reformists to resign as CPSU general secretary. Third, Taiwan was at this time energetically pursuing "pragmatic" (aka dollar) diplomacy in pursuit of diplomatic recognition, establishing relations with eight small developing countries in 1989–91, and as the former satellites lost no time recognizing South Korea upon their self-emancipation it was clear that they might also recognize Taiwan itself unless the PRC quickly buried the ideological hatchet. Upon the December 1991 dissolution of the Soviet Union into fifteen republics, twelve of which promptly agreed to join the Commonwealth of Independent States (CIS), China promptly recognized all of them (now diplomatically addressed as "Messrs.," rather than "comrades"). Part of the reason for the PRC's quick adaptation was that otherwise, many alternatives seemed open to the new democratic Russian Federation: it then seemed feasible to resolve the old Russo-Japanese territorial dispute (involving three small islands and a tiny archipelago north of Hokkaido) and sign a peace treaty with Japan, which had considerable trade complementarity with the Russian Far East; South Korea had just granted Moscow a US$3 billion concessionary loan (in gratitude for recognition), and Taiwan briefly established consular relations with Latvia and very nearly exchanged ambassadors with the Ukraine and Outer Mongolia before being deterred by PRC diplomats. The new line in the Kremlin under Yeltsin and Kozyrev was anticommunist and pro-Western. To Chinese Kremlinologists these were traitors to socialism, while for their part the latter suspected the CCP of supporting the August 1991 coup conspirators and lost no time in signing a partnership agreement with Bill Clinton. Beijing also voiced concern lest successful reform in the new Russia lure Western FDI away from China and thereby undermine performance-based CCP legitimacy.

Yet Moscow's new international prospects under bourgeois democracy proved greatly exaggerated. The decisive domestic factor was that the Russian "double bang" of marketization and privatization failed miserably to revive the economy, which went into free fall for the next decade: real GDP declined 13 percent in 1991; 19 percent in 1992; 12 percent in 1993; and 15 percent in 1994, culminating in the collapse of the ruble in 1998. The health system and transportation system collapsed, even the birth rate shrank. Under the circumstances the leading Western industrial powers, still overburdened with debt in the wake of the Star Wars arms race and worldwide recession following the second oil price hike, were far less munificent with financial support than had been expected. Only Germany, now reunified thanks to Gorbachev's refusal to invoke the Brezhnev Doctrine to defend the Berlin Wall, made substantial subventions to Russian economic readjustment (more than US$20 billion in 1993 alone), cultivating a relationship that has made Germany Russia's top trade partner ever since. In the West, after Russian arms were discredited in the Gulf War (in which Moscow played no diplomatic role), Russia was demoted from bipolar nemesis to diplomatic nonentity, excluded from any role in resolving the imbroglio surrounding the ethnic disintegration of Yugoslavia, and finally invited to the "Group of Seven" but initially only as observer. The expansion of NATO to include former Russian satellites in Eastern Europe and even former Russian republics in 2004 infuriated the Russians, who were firmly convinced the West had promised no post-cold war expansion beyond Germany. Yeltsin's emergent political rivals, both on the left (Zyuganov and the revived Communist Party, the CPRF) and the right (for example, Lebed) challenged his nationalist bona fides and urged a shift from West to East, arguing on geostrategic grounds in favor of a more "balanced" international posture between East and West.

Even in the East, hopes of new breakthroughs were quickly dispelled: negotiations with Japan premised on a territorial compromise implementing Khrushchev's (never implemented) 1958 agreement (splitting the four: giving up two now, with the other two to be negotiated later) aroused unexpectedly firm military and local opposition, coming as it did after the Union had already imploded, leading Yeltsin to postpone his visit twice and not even to moot a proposal when he finally arrived in Tokyo in October 1993.

With regard to Korea, Russia's role as the first socialist patron to abandon the Democratic People's Republic of Korea embittered Pyongyang even more than Beijing's subsequent shift in the same direction, precluding Russian involvement in the four-power talks, and South Korean businessmen saw little intrinsic value (and considerable risk) in Siberian infrastructure investments after the disintegration of the USSR. Thus the 1994 proposal to enlarge NATO to include three former satellites in Eastern Europe, implemented in 1997 in apparent appreciation of American election-year constituency concerns (as earlier with Cuba) rather than any realistically perceived security threat, was merely a continuation of this adverse current. The West was ignoring Russia and sanctioning China (for Tiananmen), so the two turned to each other. The semiannual bilateral talks were resumed, this time including the newly independent Central Asian states bordering China in a tandem diplomatic delegation called the "Shanghai 5" (Russia, China, Kazakhstan, Kyrgyzstan, and Tajikistan). After several years' negotiations, this team agreed with Beijing in August 1986 to a set of confidence-building measures on their shared borders, including the regular exchange of information on military exercises and limits on the size of such exercises to no more than forty thousand troops. At a second joint summit the following year (April 1997), Russia and the Shanghai 5 agreed to reduce the size of its forces on the one hundred–meter border zone by 15 percent and place limits on a wide range of ground, air defense, and aviation equipment and personnel.

Ironically, two nations that had never been able to agree on the same ideology now found it possible to cooperate smoothly without one. One reason for this is that the ideological accord having irrevocably broken down, cooperation was now premised on more modest premises, making it more feasible to achieve: what was ideologically "right" for one side did not necessarily have to be right for the other. Thus they established a "constructive partnership" in September 1994, then a "strategic cooperative partnership" in April 1996 (a month after China's confrontation with the United States over Taiwan and immediately following Clinton's confirmation of a beefed-up Japanese-American Security Alliance), finally formalizing the relationship in a "Treaty of Good Neighborly Friendship and Cooperation" in July 2001 (reportedly at Beijing's initiative).[13] A "partnership" [*huoban guanxi*], has become a very informal, nonexclusive expression of mutual commitment in the diplomatic vocabulary of both powers, as China formed partnerships with Pakistan, France, Germany, the European Union, Japan, Korea and the United States, while Russia claimed partnerships with the United States, Japan, Iran, and India. Yet, for both, the Sino-Russian partnership has remained pivotal, an entry ticket back to what Jiang Zemin called "great power strategy" [*da guo zhanlue*]. Though third parties are never mentioned, the strategic utility of the partnership is implicitly tied to its greater geopolitical leverage vis-à-vis the American superpower, which had emerged from the cold war with more international power than either country deemed safe. Both sides stress that neither the partnership nor the 2001 Friendship Treaty is an "alliance," with an agreement only to consult but no obligation to military engagement in case of a threat to either side, and both disavow any security implications for a third party (that is, the United States), from whom both stand to gain more in economic terms than from their relationship with each other. Without alliance commitments, without mutually agreed strategic goals or opponents, just how meaningful is this "partnership"?

Sino-Russian Relations in the Twenty-First Century

While both sides would no doubt agree that the cross-border peace that has been sustained since 1970 is preferable to the alternative, and that the border settlement and confidence-building measures have put peace on a firmer footing than ever before, the partnership has also fallen somewhat short of expectations—particularly in the first decade of the new century, as some of its presumed support bases seem to have eroded substantially. But it is a very mixed picture: one might perhaps say the relationship has simply "normalized." For a more systematic assessment, let us sequentially examine the partnership's three most central pillars: territorial, domestic, and international.

From a formal legal perspective, the territorial issue has been resolved completely. The border delimitation and demarcation processes proceeded once the basic principles were agreed through the 1990s, and by the beginning of the next century the western boundary had been agreed and confirmed in three treaties, while the entirety of the Sino-Russian boundaries was also covered by treaty, setting aside a few disputed areas: Bear [*Heixia*] Island near Khabarovsk, and another island on the Argun River. Then in 2004 the two sides suddenly announced that continued negotiations had produced solutions to these last two "set aside" problems as well. The comprehensive agreement was formalized in a new treaty in Vladivostok in 2005; though details have not been made public because they involve sensitive (Russian) concessions, Bear Island was in effect split, and a small upstream channel of the Amur became Chinese. Mutual gradual border demilitarization to the minimal number of troops required for peaceful border patrolling (now numbering some two hundred thousand) has permitted both sides to shift strategic priorities, as China transfers forces to Taiwan and the South China Sea and Russia addresses the security threat created by the expansion of NATO in the West. But as Bobo Lo puts it, the paradox here is that while the territorial issue is now formally resolved, it has not relieved Russian anxieties—the Russians continue to fear mass Chinese immigration, Chinese exploitation of natural resources, a Chinese takeover of retail trade, and so forth—paranoid fears, but not entirely without foundation.[14]

On the positive side, the partnership has certainly been sedulously cultivated at the elite level. Since 1992 there have been dozens of high-level diplomatic exchanges and summit meetings (for example, eight presidential summits during Yeltsin's tenure) have been held on an annual basis; these have resulted in hundreds of agreements, among the most important of which were the 1991 agreement to delimit the eastern borders along the thalweg and initiate border demarcation (completed in 1997), the 1992 summit agreement gradually to demilitarize the border, the September 1994 agreement to detarget strategic weapons, mutual nonaggression and non-first-use of nuclear force; and the 1997 agreements on trade, oil and gas development and cultural cooperation. The year 2006 was declared the Year of Russia in China, and the following year the Russians declared the Year of China in Russia, prompting a series of exhibitions and friendship rituals. Yet it remains a top-down relationship that has never caught fire at the mass level: for example, according to public opinion surveys conducted in 2005 only 8 percent of Russians now view China as a friend, while 45 percent deemed it an adversary (though 47 percent also considered China a model for economic success).[15] Suspicion has been particularly rife in the Russian Far East, a vast resource-rich region with a shrinking population of now less than 7 million that has inveighed against Russian territorial concessions in the border settlement and fears Chinese demographic inundation. Even among elites there is suspicion of China's rise on the Russian side and cynicism about Russia's decline on the Chinese side: Chinese complain of the Russian refusal to sell their latest weaponry or their oil companies or to build promised pipelines; the Russians complain of Chinese intellectual property rights piracy (not to mention weapons smuggling), shoddy exports, uncontrolled emigration, or pushing Russia into the role of "resource appendage" by importing only raw materials. In one of history's great rank reversals, the "big brother" and former superpower has fallen far behind China economically (in aggregate but not per capita terms), despite Russia's economic recovery (thanks to a worldwide energy shortage and price spiral) since the turn of the millennium. While this has roused Russian anxieties, it also inspires admiration—not for "socialism with Chinese characteristics" but for the China model of successful adoption of capitalist economy in an authoritarian political context.

The partnership's greatest value is bilateral, turning what is still the world's longest land border from a military landmine and budgetary black hole into a thriving economic thoroughfare.[16] After all, the two are geographically condemned to be neighbors, and it makes more sense pragmatically to be good neighbors than bad. Yet even bilaterally there are persisting difficulties.

Bilateral trade has long been problematic—if politics is the locomotive of the relationship, economics has been the caboose. After a virtual freeze during the thirty-year dispute there was an initial upsurge in the early 1990s, to fill the vacuum left by the Tiananmen sanctions (the value of all Western investment in China dropped 22 percent during the first half of 1990) and the collapse of the centralized Russian distribution system and disappearance of subsidies; while total Soviet foreign trade dropped 6.4 percent for 1990, Sino-Soviet trade volume increased to US$5.3 billion, a quarter of which was border trade. Several Special Economic Regions were established in emulation of China's thriving Special Economic Zones in the southeast, more than two hundred cooperative projects were initialed between localities of the two countries, and China dispatched some fifteen thousand citizens to the Soviet Far East for temporary labor service. But these steep early rates of commercial growth could not be sustained, despite Yeltsin's announced goal of raising it to US$20 billion by the millennium; the 1991–92 economic crisis in the Russian Far East left Russians unable to repay Chinese exporters, and the Russians complained of shabby product quality and disruption of their retail networks. Visa-regime negotiation in 1993 (designed to control shuttle trade, a source of underground migration) and Moscow's subsequent imposition of border duties, cuts on transport subsidies, and restrictions on organizations entitled to engage in foreign trade caused trade to plunge by nearly 40 percent in the first half of 1994. In 1995 it began to recover, reaching US$5.1 billion that year and US$6.85 billion in 1996, but in 1997 it sank to US$6.12 billion, and dropped further in 1998, particularly after the November devaluation of the ruble. Trade began to grow more vigorously after 2000, as the Russian economy recovered as an energy exporter: though it failed to reach the goal of US$20 billion announced at the 1996 summit, by 2000 it was up to nearly US$8 billion, $10.7 billion in 2001, US$12 billion in 2002, US$15.8 billion in 2003, reaching US$29 billion by 2005 (the Russian figure was US$20 billion, apparently due to Russia's refusal to count shuttle trade, which it prohibits). China by 2006 was Russia's fourth biggest trade partner while Russia was China's eighth biggest. Trade fell sharply in 2007, due in part to a weapons buying strike by Beijing as a way of pressing Russia to sell more advanced weaponry,[17] but it rebounded smartly in 2008, increasing by 38.6 percent over the previous year to reach US$55.9 billion (with realistic hopes of reaching US$60 billion by 2010). Meanwhile the balance of trade has shifted from Russia to China: Russia now has a deficit of US$13.6 billion, its biggest trade deficit. Given the heavy state role in the economy and mercantilist tendencies on both sides, this is a sensitive issue. In terms of trade composition, Russian complaints about being derogated to the position of raw material supplier seem statistically justified: the proportion of raw materials has risen from 10 percent of Russian exports to 20 percent in 2003, to 30 percent in 2004, and seems likely to increase further, thanks to timely recent Chinese "loans" to hard-pressed Russian energy suppliers (and to the decline in Chinese weapons purchases).[18]

The most immediate beneficiary of expanded trade is ironically the region that has complained most vociferously about the relationship, the Russian Far East (RFE). This resource-rich but climatically forbidding region boasts only about 4.9 percent (6.5–7 million) of the Federation's approximately 148 million population, most of whom live along a narrow beltway just north of the border—facing some 120 million Chinese on the southern side of the Heilongjiang/Amur. The RFE grew in the late nineteenth century when it was on the frontier, and subsequently thrived as the ward of the state, with prison camps and defense installations, but has languished since the collapse of the Soviet Union. The region experienced its first population contraction of 250,000 in 1992 and has continued to shrink through out-migration in the context of reduced central subsidies, massive unemployment in the military-industrial sector in the wake of Russia's peace dividend, and the collapse of the Soviet infrastructure network. Against this background, the influx of Chinese workers or traders (allegedly including large numbers of criminals, prostitutes, and other riff-raff) was functionally useful but incited populist alarm. According to Chinese statistics, border crossings amounted to 1.38 million in 1992 and 1.76 million at their peak in 1993—but for the Russians, the central issue was not how many were crossing but how many stayed: unofficial Russian estimates of Chinese illegal residents run as high as one million in the Far East and six million nationally, versus Chinese official estimates of approximately 250,000. In light of these trends, the future seems apt to feature a dialectic between a growing Russian need for supplemental labor to realize the economic potential of the Far East in the wake of continuing population decline and Russian fears of a Chinese demographic threat. For the present, the latter seems to have priority: in 2008 Russia passed laws barring non-Russians from making cash transactions in Russian markets and Beijing cooperated by enforcing tough visa requirements on Chinese shuttle traders, resulting in a sharp decline in Chinese traders (but also reported shortages in Russian markets).

One facet of the economic exchange that had battened on the post-Tiananmen sanctions was that of military technology and equipment. Deprived of American and European arms since the post-Tiananmen sanctions, the Chinese returned to Russian arms merchants, from whom much of their original hardware came and which hence offered advantages in terms of compatibility of parts. Soviet global arms sales had dropped "catastrophically" in the wake of the 1991 Gulf War, when the Soviet war equipment used by the Iraqis was seen to be so completely eclipsed by high-tech American weaponry. Inasmuch as military equipment was the second largest item in the Soviet export repertory (after petroleum products), continued Chinese interest was particularly welcome at this point, and Russian strategic monitoring of arms exports relaxed accordingly.[19] Negotiations for the purchase of Sukhoi SU-27 fighters, under way since early 1990, culminated in the purchase of twenty-six at a "friendship" price of more than US$1 billion (about 35 percent of which China could pay in hard currency, the rest in bartered goods), with an option to buy an additional forty-eight. In March 1992 China also took delivery of the highly sophisticated S-300 antiaircraft missile system and SA-10 antitactical ballistic missile missiles. The first contingent of Chinese pilots was sent to Moscow in June 1992 to undergo a one-and-one-half-year training course, and by 1993 more than one thousand Russian experts were based in China by "private" contractual arrangement, helping to modernize Chinese nuclear and missile capabilities.[20] The 1995–96 confrontation over the Taiwan Strait whetted Chinese appetites for further acquisitions, and in November 1996 the two sides signed a bilateral defense cooperation pact, resulting in China's purchase of thirty to fifty SU-30 multipurpose fighters, four diesel-powered (Kilo-class) submarines, and two Sovremenniy-class destroyers with accompanying Sunburn antiship missiles designed to counter U.S. Aegis-equipped ships. By early 1997 China was the leading purchaser of Russian arms, machinery, and equipment, rivaled only by India, purchasing nearly 70 percent of its arms imports there (totaling US$3.3 billion from 1994–99). Yet a crisis of confidence has since 2005 stalled this relationship. Upset by the private corporate agreement to license Chinese production of SU-27s, the Russian Foreign Ministry reportedly blocked sales of Tu-22 Backfire long-range bombers and Su-35 fighters, though the Chinese have been able to purchase Russian refueling technology to give Chinese bombers a range of more than one thousand miles. Russian technical assistance also contributed significantly to China's program to launch satellites and manned space flight. But questions began to be raised (by Westerners but also by their own strategists) of the wisdom of rearming a once and possibly future security risk, the Russians have been trying to shift Chinese interest to the purchase of nonlethal technology; thus some 25 percent of the Chinese commercial aircraft pool is now Russian.[21] But in the past few years there has been a sharp decline in arms sales: in 2005 the Chinese obtained a fifteen–year licensing agreement contract to produce two hundred Russian SU-27SK fighters as J-11As, but the Russians subsequently discovered that Chinese had illegally copied the design to produce the aircraft indigenously as the J11B, and so they canceled the deal; for their part, the Chinese complain that the Russians do not sell them the latest weaponry that they sell to India. The Russian counterargument is that the Indians agree to buy weapons off the shelf without trying to appropriate the technology, and moreover the Indians have persuaded them if they sell to China it will soon fall into Pakistani hands.

How firm is the political base of the relationship? Still not strong enough to drive it, it would appear. Domestic constituencies have shifted over time, from the committed socialist reformers of the 1980s to a "red-brown" coalition of communists and nationalists in the aftermath of Tiananmen to Putin's power pragmatists of the 2000s. The collapse of the communist bloc threw both opponents and proponents of the relationship into temporary disarray—whereas before that time, the relationship had been endorsed by reformers on both sides of the Ussuri and opposed by the old guard, since then there was an ironic reversal of roles: China's reform bloc became more wary of the partnership because, by raising the old specter of Sino-Soviet alliance within a "strategic triangle," it threatened to alienate China from the West, it's largest market and source of technology transfer. Meanwhile in Russia, the fact that the CCP was able to crush liberal opposition and prevail while communism was self-destructing elsewhere inspired the forces of orthodoxy that had once been among China's most vociferous critics.[22] The pro-China stance of the CPRF, since the 1995 elections the most powerful party in the Duma, reflects this group's ideological assumptions. At the same time the former pro-China liberals, including scholars such as Lev Delyusin and former diplomats such as Yevgeniy Bazhanov, though on guard against any blind nostalgia for fraternal solidarity, remain basically sympathetic to the PRC. The now marginalized anti-China bloc consists of two quite disparate currents: the radical pro-Western bloc, intellectually led by the Moscow Institute of Foreign Relations (affiliated to the Russian Foreign Ministry) and linked politically to such figures as Yegor Gaydar and the Yabloko movement; and radical nationalists such as Vladimir Zhirinovsky (whose Liberal Democratic Party had an unexpected electoral success in 1993), who regard China as an alien security threat. The local political leaders of contiguous regions of the Russian Far East, particularly Primorskiy and Khabarovskiy krays, share some of this rabid nationalism in their obsession with the border threat and inflated estimates of the problems of smuggling and illegal migration, but Putin brought them to heel by making their positions appointive rather than elective and transferring the most vocal rabble-rousers out. At the same time, the economic prosperity of their domains has become so closely linked to that of the PRC that there is an objective need for good economic relations (though economics and politics are not necessarily correlated). At the top, a pragmatic majority under Putin and Medvedev has since the mid-1990s favored a "balanced" or Eurasian, pro-China tilt.

The partnership has much more limited international leverage than during the heyday of the Sino-Soviet alliance in the 1950s. The endorsement of multipolarity and antihegemonism in the partnership documents clearly hints at a shared intention to counterbalance U.S. interests in the region, as evinced by apparently coordinated verbal support of Yugoslavia during the 1999 U.S. bombing campaign and opposition to the Iraqi invasion in 2003; as the Chinese joined the Russians in opposition to NATO expansion, the Russians joined the Chinese in opposition to American plans to install Theater Missile Defense (TMD) systems in Japan and Taiwan. But whether two against one suffices to override an American-led coalition depends on the circumstances. On the one hand, joint Russian-Chinese opposition (that is, implicit veto threat on the Security Council) to UN intervention in Kosovo in 1999 at least obliged the United States to resort to an alternative IGO vehicle, NATO. And joint Russian-Chinese opposition to escalating pressure on North Korea in 1993 or on Burma after the arrest of Daw Aung San Suu Kyi seems to have thwarted any notion of invoking UN sanctions. Yet quite often, Sino-Russian collaboration has been insufficient: joint opposition to American missile defense failed, as Bush withdrew from the ABM treaty anyhow and in the Far East, the Japanese have made substantial contributions to an effective TMD despite Chinese objections. Joint opposition to the American invasion of Iraq (indeed, including Western European opposition) proved equally unavailing. The partnership has provided certain payoffs to each partner. It implicitly enhances China's position vis-à-vis India and Vietnam by reducing the probability that Moscow will support them in any confrontation with the PRC. To Moscow, perennially unsuccessful in resolving its border dispute with Japan, Beijing remains the key to entrée to the dynamic Pacific Rim. The partnership has already provided access to Hong Kong (where Russia now has a consulate) and to membership in ASEAN's Regional Forum, to APEC in 1998, and to Russia's prospective entry to the WTO. Russia has played the same role for Beijing with regard to the three Central Asian republics bordering Xinjiang, all of whom remain CIS members well integrated into the Russian security apparatus. In a team-negotiating format arranged by Moscow, China reached border agreements (and the initiation of border demarcation) with all of the bordering Central Asian republics. China has become Kazakhstan's largest trade partner and in 1997 agreed to invest US$9.7 billion there (China's largest FDI project, the equivalent of half of Kazakhstan's GNP) to build oil and gas pipelines from the Caspian oilfields to the Xinjiang region.[23] The Central Asians have in turn promised to control Uighur acolytes of an independent "Eastern Turkestan" (viz., Xinjiang) on their territory. The Chinese, who unlike the Americans have recognized Russia's leading role in the CIS, have limited their interest to trade (particularly energy), which they have continued to pursue in pipeline deals with Kazakhstan and more recently with Iran. This has resulted in a certain tension over the future role of the Shanghai Cooperative Organization (SCO). Russia thinks the organization should focus on fighting (Islamist) terrorism, while China's aspiration has been to extend it to the field of economic cooperation, particularly energy extraction. In the wake of the worldwide 2008–2010 financial crisis, China's offers to invest its enormous cache of foreign exchange in tied loans and joint ventures are likely to be welcomed in Central Asia, further escalating Russian anxieties.

From the Russian strategic perspective, Asia has gained importance since the cold war, following secession of the protective glacis of Eastern European satellites, the Baltic states, Ukraine and Belorussia: though the populace still prefers to identify itself as "Western," the Russian Federation now defines itself geopolitically as a land bridge between Europe and Asia. Like many other countries, Russia has inaugurated informal trade relations with Taiwan (Taiwan opened its trade office in Moscow in 1994, and Moscow opened its office in Taipei in 1996) while formally recognizing the PRC, and trade relations with Taiwan have expanded: by 1997, Taiwan had become Russia's fourth-largest trading partner in Asia. Within Asia, given the intractability of the territorial issue with Japan, India and China are Russia's twin pillars—one in the south, the other in the east. Russia expressed interest in consolidating this strategic triangle, but the weak link has been the Sino-Indian relationship, which has remained far weaker than the Indo-Russian link. On the one hand, bilateral trade has been increasing; on the other it is imbalanced, and the two are competing in third-party markets and in contracting commodity import arrangements. While they work together to block global emission-control initiatives inimical to their interests as developing economies and for a restructuring of the postcrisis world financial structure, China quietly seeks to block India's bid for a permanent seat on the UN Security Council, an Asian Developmental Bank loan, or India's inclusion (with U.S. support) in Nuclear Suppliers Group commerce—and border talks have stalled. Finally, both compete on the market for Russian weapons they may conceivably use against each other (though in each case the primary threat is anticipated from elsewhere). Yet in negotiations over global financial reform and the increasingly important "global warming" discussions, the BRIC (Brazil, Russia, India, China) and BASIC (Brazil, South Africa, India, China) caucuses have been able to coalesce in pursuit of their shared interests.

Conclusions

The Sino-Russian relationship has by all accounts been a complicated one, fostering historically justified mutual suspicions. Yet as we have emphasized here, there have also been periods of cooperation and relative amity. During the long period of revolutionary civil war from 1927–49 the Soviet Union was a staunch supporter of the embattled CCP, contributing to its ultimate resurrection and improbable victory. True, much Soviet advice failed to take Chinese interests and circumstances into account and was hence ill-conceived, sometimes disastrously so, but after all, they continued to support their Chinese comrades when no one else would. And in the full flush of revolutionary victory these two Communist Party-states formed a comprehensive alliance designed to facilitate China's rapid economic modernization and together conceive a strategy aiming for world revolution. And they in fact contributed considerably to the accomplishment of the first goal though not much to the second. Even after both revolutions had exhausted themselves in the late twentieth century they were able once again to overcome their suspicions and cooperate in reorienting their respective political economies.

So what are we to make finally of the current period of wary cooperation—is this simply a temporary respite in an historical cycle of conflict and relaxation, a convenient recess between rounds? Or is there something more to it than that? There are both similarities and differences among the two periods of cooperation closely considered here. (The period of cooperation between the USSR and the CCP in the prerevolutionary period does not really count, as this consisted of state sponsorship of a clandestine foreign insurgency [against a government with which Moscow maintained amicable ties] rather than a relationship between two sovereign states.) One similarity is that in both cases the two have values in common and foes they wish to defend against—a shared adversary—though the specifics are different in the two periods. In the first period what the two held in common were Marxist-Leninist revolutionary values, and the opposition both perceived to this was the bourgeois reactionary "camp," led by the United States. In the latter case what they have in common is more vaguely defined—a common authoritarian heritage and enduring quasi-socialist political culture, the opposition to which is not international capitalism, of which both now partake, but meddlesome human rights liberalism. A second shared factor in both periods is the longest land border in the world—albeit considerably shorter in the second period since the independence of the three Central Asian border-states. Though there are Uighur peoples in China, Kyrgyzstan, and Kazakhstan, in neither case do they have sufficient purchase on their governments to lay claim to co-ethnics on the Chinese side of the border, but the imperial experience has created grievances and territorial irredenta, particularly on the Chinese side. In both periods the border has been a significant issue, one that though now formally resolved still contains the potential for friction. Third, in both periods the relationship has been an asymmetrical one. In the first period, the Soviet Union was technologically superior to China, and both the Russians and the Chinese perceived the relationship in these terms. In the more recent period the relationship has been somewhat more symmetrical: although China had a larger absolute GDP as soon as the USSR disintegrated into fifteen independent states and has been increasing its lead since, the Russian Federation retains a higher per capita GDP and remains militarily and technologically ahead of the PRC. Fourth, both periods of cooperation have been plagued by serious problems with the relationship. There are deep historical roots to this sense of primeval dread that have not entirely been outgrown. In the first case the major differences were conceived in terms of ideological worldviews, which did not permit any deviance given the narrow conception of scientific "correctness" and the conviction that history moves in the same developmental direction for all. In the second case this zero-sum mentality has been alleviated by the Russian rejection and the more pragmatic Chinese interpretation of Marxism-Leninism, but there are still legitimate grievances on both sides, now more specifically and empirically defined.

There are also significant differences between the two periods of friendly cooperation. First, the second period, though still very central in the foreign policy horizons of both countries, is more modestly conceived, with significantly lowered, "live and let live" expectations on both sides. Nowhere is this demonstrated more clearly than in the low-key reaction to the deterioration of some of the pillars of the relationship since 2005. Despite the apparent halt of Russian weapons sales, disagreements about the construction of oil pipelines, Russian displeasure over China's economic surge into Central Asia, the imposition of strict visa requirements on Chinese shuttle traders, and an apparent Chinese disagreement with Russia's crackdown on Georgia, there have been no polemical recriminations or public protests; in fact, neither side has made much of any of this. Second, the border issue has been far more completely and satisfactorily resolved in the latter case. Although anxieties persist, particularly on the Russian side, there is no visible prospect of a return to border fortifications and bilateral arms race. Over time, both sides seem to have become cognizant of the considerable fiscal advantage of adjusting cross-border relations smoothly enough to be able to avoid fortifying the border at great, avoidable cost. Third, although the relationship is now more symmetrical than during the alliance period, Chinese economic progress has been so vigorous as to turn the economic tables with astonishing swiftness. While Russia retains its lead in per capita incomes and levels of scientific and military technology development, it may be only a matter of time before this too is lost. Hitherto the Chinese have handled this power transition with diplomacy and even deference, but as the Chinese grow richer and more confident this could spark hurt feelings and eventually even lead to a revived sense of "China threat." Finally, the common values the partnership is meant to protect are far more vaguely defined in the second period, as is the common enemy against which it is to be mobilized. The term "strategic partnership" may be an overstatement in view of the apparent lack of any concerted international strategy (indeed, both deny any shared strategy or common foe). The original Sino-Soviet alliance was certainly conceived in terms of such a joint strategy, although there was increasing disagreement about what it should be, but since the cold war, though Moscow has been inclined to brandish the threat of a triangular veto of U.S. unilateralism, there have been few issue areas in which such concertment has succeeded. China's concern with NATO expansion is largely rhetorical, as is Moscow's concern about the recovery of Taiwan—what resources would either be willing to bring to bear on behalf of the other's achievement of such cherished national goals? In sum, while both clearly value their more amicable relations, "good neighbors" would perhaps be a more apt description than "strategic partners."

7 The Rivalry Between the Two Koreas

Samuel S. Kim

Inter-Korean Rivalry Conceived and Applied

Not unlike any rivals or rivalries in world politics, the rivalry between the two Koreas—the inter-Korean rivalry (IKR)—reflects and effects a variable mix of sui generis and nomothetic features. First, the IKR is a rivalry between two divided incomplete nation-states, and as such, it is both intrastate and interstate rivalry. Indeed, half Korea plus half Korea in 1945 morphed into two "states," with two systems in 1948, siring two incomplete nation-states. Such divided nations are primed for zero-sum and often-violent fratricidal politics of national identity mobilization to maximize their exclusive security and legitimacy. In short, the Korean division was made to order for the initiation of strategic rivalry of a special kind—a legitimacy-cum-identity war.

Second, the IKR is far more than dyadic rivalry; it is and becomes the vortex of multiple strategic rivalries. While geography matters in the shaping of any state's foreign policy, this is especially true for the foreign policies of the two Koreas and their three powerful neighboring states. The geographical location of the Korean peninsula, tightly enveloped by the three big neighboring powers, doomed pre-1945 Korea as a shrimp among whales and transformed Korea as the battleground of great-power hegemonic rivalries. Each of the Big Four of Northeast Asia (NEA)—China, Russia, Japan, and the United States—has come to regard the Korean peninsula as the strategic crossroads of the NEA security complex and therefore as falling within its own geostrategic ambit.[1] The Korean peninsula, divided or united, shares land and maritime borders with China, Russia, and Japan, uniquely situating it within the geopolitics of NEA. With the Korean peninsula as its strategic pivot, NEA is the one and only international region or subregion where the Big Four uneasily meet and interact and where their respective interests coalesce, compete, or clash in an unpredictable situation-specific way. Crowded by all four great powers, Korea's unique place in the geopolitics of Northeast Asia remains at once a blessing, a curse, and a Rorschach test.

Third, the IKR is a highly militarized one. Even today, almost six decades after the Korean War "ended" with an armistice accord, the so-called demilitarized zone (DMZ) easily stands out as one of the most heavily fortified conflict zones in the post-cold war world, where 1.9 million military personnel—including 28,500 U.S. troops—confront each other, armed to the teeth with the latest weapons systems. Indeed, the Korean situation has acquired such security-deficit monikers as "powder keg," "the fuse on the nuclear powder keg in the Pacific," "the scariest place on earth," and "the last glacier of Cold War confrontation."

Fourth, the IKR is one of the longest and most consistently hostile post-World War II rivalries. As the life cycle of divided Korea turns sixty-five, exceeding the thirty-five-year Japanese colonial rule by three decades, the IKR is one of the most protracted and intense of its kind since the end of World War II, an *enduring rivalry par excellence.* Yet no divided country (including China, Germany, and Vietnam)—the four major fault lines of cold war rivalries—had been previously united as an independent political entity so continuously or so long as Korea. Unlike almost all of the 192 member states of the United Nations that include two or more ethno-national communities of significant size, throughout two millennia of history Korea has been united ethnically and linguistically, and from AD 668 until 1910, it lived under the same rule with the same territory, language, race, customs, and history, and with the same strong and powerful neighbors to envy and resent. There is thus a substantial disparity between the primordial unity of the nation and people of Korea and its more recent divided status as two incomplete states, giving rise to continuing asymmetries between the rising expectations for Korean reunification and the limited integrative capabilities and compatibilities on the ground. Like conjoined twins attached at the hip, each half of Korea has operated with the knowledge that both its every move and its national identity are reflected in its ideologically opposed doppelganger.

The geopolitical and geoeconomic attributes of the two Koreas—including the asymmetries of the IKR, the geostrategic location, and the divided polity—make examining the protracted IKR both interesting and challenging for theory, policy, and comparative analysis. Following three major types of strategic rivalry with some situation-specific modifications,[2] I seek below to track and explain the turbulent trajectory of the IKR along three separate but mutually interconnected and interdependent domains: legitimacy/identity, military/security, and functional (economic, social, and humanitarian).

The Legitimacy/Identity War

For more than a hundred years, especially between 1894 and 1945, owing to its geographical location and small size, the Korean peninsula morphed into a highly contested strategic terrain that absorbed and reflected wider hegemonic rivalries and even sanguinary wars involving, to varying degrees, imperial Japan, czarist Russia, the Soviet Union, Qing China, the People's Republic of China (PRC), and the United States—variations on the Big Four of contemporary Northeast Asian international relations. In the process, Korea was conquered, colonized, liberated, and divided, spawning a three-stage mutation of Korea's stunted national identity as a shrimp among whales from Chosun (Yi) Korea (1392-1910) to Colonial Korea (1910-45) to Divided Korea (1945-present). Both Koreas emerged from this checkered history determined to put an end to the proverbial shrimp-among-whales status. The turbulent trajectory of the IKR in the post-World War II era can be telegraphed and epitomized by a series of major internal and external systemic shocks:[3]

- Shock I (External): The Korean division in August 1945 that planted the seeds of the IKR;
- Shock II (Internal + External): The establishment of the U.S.-backed government (ROK) in the South and the USSR-backed government (DPRK) in the North in the latter half of 1948 that set the stage for the formal initiation of the IKR;
- Shock III (Internal + External): Kim Il Sung's initiation of the Korean War with Moscow and Beijing's support that triggered multiple strategic rivalries including most importantly a Sino-American military rivalry;

TABLE 7.1. Chronology of Inter-Korean Agreements, 1971-December 2009[a]

No.	Date mm/dd/yr[b]	Title
1	07/04/72	South–North Joint Communiqué of July 4, 1972
2	12/13/91	Agreement on Reconciliation, Non-aggression, and Exchanges and Cooperation Between South and North Korea (The Basic Agreement)
3	01/20/92	Joint Declaration of the Denuclearization of the Korean Peninsula
4	02/19/92	Agreement on the Composition and Operation of Subcommittees from South–North High-Level Negotiations
5	03/19/92	Agreement on the Establishment and Operation of a South–North Joint Nuclear Control Commission
6	05/07/92	Agreement Regarding the Establishment and Operation of a South–North Joint Military Commission
7	05/07/92	Agreement Concerning the Establishment and Operation of South–North Liaison Offices
8	05/07/92	Agreement on the Establishment and Operation of a South–North Joint Commission for Exchanges and Cooperation
9	09/17/92	Agreement on the Composition and Operation of a South–North Joint Reconciliation Commission
10	09/17/92	Protocol on the Implementation and Observance of Chapter 3, South-North Exchanges and Cooperation, of the Agreement on Reconciliation, Nonaggression and Exchanges and Cooperation
11	09/17/92	Protocol on the Implementation and Observance of Chapter 2, Nonaggression, of the Agreement on Reconciliation, Nonaggression and Exchanges and Cooperation
12	09/17/92	Protocol on the Implementation and Observance of Chapter 1, Reconciliation, of the Agreement of Reconciliation, Nonaggression and Exchanges and Cooperation
13	06/28/94	Agreement for the Holding of a Summit Meeting between South and North Korea
14	07/02/94	Agreement of the Procedure for Holding a Summit Meeting between South and North Korea
15	04/08/00	South–North Agreement (on Summit Meeting)
16	05/18/00	Agreement on Working Procedures for Implementing the April 8 South–North Agreement on Inter-Korean Summit
17	06/15/00	South–North Joint Declaration
18	06/30/00	Agreement to Exchange Visits by Separated Families, Establish and Operate a Reunion Center and Repatriate Unconverted Long-Term Prisoners
19	12/16/00	Agreement on Procedures for Resolution of Commercial Disputes between the South and the North
20	12/16/00	Agreement on Prevention of Double Taxation of Income between the South and the North
21	12/16/00	Agreement on Clearing Settlement between the South and the North
22	12/16/00	Agreement on Investment Protection between the South and the North
23	08/28/02	Agreement on North Korea's Participation in Pusan Asian Games (Asiad)
24	08/30/02	Agreement at the Second Meeting of the Inter-Korean Economic Cooperation Promotion Committee
25	09/08/02	Agreement at the Fourth Inter-Korean Red Cross Meeting
26	09/17/02	Agreement on Provision of Materials for Inter-Korean Linkage
27	09/17/02	Agreement Reached at the First Round of Working-Level Talks on Inter-Korean Railways and Highways
28	11/09/02	Agreement at the Third Inter-Korean Economic Cooperation Promotion Committee
29	01/22/03	Agreement Made at the Third South-North Korean Red Cross Working-Level Contact

TABLE 7.1. Chronology of Inter-Korean Agreements, 1971-December 2009[a] (continued)

No.	Date mm/dd/yr[b]	Title
30	01/25/03	Agreement Made at the Second Meeting of Working-Level Consultations on the Connection of South-North Railways and Roads
31	01/27/03	An Interim Military Guarantee Agreement for the Use of Temporary Roads between South-North Control Zones in the Eastern and Western Coastal Districts
32	05/23/03	Agreement reached at the end of the Fifth Meeting of Inter-Korean Economic Cooperation Promotion Committee
33	06/09/03	Agreement on Connection of Inter-Korean Rails and Roads
34	07/04/03	Third Meeting Agreement on Connection of Inter-Korean Rails and Roads
35	07/31/03	Agreement of Second Meeting of Inter-Korean Consultation on Economic Cooperation System
36	08/28/03	Agreement reached at the end of the Sixth Meeting of the South–North Economic Cooperation Promotion Committee
37	10/28/03	Agreement of Seventh Working-Level Contact on Connection of Inter-Korean Railways and Roads
38	11/08/03	Agreement of Seventh Meeting of Inter-Korean Economic Cooperation Promotion Committee
39	11/21/03	Agreement from the Second Inter-Korean Red Cross Talks
40	12/05/03	Agreement at the 8th Working-Level Contact for the Inter-Korean Railroads and Road Reconnections
41	03/05/04	Agreement at the 8th Meeting of the Inter-Korean Economic Cooperation Promotion Committee
42	06/05/04	Official Signature and Exchange of the Inter-Korean Maritime Agreement and Subsequent Agreement (June 5, 2004)
43	07/12/05	Agreement at the 10th Meeting of the Inter-Korean Economic Cooperation Promotion Committee (July 12, 2005)
44	07/27/05	Agreement from the First Round of the Consultative Meeting of Inter-Korean Working-Level Fishery Cooperation (July 17, 2005)
45	07/30/05	Agreement from the 5th Working-Level Consultative Meeting on Inter-Korean Road and Railway Reconnection (July 30, 2005)
46	08/05/05	Nine Agreements on Inter-Korean Economic Cooperation to Come into Effect (August 5, 2005)
47	08/19/05	The Agreement at the First Round of the Inter-Korean Agricultural Economic Cooperation (August 19, 2005)
48	08/25/05	Joint Statement of the 6th Inter-Korean Red Cross Talks
49	10/14/05	The Agreement on the Implementation of Video Reunions between Separated Families (October 7,2005)
50	10/31/05	The Joint Statement of the 11th Meeting of the Inter-Korean Economic Cooperation Promotion Committee (October 28, 2005)
51	02/28/06	Agreement on the 7th South-North Red Cross Talks (February 23, 2006)
52	06/08/06	The Agreement of the 12th Meeting of the Inter-Korean Economic Cooperation Promotion Committee (June 6, 2006)
53	10/05/07	Declaration on the Advancement of South-North Korean Relations, Peace and Prosperity
54	11/16/07	Agreement on the First South-North Prime Ministerial Talks on Implementing the Declaration on the Advancement of South-North Korean Relations, Peace and Prosperity
55	12/06/07	Agreement at the First Meeting of the Joint Committee for Inter-Korean Economic Cooperation
56	01/02/08	Agreement at the First Meeting of the Committee for the Promotion of the Special Peace and Cooperation Zone in the West Sea

[a] Agreements between DPRK and KEDO (of which the ROK is/was a member), as well as numerous "joint press statements," are excluded.
[b] Date signed or entered into force.
SOURCE: The ROK Ministry of Unification available at http://www.unikorea.go.kr.

- Shock IV (External): What is known in Asia as the "Nixon in China Shock" in 1971–72 that brought about the first-ever inter-Korean dialogue and the ·South-North Joint Communiqué of July 4, 1972 (see Table 7.1);
- Shock V (External): A series of momentous changes from 1989 to 1991 including the end of the cold war, German reunification, Moscow-Seoul normalization, and the collapse of the Soviet Union that ushered in a third cycle of inter-Korean dialogue and two major inter-Korean accords (see Table 7.1);
- Shocks VI-VII (Internal + Internal): President Kim Dae Jung's Sunshine Policy and President Roh Moo-hyun's Policy of Peace and Prosperity that led to two inter-Korean summits and two summit declarations setting the stage for progressive termination of the legitimacy/identity war and the IKR;
- Shock VIII (Internal): The rise of conservative Lee Myung-bak administration that seemed determined to trash the 2000 South-North Joint Declaration and the 2007 Declaration on the Advancement of South-North Relations, Peace and Prosperity, a great leap backward for the termination of the IKR.

The politics of competitive legitimation and delegitimation on the divided Korean peninsula started in August 1945 with the two Koreas taking separate state-making, identity-forming, and legitimacy-seeking paths under the sponsorship of the two competing superpowers (Shock I). For colonial Korea, World War II ended with a double irony. On August 15, 1945, Korea was liberated and divided at one and the same time, resulting in two separate systems, two incomplete nation-states. The Korean division along the thirty-eighth parallel was initially imposed on August 15, 1945, by President Harry Truman as part of an ad hoc U.S. zonal plan for dividing up Japanese troop surrender arrangements in the wake of Japan's unconditional surrender on that same day.

This was the beginning of a legitimation-cum-identity crisis that continues to impact both the domestic and international politics of divided Korea. The establishment of the ROK on August 15, 1948, and its repeated claim to represent the entire Korean peninsula and people as the sole legitimate government, based on UN-supervised elections and a General Assembly Resolution of December 12, 1948, gave rise to Pyongyang's first identity/legitimacy challenge (Shock II). In a less than a month, Pyongyang reciprocated by establishing the DPRK, claiming to represent all of Korea based on the 1948 election of a "People's Assembly."

By any reckoning the Korean War (Shock III) was the single greatest system-transforming event in the early post-World War II era. The nascent rivalry between the two Koreas escalated to a full-scale international war even as it catalyzed multiple strategic rivalries. As well, the Korean War served as the most important determinant in shaping the character not only of the two Koreas but also of great-power politics in Northeast Asia and beyond. The war had the decisive catalytic effect of institutionalizing the rules of the cold war zero-sum rivalries, thereby congealing patterns of East-West conflict across East Asia and beyond.[4] The United States owes to the Korean War the crystallization of its cold war identity, which in turn gave birth to an American strategic culture that thrived on a Manichaean vision of global bipolarity and the omnipresent communist threat. Similarly Soviet strategic culture, until the latter half of the 1980s, was anchored in and thrived on its own cold war identity. The simplicity of a stark bipolarized worldview provided an indispensable counterpoint for the quest for superpower status in the region dominated by American hegemony.

For both Koreas, the war initiated a decisive shift in identity politics from the competition of multiple identities to the dominance of the cold war identity. As a consequence, the collective ethnonational identity of Korea as one whole nation was radically fractured beyond easy repair.[5] As well, the war was the defining event of North Korean identity formation. Whereas the 1950 invasion etched into the minds of the American policymaker and public an image of North Koreans as aggressive communists who must be deterred and stopped at any cost, North Koreans view the United States intervention in the Korean War and subsequent military presence on the Korean peninsula as yet another example of great-power interference in Korean affairs.

For nearly two decades after the "end" of the Korean War, the two Koreas talked about and sometimes acted out their competing hegemonic unification visions only in the context of the overthrow or replacement of one system by the other. The domestic politics of the two Korean states were formed in binary opposition to each other. Over the course of their mutually antagonistic existence, both the ROK and the DPRK have sought to claim legitimacy over the entire Korean peninsula and have necessarily had to deny the legitimacy of the other state. But the politics of competitive legitimation and delegitimation has also had significant ramifications within the states and societies of the two Koreas, effects that produce positive feedback and then impact the style and substance of both international relations and inter-Korean relations.

At the international level, this has led to global competition for diplomatic recognition and for sole UN membership, in addition to the more obvious competition for military superiority. In this frantic international race for diplomatic recognition, both Koreas abandoned the Hallstein Doctrine (or the Beijing Formula), thereby opening the way for dual recognition. Not a single country recognized both Seoul and Pyongyang in the 1950s and 1960s, but by 1976 some forty-nine countries had already done so without incurring diplomatic severance from Pyongyang or Seoul. By 2005 the number of states recognizing both Koreas reached one hundred fifty-two, or 80 percent of UN membership.[6]

After Shock V (the Nixon-in-China shock) and the ensuing Sino-American rapprochement in the early 1970s, the two Koreas in a panic reaction held the first-ever inter-Korean dialogue and produced the first-ever joint communiqué (South-North Joint Communiqué of July 4, 1972), in which they both agreed to uphold three principles: (1) unification achieved through independent efforts; (2) unification achieved through peaceful means; and (3) national unity sought by transcending differences in ideas, ideologies, and systems. The second cycle of talks, running from September 1984 through February 1986, involved a flurry of contacts and exchanges in various functional and humanitarian fields and reaffirmed the three principles of unification. Catalyzed by Shock V, the third cycle was more promising than the first two. It jumpstarted inter-Korean trade, guided the entry of the two Koreas into the United Nations as two separate but equal member states, and led to the drafting of two documents: the North-South Basic Agreement (officially known as "Agreement on Reconciliation, Nonaggression, and Exchanges and Cooperation between the South and the North"), and the "Joint Declaration of the Denuclearization of the Korean Peninsula."

One positive and enduring legacy of the third cycle of inter-Korean dialogue is dual and simultaneous entry of the two Koreas into the United Nations. In regard to the politics of competitive legitimation and delegitimation, no other global institution matches the importance of the United Nations. It is there that Seoul and Pyongyang, having searched the world over for a forum, can readily find an arena commanding global audiences and global primetime in their long march to absolute one-nation international legitimation. If national identity changes through processes of social interaction in international institutions, as social constructivists argue, then, the United Nations more than any other international intergovernmental organization provides a social and institutional context to explore change and continuity in the identity politics of the two Koreas.

The conservative Kim Young Sam administration (1993–97) had little to show for improving inter-Korean relations. Two inter-Korean accords (Agreement Nos. 13–14 in Table 7.1) on holding an inter-Korean summit meeting in the second half of 1994 were no more than a reluctant, pro forma and post hoc acceptance of what former President Jimmy Carter had already managed to obtain in his "summit" meeting with President Kim Il Sung. But the scheduled summit was aborted by Kim's sudden death on July 8, apparently of a heart attack. What will be remembered is Kim Young Sam's incredulous response to the news of Kim's sudden death by raising Seoul's national security/threat alert level as if the paralyzed country was about to launch another war. Kim Young Sam may also be remembered, at least until the coming of the conservative Lee Myong-bak administration in early 2008, as the one and only South Korean president who jumped on the collapsist bandwagon, depicting North Korea as a "broken airplane" headed for a crash landing that would be followed by a quick reunification by Southern absorption. During his presidency the legitimacy war accelerated and intensified.

With the election of progressive opposition-party leader Kim Dạe Jung as ROK president in December 1997 came the single greatest blow (Shock VI) to the legitimacy war and the beginning of the peaceful end to the IKR. In his inaugural address, President Kim Dae Jung initiated a new grand strategy of opening to North Korea—the Sunshine Policy—with a pledge not to undermine or absorb the DPRK (that is, German-style unification by absorption). The twin pillars of the Sunshine Policy were the separation of politics from economics and the use of the principle of flexible reciprocity. The Sunshine Policy was also based in part on explicit recognition of the ineluctable reality on the ground that undermining the DPRK is not a viable policy option because of the disorder and destruction that would follow from a Northern collapse. Speaking to one of the major fears in Pyongyang in the post-cold war era, Kim Dae Jung's repeated pledges that the South has no intent "to undermine or absorb North Korea" stand out as one of the most significant steps toward accepting identity difference as an integral part of the peace process.[7]

The Sunshine Policy created the appropriate conditions—both in South and North Korea—for the historic inter-Korean summit of June 13-15, 2000. Revealingly, the first-ever inter-Korean summit was initiated and executed by the Koreans themselves in the absence of any external shock or great-power sponsorship. All previous inter-Korean dialogues were sparked by momentous changes and events external to the Korean peninsula. The 2000 Summit would not have been possible without President Kim Dae Jung's initiation of the Sunshine Policy in his inaugural address in February 1998 and his Berlin Declaration in March 2000.

Despite all the South's unification pomp that surrounded the historic summit, and despite the ritualistic pronouncement in the North that these were "the greatest successes in the reunification movement since the country was divided into two parts over half a century back," a great paradox surfaced when President Kim Dae Jung and Chairman Kim Jong Il embraced each other before global television audiences. While their hug symbolically signaled their acceptance of each other's legitimacy, neither of them enunciated a belief that reunification would be coming in the near future. Kim Dae Jung, in fact, predicted that it would take twenty to thirty years for the divided Korean peninsula to achieve national reunification, even as North Korea declared for the first time that "the issue of unifying the differing systems in the North and the South as one *may be left to posterity to settle slowly in the future*."[8] Equally tellingly, the front page of the June 15, 2000, issue of *Rodong Sinmun*, the official organ of the Korean Workers' Party, showcased the South Korean leader to the domestic audience for the first time as "Daehan Minkuk Daetongryong Kim Dae Chung" (Republic of Korea President Kim Dae Jung) and as the cosigner of the North-South Joint Declaration. The summit seemed to have brought the two Koreas down to earth from their respective dreamlands of hegemonic unification, to a position of peaceful coexistence as two de facto, if not fully de jure, sovereign states. And the fact that inter-Korean relations have continued on the rapprochement tract in the face of military tensions ranging from naval clashes to missile tests to nuclear weapons programs testifies to the suppressive impacts of the leadership factor in the legitimacy/identity war.

The peace facilitative impacts of Shock VI (President Kim Dae Jung's Sunshine Policy) have been made manifest in all three dimensions of the IKR, especially in the termination of the fifty-year legitimacy/identity war. Here we find proof positive of Diehl and Goertz's rivalry theory that "shocks can occur in two forms, dramatic changes either in the international system or *the character of the actor/state*," setting the stage for the beginning of new rivalries and the end of existing rivalries.[9] Kim Dae Jung's election as ROK president in late 1997 constituted a "regime change" of the first magnitude in both systemic and policy terms. He reflected and effected an almost perfect combination of Mr. Democracy (projecting South Korea's political identity as the first third-wave democracy in East Asia to accomplish a peaceful transfer of power from the conservative ruling party to a progressive opposition party) and Mr. Peace Maker (the first incumbent head of state in Asia to win the Nobel Peace Prize in late 2000).

That the 2000 summit set the stage for the peace-facilitative and rivalry-suppressive processes can be seen in both perceptual and policy terms. The Sunshine Policy coupled with President Bush's "axis of evil" speech seemed to have worked as a force-multiplier in catalyzing dramatic perceptual shifts in Seoul and Pyongyang. As shown in Figure 7.1, South Koreans' perception toward North Korea registered dramatic shifts during the Kim Dae Jung administration with positive (no-threat) perception increasing from 36.9 6 percent in 1995 to 52.5 percent in 2003 and to 64.9 percent in 2005 while negative (threat) perception declined from 59.6 percent in 1995 to 36.8 percent in 1999 and further down to 31.1 percent in 2005. In mid-February 2002, only a few weeks after the infamous "axis of evil" speech, the *New York Times* reported that even before Bush departed for a trip to Asia, the predominantly conservative South Korean press "was filled with denunciations of his inclusion of North Korea as part of the 'axis of evil,' protesting that Mr. Bush was undercutting years of diplomacy aimed at luring the Stalinist North out of its frightfully armed shell with economic incentives."[10] A 2002 poll indicated that 62 percent of South Koreans considered the "axis of evil" comment as "an excessive statement to escalate tensions in the Korean peninsula," whereas only 31 percent regarded it as "a proper statement to indicate the North Korean threat."[11] According to two South Korean scholars, "The perception of a reduced threat from North Korea made for a new way of thinking about North Koreans as 'brothers' in need of support and cooperation, rather than as intimating 'enemies' who should be contained."[12] North Korea's elite perception seems to have changed significantly as made evident in the 2003 New Year Joint Editorial: "It can be said that there exists on the Korean Peninsula at present only confrontation between the Koreans in the north and the south and the United States."[13]

Since the 2000 summit meeting, forty-two inter-Korean agreements have

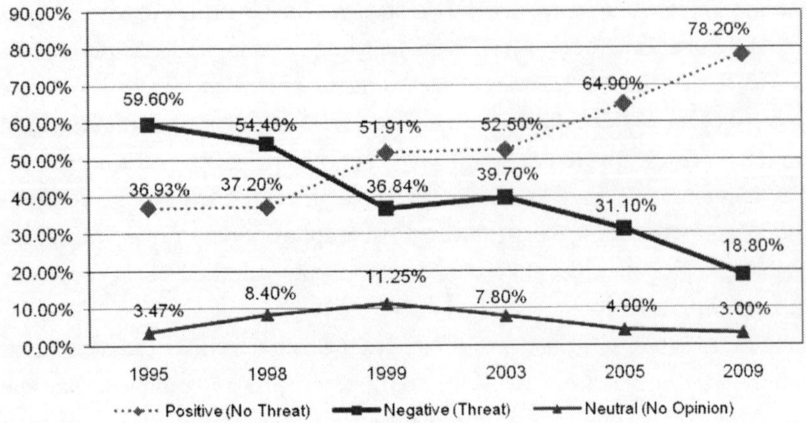

FIGURE 7.1 Changes in South Korean perception toward North Korea, 1995–2009.
SOURCE: Adapted from Kang Choi and Joon-Sung Park, "South Korea: Fears of Abandonment and Entrapment," in Muthiah Alagappa, ed. (Stanford: Stanford University Press, 2008), 386; and Korean Institute for National Unification (KINU) http://ww.kinu.or.kr.

been signed between the two Koreas—seventeen during the Kim Dae Jung administration, twenty-five during the during the Roh Moo-hyun administration—but none yet during the first half (thirty months) of the Lee Myung-bak administration (February 2008–August 2010), as listed in Table 7.1. President Roh Moo-hyun carried out the Sunshine Policy under a new rubric of Policy of Peace and Prosperity with greater vigor. From October 2–4, 2007, the second Inter-Korean summit was held in Pyongyang, resulting in an eight-point agreement—"Declaration on the Advancement of South-North Korean Relations, Peace and Prosperity."

The 2007 summit was the major follow-up step toward a functional working peace system. This is evident when we compare the summit declaration of June 15, 2000, and that of October 4, 2007. The Joint Declaration from the 2000 summit has nothing to say about military and security matters, but the 2007 summit produced a more substantive "Declaration on the Advancement of South-North Korean Relations, Peace and Prosperity," which includes several tension-reduction and confidence-building agreements. While the 2000 declaration stated in very general terms the need for balanced development of the national economy through economic cooperation, the 2007 declaration contained a greater range and scope of economic agreements. Most symbolically and perhaps most significantly, whereas in 2000 President Kim Dae Jung traveled to Pyongyang by flying over or around the DMZ, in 2007 President

Roh punctured a huge peace hole in the DMZ by traveling across into the North by car. On his way to Pyongyang, he got out of his limousine with the First Lady and walked the Military Line of Demarcation that separates the two countries inside the demilitarized zone (DMZ), underscoring the artificial nature of the line.[14]

From the outset, the conservative Lee Myung-bak administration took a great leap backward with a hostile stance toward Pyongyang (Shock VIII) seemingly determined to trash the 2000 South-North Joint Declaration and the 2007 Declaration on the Advancement of South-North Relations, Peace and Prosperity. The most Lee had to offer was a "Grand Bargain" nuclear proposal—"Unilateral Disarmament first, Grand Goodies later"—and a patronizing development plan for the North, "Vision 3000." Lee's posture served to energize the hardliners in Pyongyang while weakening pro-dialogue factions.

Whereas the inter-Korean psychological warfare has virtually vanished since the 2000 summit, the hard-line Lee administration seemed determined from day one to resuscitate this form of the legitimacy war. It has been uncovered that the Lee administration had already set aside several billion won to produce and broadcast propaganda materials in preparation for a North Korean collapse. This is nothing short of an opening salvo of a legitimacy war for Korean reunification via absorption (German-style unification by absorption) aimed at North Korean citizens. As well, it seemed made ready for attacking North Korea on a different level from "contingency plans" (see below), but from Pyongyang's perspective it could be seen as the continuation of regime-destroying war by another name.

All of this happened well before the sinking of the ROK Navy corvette *Cheonan* on March 26, 2010, when this warship was severed in two and sank off the country's west coast near Baengnyeong Island. Forty-six crew members died, and fifty-eight of the one hundred and four crew members were rescued. A South Korea-led investigation carried out by a team of experts from South Korea, United States, United Kingdom, Canada, Australia, and Sweden—except some Swedes the so-called "international" team was drawn almost exclusively from South Korea's cold war allies and all belligerents in the Korean War—presented a five-page summary of the Joint Investigation Group (JIG) report on May 20, 2010, concluding that the warship had been sunk by a North Korean torpedo. The findings of the JIG's summary report have been disputed by China, by the Russian

Navy's investigation, and by other prominent sources, and Pyongyang has denied any involvement.

Irrespective of the actual cause of the sinking,[15] the JIG's summary report and the breathless mainstream media coverage on the fly completely skate over the background condition and context of the Cheonan incident. South Korea and the U.S.-led United Nations Command (UNC) claim that the Northern Limit Line (NLL)—which runs just north of Baengnyeong Island—is the demarcation line between North and South. Whereas the NLL was unilaterally established by the United States, neither the DPRK nor the international community has ever recognized it. As such the NLL has no standing in international law. For Pyongyang to accept the NLL is to give up its access to lucrative fishing grounds and constrains its ability to develop its only deep-water port on its southwestern coastal city of Haeju. The past decade has seen three brief but bloody naval skirmishes in these contested waters. In November 2009, the simmering tensions erupted into a deadly skirmish when a North Korean patrol boat crossed the NLL, and a South Korean patrol boat fired warning shots. A full-scale battle broke out, ending with the North Korean ship, in flames, retreating back to its side of the NLL with at least one of its sailors dead.

One of the most important provisions in the eight-point accord signed by President Roh Moo-hyun and Chairman Kim Jong Il at the end of their summit on October 5, 2007 (Agreement No. 53 in Table 7.1), was to discuss various confidence-building measures "to avoid accidental clashes" by establishing "a special peace and cooperation zone in the West Sea encompassing Haeju and vicinity in a bid to proactively push ahead with the creation of a joint fishing zone and maritime peace zone." Within days of Lee Myung Bak's election as president two months later, his transition team backed away from the 2000 and 2007 summit accords. In March 2008, barely a month after Lee took office, Pyongyang accused Seoul of sending three naval vessels across the demarcation line, and then test-fired short-range missiles in response. At the same time, Pyongyang urged that the armistice agreement be replaced with a permanent peace treaty as part of six-party talks on denuclearization, a step Seoul resisted. When viewed against such a backdrop of the ongoing maritime boundary dispute between the two Koreas, "trespass" is and becomes in the eyes of the beholder. It seems clear that President Lee's efforts to trash the 2000 and 2007 summit accords and rewrite the new rules of the North-South relationship in a unilateral zero-sum way served as the chief catalyst of a new cycle of escalation that led to the sinking of the Cheonan.

On May 24, 2010, four days after the release of the JIG's summary report, the Lee administration with an eye to the June 2nd local elections announced five key sanctions measures against North Korea: (1) complete ban of navigation by North Korean vessels in the ROK's territorial waters; (2) suspension of inter-Korean trade; (3) prohibition of South Korean citizens' visits to North Korea; (4) prohibition of new investment in North Korea; and (5) suspension of assistance to North Korea. And yet, despite Seoul posting strong economic growth after a swift recovery from the global financial crisis (6.5 percent in 2010 from 0.2 percent in 2009) and opinion polls predicting an easy win for the ruling Grand National Party (GNP), aided and abetted by the strong "North wind" of the Cheonan incident, Lee's timing of the release of the JIG's summary report to scare South Korean citizens into voting conservative backfired badly with the unexpected rebuff and a significant swing away from the GNP of President Lee, in favor of the center-left opposition Democratic Party (DP). Paradoxically, a "silver-lining" exemption in the May 24 Sanctions Measures is the foundational principle and accomplishment of a "peace by pieces" working peace system of the Sunshine Decade—the Kaesong Industrial Complex (see below).

The Military Rivalry

The most salient feature of the Inter-Korean military rivalry is the extent to which it has been overshadowed by the U.S. factor, especially the military presence, on the Korean peninsula over the years. While Chinese troops had withdrawn from the North in 1958, 28,500 U.S. troops still remain in the South more than a half century after the Korean War "ended" (down from 32,500 in 2003). As earlier noted, the Korean War (Shock III) instantly catalyzed multiple strategic rivalries. But while the Sino-American military rivalry has been on a declining trajectory since the early 1970s, the DPRK-U.S. military/nuclear confrontation has continued with Seoul playing second fiddle. Despite or perhaps even because of Pyongyang's long-standing demand for negotiating the armistice accord into a peace treaty, in Washington's strategic thinking, the Korean War Armistice Agreement (KWAA) of July 27, 1953, is still viewed and acted out as the untouchable linchpin of the U.S. alliance system in Northeast Asia. As such it is "virtually hearsay even to raise the issue, let alone discuss a detailed road plan toward ending the armistice."[16] Consider the on the fly dismissal of the DPRK's latest official and detailed proposal to quickly negotiating "peace treaty for terminating the state of war, a root cause of the hostile relations."[17]

Under the shadow of the U.S. military presence the inter-Korean military rivalry has continued in all dimensions of strategic doctrine, arms race, force structure and deployment, and conflict behavior. During the long cold war years, the grand strategies of the two Koreas were anchored in mutually antagonistic identities centered on alliance maintenance for security, development, and legitimacy/identity. Still, Pyongyang's main security concern was not so much to balance against or bandwagon with the United States as it was to maximize military and economic aid from both Moscow and Beijing. Ironically, here it was the Sino-Soviet conflict, not the superpower rivalry, that enhanced "the power of the weak." In its security behavior Pyongyang demonstrated a remarkable unilateral zigzag strategy in its relations with Moscow and Beijing, taking sides if necessary on particular issues while attempting to extract maximum payoffs in economic, technical, and military aid, but never completely casting its lot with one against the other. On the other hand, Seoul's abiding security concerns had more to do with allied abandonment than allied entrapment.

In the post-cold war era, especially during the Sunshine Decade (1998–2007), Seoul has made a subtle but significant shift away from the fear of allied abandonment (Seoul's cold war strategic nightmare) to the fear of allied entrapment in the U.S.-ROK alliance. While no longer fearing abandonment of its own security interests in Washington's pursuit of a separate deal with Pyongyang, Seoul's security dilemma was centered on entrapment by the Bush administration's regime-change strategy that could suck Seoul into a military conflict escalation of not its own making. In March 2005 President Roh publicly declared, "We will not be embroiled in any conflict in Northeast Asia against our will. This is an absolutely firm principle we cannot yield under any circumstances."[18] The strategy out of Pyongyang in the North has also shifted from Kim Il Sung's "magnificent obsession" (that is, the quest for absolute international legitimation and reunification on his terms) to a security-cum-survival strategy, whatever it takes.

And yet, the inter-Korean arms race has continued unabated in all aspects of military manpower, arms acquisition, and military spending. Immediately following the 1953 KWAA, Seoul with 580,000 troops had a decisive superiority over Pyongyang with 260,000 troops in overall military manpower. At the peak of inter-Korean military tension in 1970, Seoul's military manpower increased to 645,000 while Pyongyang almost doubled its overall military manpower to 438,000. While Seoul's armed forces manpower strength has stabilized at 650,000 since the early 1980s, Pyongyang has continued to increase its force level, reaching 1.1 million in 1992.[19] In the post-cold war years, the two Koreas' overall military manpower has stabilized at 1.85 million (655,00 for the ROK and 1,190,000 for the DPRK as of December 2008),[20] commanding among the largest active armed forces in the world.

Pyongyang's numerical superiority in overall military manpower has been progressively offset by Seoul's rapidly growing superiority in military expenditure and the quality of weapons systems. As late as 1975, North Korea's military spending (US$1.28 billion) was greater than South Korea's (US$1.08 billion), but since the mid-1970s, Seoul increased its military share of GDP from about 4 to 6.3 percent and continued at levels of about 5 percent until the late 1980s. Despite the declining percentage in the 1990s, South Korea's expanding economy assured ever larger shares for the defense sector with an overall 81 percent increase in military spending from 1999 to 2007.[21] Even though Pyongyang's military spending has been rising in absolute terms (to about US$470 million in 2006), it cannot compete with the Southern rival spending more than fifty-two times its military spending (US$24.6 billion in 2006).[22] Once again, Seoul has recently launched a large-scale military modernization program for a more robust and self-sufficient defense. Tellingly enough, three major spikes in Seoul's military spending and modernization all correspond more closely with perceived or actual changes in U.S. military posture in the region than with perceived or actual threats from the North.[23]

With its socialist command economy shifting its gears from a low growth rate of 2.4 percent in 1989 to a negative growth rate of -3.7 percent in 1990 and deteriorating technological base, Pyongyang found it virtually impossible to match Seoul's growing power superiority.[24] Indeed, it has become increasingly evident that despite its numerical advantage in military manpower and some categories of conventional weapons systems (for example, tanks, field artillery, combat vessels, landing vessels, and combat aircraft), Pyongyang's military is essentially of 1950s vintage and Seoul is far superior in overall military capabilities, which mainstream bean counting obscures more than clarifies.[25] Pyongyang's intense arms race in conventional forces with Seoul developed in tandem with the progressive decline of the North Korean economy with the paradoxical consequences of weakening both economic and military power. In short, the two Koreas were in rough parity in overall military capabilities during the first two decades following the "end" of the Korean War, but the next three decades witnessed North Korea's military training, equipment, and overall military quality steadily deteriorating relative to the South.[26]

From Pyongyang's perspective, the strategic situation even in inter-Korean terms cannot but appear dangerous, given Seoul's growing military superiority over Pyongyang, let alone Washington's nuclear threats. Faced with such existential threat, the DPRK like any state in a similar situation can try to increase its military capability internally (internal balancing) or seek an alliance with powerful states (external balancing). Alliances form as a means of external balancing. Alongside internal balancing through the aggregation of arms build-up and now defunct overseas territorial aggrandizement, they are one of three means of enhancing power and/or security.

It is worth noting in this connection the impact of Shock V on the evolution of Pyongyang's military thinking and strategy. The growing sense of socialist betrayal and abandonment fears and the urgency of securing self-reliant existential deterrent were accentuated by the sudden loss of the Soviet nuclear umbrella. When the Kremlin announced in September 1990 that it would normalize relations with Seoul, the DPRK said in a prophetic memorandum that Moscow-Seoul normalization would mean an end to the DPRK-USSR alliance and that Pyongyang would have "no other choice but to take measures to provide for ourselves some weapons for which we have so far relied on the alliance."[27] As if to add insult to injury, the Sino-DPRK alliance too morphed into a paper tiger with PRC-ROK normalization two years later.

If we add, as we must, the U.S. military power in the overall correlation of forces across the DMZ, we begin to understand the logic of Pyongyang's attempts to level the playing field by building up asymmetrical capabilities. Developing asymmetrical capabilities such as ballistic missiles and weapons of mass destruction serves as existential deterrent *sine qua non* in its survival strategy. North Korea is not unique in this respect. For states with existential threats, nuclear weapons constitute "bedrock weapons of the weak" in a condition of asymmetric power relationships and the ultimate security insurance to guarantee regime survival.[28] Throughout the 1990s and into the twenty-first century, Pyongyang's nuclear card has consistently been a very fungible instrument for negotiating regime security-cum-survival. In the face of Shock V, nuclear weapons became *faute de mieux* "the most efficient means by which to optimize across security needs, abandonment fears, and resource constraints."[29] North Korean nuclear and missile strategy also illustrates with particular clarity that when the enactment of a national identity is blocked in one domain, the state seeks to compensate in another.

Even in inter-Korean terms, the military rivalry on the Korean peninsula reflects and effects "an asymmetrical power balance between the South's conventional power superiority and the North's asymmetric power advantage (derived from its long-range artilleries and WMDs), leading to a 'balance of terror' that sustains the current armistice."[30] Despite the occasional incidents and pin-pricks, as David Kang argues, the explanation for a half-century of stability and peace on the Korean peninsula is actually quite simple: "Deterrence has been clear and unambiguous."[31]

With the inauguration of the Lee Myung-bak administration in February 2008 came the great-leap-backward shock (Shock VIII) in the form of OPLAN 5029, with profound implications for the inter-Korean military rivalry. From the beginning, Lee Myung-bak has pushed hard to convert the concept plan (CONPLAN 5029) into an operational plan (OPLAN 5029), and it was completed at the annual meeting of U.S. and ROK military chiefs held in Washington on October 16, 2008. While CONPLAN 5029 is characterized by somewhat abstract content about what general course of action would be taken by South Korea and the United States in the event of a particular emergency situation taking place in North Korea, OPLAN 5029 would provide much more specific plans for the use of military forces, including the mobilization and positioning of troops at the battalion level and higher, to respond to various types of internal instability in North Korea—a civil war, an outflow of WMD, the kidnapping of South Korean citizens, a mass influx of refugees, or a natural disaster. OPLAN 5029 is nothing short of a plan for U.S.-ROK Combined Forces Command to prepare-and bring about—the collapse of North Korea. No wonder the Roh Moo-hyun administration unit vetoed the U.S. proposal to turn the hitherto conceptual plan (CONPLAN 5029) into an operational plan (OPLAN 5029) at its National Security Council meeting on April 15, 2005, for infringing upon Seoul's sovereignty. No wonder North Korea's on-the-fly response was: "The U.S. 'OPLAN 5029–05' unlike the previous 'plans' is chiefly aimed to deliberately create a war state on the Korean Peninsula and spark a military conflict on its own initiative. It calls upon the South Korea-U.S. 'Combined Forces Command' to replace the U.S. Pacific Command not only in working out plans but in carrying out operations."[32] What is surprising is that even the conservative *Korea Times* attacked OPLAN 5029 as "just another case of the Lee Myung-bak administration's 'ABR (Anything-but-Roh)' about-faces in administration and diplomacy."[33]

Despite or perhaps even because of Pyongyang's "charm offensive" since late August 2009 (seemingly aimed at restoring inflows of economic aid and trade), the inter-Korean military rivalry seemed to have relapsed into another cycle of threats and counterthreats. On October 5, 2009, Defense Minister Kim Tae-young publicly stated that Seoul had already identified some one hundred sites linked to North Korea's nuclear program and has the capacity to destroy them if necessary. In late 2009, the Lee Myung-bak administration is reported to have completed a drastically revised version of a North Korea "contingent/collapsist plan," code-named "recovery" to cope with "new realities" in the North such as Kim Jong Il's sudden death, a military coup, popular revolts or other emergencies that may cause the collapse of the military regime.[34]

Then, on January 20, 2010, Defense Minister Kim Tae-young said Seoul would have to launch "preemptive strikes" if it detects signs of possible nuclear aggression from North Korea, even as both Koreas were holding talks about improvements of the Kaesong Industrial Complex (KIC), the most important inter-Korean joint economic project.[35] Pyongyang responded with a "grabbing with two hands" approach. With one hand, Pyongyang seemed determined to pursue survival interests including the replacement of the armistice agreement with a peace treaty and inter-Korean economic cooperation, while at the same taking a "sacred war" line on anything it sees as a threat to the regime with the other hand.

Once again all of this serves as a spot-on reminder that the Cheonan crisis has been long in the making, especially since the inauguration of the hardline Lee Myung-bak administration in February 2008. Even before the release of the JIG's summary report, ROK Defense Minister Kim Tae-young testified at a National Assembly hearing on March 29, 2010, that "North Korea may have intentionally floated underwater mines to inflict harm on us." In early May 2010, Park Jin, Chairman of the Foreign Affairs, Trade and Unification Committee of the National Assembly, was dispatched to Washington as President Lee's point man to lobby for joint naval exercises with the United States in the Yellow Sea and a five-party regional security meeting excluding North Korea.

Swords into Plowshares

For more than four cold war decades, there were no direct inter-Korean economic relations of any kind. Instead, the two Koreas were locked into the politics of competitive legitimation and delegitimation, taking two different approaches to economic development. The quest for performance-based legitimation through economic development is an integral part of any polity in our times, but it has become magnified in the competition-driven politics of the two Koreas. Indeed, the battle for legitimacy, coupled with the realist concern for relative gains of the other Korea, has spurred rigorous economic rivalry.

In the late 1950s and the 1960s the political economy of North Korea seemed headed toward becoming an exceptional model island of autocentric and socialist national economy in the sea of the capitalist world system. Between 1953 and 1960, for example, North Korea's GNP closed the gap with South Korea despite the 1:2.1 demographic ratio, and in per capita income the North remained ahead of the South into the mid-1970s.[36] Starting in the late 1970s, however, Pyongyang's political economy began to show signs of a confidence crisis with its socialist economy on a declining trajectory. To a great extent, the South Korea factor has both reflected and effected Pyongyang's growing promise/performance gap in economic development. In such a protracted rivalry as the politics of competitive legitimation of the two Koreas, the fittest is the one that is most adaptable, as in a neo-Darwinian struggle for survival. Lacking constitutional claims to legitimacy, both Presidents Park Chung Hee (1961–79) and Chun Doo Hwan (1980–87)—military dictators turned into presidents—took a performance-based approach to legitimation, following three closely interconnected and synergistic developmental strategies: (1) a state-guided export-oriented (and import-substituting) strategy of economic development, exploiting the country's geostrategic American connection to the fullest to maximize payoffs and minimize penalties; (2) a "development first, reunification later" strategy; and (3) a strategy of "bleeding North Korea dry" in the arms race, rejecting any discussion on mutual reductions of military forces on both sides of the DMZ.

As it turned forty in September 1988, the DPRK seemed in the straits of a middle-age identity crisis, with few genuine friends left and little cause for celebration. What was happening on the other side of the peninsula in 1987-88 underscored this crisis by revealing striking contrasts and gaps in the political economies of the two Koreas. In foreign trade, Seoul's annual volume in

TABLE 7.2 Comparison of Major Economic Indexes of North and South Korea (as of December 2007)

Sector/Category	*Unit*	*North Korea* (A)	*South Korea* (B)	*A:B*
Population	1 million	23.2	48.5	1:2.1
Arable Land (% of land area)	%	23.3%	16.6%	1:0.7
Nominal GNI	US$ billion	26.7	971.3	1:36.4
Per Capita GNI	US$	1,152	20,045	1:17.4
GDP Growth Rate, 1998-2007 (annual average)	%	2.0%	4.0%	1:2.0
Total Foreign Trade	US$ billion	4.8	728.2	1:152
Exports	US$ billion	1.69	371.6	1:218
Imports	US$ billion	3.08	356.6	1:115
Trade Balance	US$ billion	-1.398	15.0	
Foreign Exchange Reserves	US$ billion	262.2		
Trade as Share of GDP (%)	%	17.6%	75.0%	1:4.3
Scale of Assessment for UN Budget	%	0.007%	2.173%	1:310

SOURCES: The ROK Ministry of Unification at http://unikorea.go.kr; and UN Doc.ST/ADM/SER.B/709.

1987 amounted to US$88 billion as against US$4 billion for Pyongyang, an insurmountable ratio of 22:1. For the banner Olympic year of 1988, South Korea managed to achieve an impressive 12.1 percent economic growth rate, as against North Korea's 2.4 percent economic growth rate. As if to add insult to injury, Moscow's aid to Pyongyang dropped from US$260 million in 1980 to US$6 million in 1986, the last year of Soviet aid, and the next three years registered negative: -US$33 million for 1987, -US$41 million for 1988, and -US$16 million for 1989.[37] As shown in Table 7.2 below, North-South gaps in key economic indicators grew progressively wider from the late 1980s to 2007.

Against this backdrop and Shock V, inter-Korean trade kick-started on November 21, 1988, when forty kilograms of North Korean clams arrived in Pusan, the first realization of economic exchange between the two Koreas. In January 1989, South Korea imported paintings, pottery, woodworking, and industrial art from the North, beginning a trade that totaled US$18.7 million for that year. Since those meager and largely symbolic beginnings, inter-Korean trade has continued to grow, expand, and diversify, so that 2002 saw US$642 million worth of inter-Korean trade—US$344 million worth of transactional trade and an additional US$298 million of nontransactional trade (that is, border-crossing goods related to humanitarian and development projects). By 2002 the ROK became the DPRK's second-largest trading partner after China.

TABLE 7.3 North Korea's Foreign Trade by Selected Top Trading Partners, 2000–2008 (Unit: US$ 1 million)[a]

Type/Year	*2000*	*2001*	*2002*	*2003*	*2004*	*2005*	*2006*	*2007*	*2008*
World	3,178	4,257	3,264	3,317	4,177	4,956	4,817	5,972	6,928
Exports	1,319	1,171	1,291	1,266	1,561	1,568	1,909	2,535	2,801
Imports	1,859	3,086	1,973	2,051	2,616	3,388	2,908	3,436	4,127
China	488 (15)	740 (17)	739(23)	1,023(31)	1,385(33)	1,580(32)	1,700(35)	1,977(33)	2,787(40)
Exports	37 (3)	167(14)	271(21)	395 (31)	586(38)	499(32)	468(25)	584(23)	754(27)
Imports	451 (24)	573(19)	468(24)	628(31)	799(31)	1,081(32)	1,232(42)	1,393(41)	2,033(49)
Japan	464 (15)	1,292(30)	368(11)	266(8)	253(6)	194(4)	122(3)	9 (0.2)	8(0.1)
Exports	257 (19)	226 (19)	235(18)	174(14)	164(11)	132(8)	78(4)	0	0
Imports	207 (11)	1,066(35)	133(7)	92(4)	89(3)	62(2)	44(2)	9 (0.3)	8(0.2)
South Korea	425 (13)	403(9)	642(20)	724(22)	697(17)	1,055(21)	1,350(28)	1,797(30)	1,818(26)
Exports	152 (12)	176(15)	272(21)	289(23)	258(17)	340(22)	520(27)	765(30)	930(33)
Imports	273 (15)	227(7)	370(19)	435(21)	439(17)	715(21)	830(29)	1,032(30)	888(22)
Russia	46 (1)	77 (2)	79(2)	114(3)	210(5)	213(4)	210(4)	160(3)	111(2)
Exports	8 (0.6)	15 (1)	10(0.8)	3 (0.2)	5 (0.3)	7(0.4)	20(1)	34(1)	13(0.5)
Imports	38 (2)	62 (2)	69(3)	111(5)	205(8)	206(6)	190(7)	126(4)	97(2)
Balance of Trade	-540	-1,915	-682	-785	-1,055	-1,820	-999	-901	-1,326

[a]Numbers in parentheses represent percentage of a given category.

SOURCE: Adapted from Nick K. Nanto and Emma Chanlett-Avery, North Korea: Economic Leverage and Policy Analysis, Congressional Research Service 7-5700 RL32493 (January 22, 2010), 38, tab. 2.

Sixty percent of the DPRK's export trade in 2002 consisted of trade with just three top trading partners: China (21 percent); the ROK (21 percent); and Japan (18 percent). By 2008, China (40 percent) and South Korea (26 percent) as top two trading partners preempted a whopping 66 percent of Pyongyang's total trade, with Japan's share having virtually vanished (0.1 percent). Even more remarkably, in 2008 South Korea (33 percent) has overtaken China (27 percent) as North Korea's top export trade partner. See Table 7.3.

The development of inter-Korean economic relations has been cautious and speculative, marked by occasional bumps, either endogenous (for example, DPRK foot-dragging) or exogenous (for example, the Asian Financial Crisis). What is rather striking about this growth in trade after forty years of noninteraction is its persistence and expansion in the presence of the so-called DMZ, which remains one of the most heavily fortified and sensitive conflict zones in the post-cold war world. Indeed, inter-Korean functional cooperation during the past decade—economic, social, and humanitarian

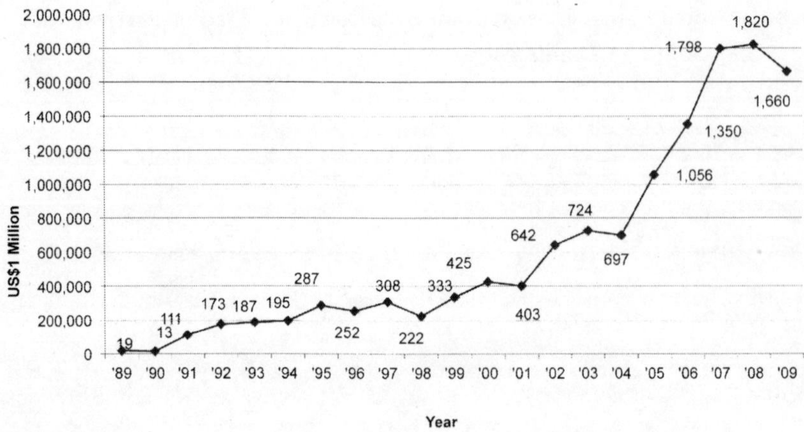

FIGURE 7.2 South Korean-North Korean trade (1989–2009).
SOURCE: The ROK Ministry of Unification available at http://www.unikorea.go.kr and *JOONGANG ILBO*, January 19, 2010.

exchanges—seems to have acquired a life of its own surviving and navigating through or around the uncharted waters of the nuclear confrontation, naval clashes, and the Cheonan crisis.

As shown in Figure 7.2, the 1994 nuclear crisis had no dampening effect as inter-Korean trade continued to grow in 1995 before receding slightly in 1996. While trade numbers fell in 1998 because of the Asian financial crisis, even the Taepodong-I missile crisis in August of that year could not derail the recovery. And despite the alleged nuclear revelations in October 2002, triggering a second nuclear crisis, the year 2003 registered a 13 percent increase (from US$642 million in 2002 to US$724 million in 2003). The inauguration of the conservative Lee Myung-bak administration in February 2008 had no major suppressive effect as inter-Korean trade continued to grow with a modest 1.3 percent increase from US$1.79 billion in 2007 to US$1.82 billion in 2008 but declined 7.7 percent in 2009 (US$1.679 billion) due mainly to the worldwide economic slowdown that sapped demand and investments. What is striking here is that the last two years of the Roh Moo-hyun administration gained an impressive 33 percent increase in inter-Korean trade, from US$1.35 billion in 2006 to US$1.79 billion in 2007.

Despite the ongoing inter-Korean military tensions and the stand-off over the Cheonan incident, the first two quarters of 2010 saw an all-time record US$994 million worth of inter-Korean trade, a 52.4 percent increase over the same period in 2009, even surpassing the previous high of US$884.79 million during the same period in 2008. With the adoption of the Sanctions Measures on May 24, 2010, however, inter-Korean trade is projected to decline by about 30 percent in the second half of 2010. But this projected decline is not as steep as expected since the KIC, which accounts for nearly 70 percent of total inter-Korean trade (up from about 50 percent in the pre-Cheonan period) is still in operation.

This resilience of inter-Korean trade in the face of continuing military standoff is the key puzzle of both theoretical and real-world significance. Beginning with a brief review of IR theoretical literature on the pacific benefits of trade and the role of economic interdependence in preventing or mitigating armed conflict, I argue that inter-Korean economic interaction defies standard commercial liberal explanations because of the sui generis character of the relationship between the ROK and the DPRK—at once a little more and a little less than two separate but formally sovereign states. Rather, a more synthetic and eclectic theory of inter-Korean economic relations is needed, one that can be specified by looking at developments in inter-Korean relations through the lenses of conflict management and functional cooperation, with nods also to traditional liberal and realist theories.

The starting point for understanding interstate economic relations are the liberal theories that rely on a critical threshold assumption that states are deterred from conflict by fear of losing the welfare gains that come with expanded trade and economic interdependence. Most often cited is Immanuel Kant's proposition that "the *spirit of commerce* sooner or later takes hold of every people, and it cannot exist side by side with war."[38] Economic interdependence, democracy, and international organizations constitute Kant's three-cornered construct of the structure of "perpetual peace." Most recently, Bruce Russett and John Oneal and others have folded the economic interdependence argument into the theory of the democratic peace to suggest the appropriateness of Kant's formulation of perpetual peace in world politics.[39]

The premise is that higher levels of trade will make conflict increasingly costly.[40] While the liberal analysis is usually intended for the systemic level, it can be applied at the dyadic level on the Korean peninsula. As the DPRK becomes increasingly reliant on trade with the ROK, it becomes increasingly costly for the North Korean government to undertake any actions that would damage this trade (and the aid coming from the South that is subsumed under "trade"). Badly in need of trading partners, the benefits to military action would need to be perceived as substantial in order for North Korea to undertake an endeavor that might interrupt these flows.

The liberal argument gives insight into why North Korea would not act so as to hinder the growing level of trade with South Korea. However, given that trade with North Korea made up but the most meager amount (0.2 percent) of the ROK's US$861 billion of international trade in 2008 and that, in terms of quantifiable economic benefits, the ROK gains little from this trade, the liberal argument does not provide sufficient explanation as to why South Korea continues to engage in trade with the North. Nor does it explain the origins of the trading relationship after forty years of prohibition of economic interaction.

To begin answering these questions, it is important to recall that with trade comes *influence*. In his classic work *National Power and Foreign Trade*, Albert Hirschman demonstrates the "influence effect" of trade—as one country becomes dependent on trade with another country, the latter state has increasing influence in the policy design of the former state.[41] Of course, with increased gains from trade comes increased vulnerability to this effect, and a state can avoid these vulnerabilities only if it has alternate markets at its disposal. The DPRK therefore finds itself in a position that, because it needs the economic benefits of South Korean trade and aid, it must bend in some ways to Southern suggestions for policy changes and economic reforms. The ROK recognizes this as well and understands the leverage that comes with trade. However, South Korea during the Kim Dae Jung and Roh Moo-hyun administrations did not use this leverage in a manifestly realpolitik way but rather in a more constructive, engagement manner.

Contemporary realist theories of international political economy draw some of their conclusions from Hirschman's trade theory but end up in a seemingly more reductionist position. For realists, states as security maximizers have a fear of inequality that can result from trading gains; realist theorists propose, that is, that relative gains matter.[42] The realist economic analysis does not apply to the dyadic relations on the Korean peninsula. From the southern side of the DMZ, however, the absolute gains in the North are simply not large enough to matter in the way that realists propose. Because the ROK holds such a superior economic and geopolitical position to the DPRK, Seoul has no reason to be worried that trade with the North will result in a military or economic advantage for Pyongyang. By a similar logic, the DPRK cannot believe that it is improving the South Korean position through inter-Korean trade, given that it represents such a tiny fraction of total South Korean trade. Relative-gains concerns can be disregarded in favor of absolute economic gains for the DPRK, something that is regarded as desirable in both Pyongyang, for reasons of regime survival, and Seoul, for reasons of peninsular stability. By the absence of the dynamic it proposes, the realist framework of relative gains, like its liberal counterpart, provides some insight as to why trade continues on the Korean peninsula, but neither of the two mainstream international relations theories demonstrates why the ROK is involved in such trade in the first place or why it is willing not to overreact to Northern military-first policy posturing. Whether rejected or accepted, each describes a logic as to why there is an environment in which trade can persist but fails to provide a causal logic as to why it actually does.

The problem with both the liberal and the realist relative-gains views of international trade in looking at Korea is that they reflect upon the impact of trade without considering the larger questions of its origins and the possibility of its nonrealpolitik strategic use. Not surprisingly, theories that incorporate economic relations into a broader perspective provide more leverage in explaining why inter-Korean trade emerged twenty years ago and why it continues in the face of mutual security concerns. The dyadic trade being witnessed between North and South Korea can be reconceptualized by looking at it through the lenses of functionalism and conflict management.

While David Mitrany and his followers spoke of functionalism as being built at the international level, the ideas certainly have applicability at the dyadic level. Viewed in a functionalist manner, Inter Korean economic relations can better be seen as part of a conscious plan—clearly on the part of the ROK and conceivably on the part of the DPRK—to develop ties between the North and the South, to promote contacts and interaction, and to bridge the social and cultural gap that has grown between two halves of a divided people over six decades of hostile interaction. Inter-Korean economic relations are in many ways not at all about economics but about reconciliation and the reduction of political and military tensions. The influence inherent in inter-Korean economic relations, while in some ways threatening to the weaker North Korea, also contributes to confidence-building measures that are a part of dealing with the larger security issue.[43]

Coherent with a broad functionalist scheme is the conflict management approach.[44] Conflict management allows for dyadic interactions at multiple levels. Therefore, whereas the liberal and realist frameworks seem to suggest a direct causality between economics and security, keeping an eye on conflict management lets economic relations continue in the face of contrasting developments in the traditional security realm. The ROK, if operating under a conflict management perspective, can make a conscious decision to continue economic interaction in the face of the DPRK's surprise announcements about its nuclear program and in the face of naval clashes in the West Sea. These seemingly very negative pin-prick occurrences are in part mitigated by more positive occurrences elsewhere in inter-Korean relations, such as on the economic front. Conflict management dissects an all-or-nothing security environment and creates varied pathways of engagement and response.

An odd pattern emerges from looking at these theoretical considerations. In the communist state that should be driven by ideology, economics would seem to be playing the driving role in inter-Korean relations, while in the capitalist state that should be driven by economics, a functionalist gradualism and pragmatic conflict-management approach holds sway. The traditional liberal mechanism by which trade prevents conflict because of a rational cost-benefit assessment does well to explain why the DPRK cannot risk provoking Seoul to the point where it might cut off burgeoning economic relations, implying that there are limits to the patterns of its current hostility and that Pyongyang may just be testing the boundaries of cooperation. On the other side of the coin, inter-Korean trade arises as an exceptional case in realist theory in which the states are not dissuaded from engaging each other because of relative-gains concerns.

With the steady implementation of President Kim Dae Jung's Sunshine Policy and President Roh Moo-hyun's Policy of Peace and Prosperity, some South Korean nongovernmental actors began to play active third-party roles in promoting inter-Korean reconciliation. Likewise, under both liberal and progressive administrations in the Sunshine Decade, South Korean NGOs began to enjoy direct relationships with North Korean counterparts. Government-to-government restrictions on such contacts lessened, and ROK government funding of certain NGOs increased to support inter-Korean cooperation efforts. Despite the many turns and twists, inter-Korean functional cooperation witnessed impressive accomplishments between 1999 to 2007, including increased inter-Korean trade, South Koreans visiting North Korea, cross-border family reunions, an inter-Korean industrial complex in Kaesong, and more than two hundred official talks between the two Koreas.

In the first decade of the twenty-first century, the DMZ has been quietly transformed, without pomp and circumstance, into a newly minted lifeline connecting the two Koreas via the KIC. In spite of the simmering nuclear standoff and the Cheonan incident, a convoy of motor vehicles leaves Seoul every working day to bring some four hundred South Korean supervisors to manage more than one hundred and ten South Korean factories in the KIC just north of the DMZ, where together with some forty-two thousand North Korean workers produce everything from electronics and watches to shoes and utensils, providing a major source of revenue for the cash-strapped North. Multiple functional channels—electricity, transportation, and communications lines—connect the two sides across this DMZ rift.

Perhaps most revealingly, the hard-line Lee administration had to exclude the KIC from the May 24, 2010, sanctions measures. Throughout the worst of the Cheonan crisis, the KIC kept working and several South Korean managers continued to commute daily across the DMZ to the KIC. In June 2010 the KIC was reported as having a record number (forty-four thousand) of North Korean workers, up by two thousand since January 2010, even as the Lee administration is planning to allow a 50 percent increase in South Koreans staying in the KIC (rather than commuting) from the current six hundred to nine hundred.

The DMZ itself is a quiet, largely undisturbed green zone that is home to the greatest biological diversity on the peninsula. What many realists dismissed as beyond the realm of possibility only a decade ago is now happening as raw materials and finished products are passing along and through what was once considered a major invasion route. This "peace by pieces" functional cooperation provides ways of living with rather than fighting about identity differences on the divided Korean peninsula.

Whither Inter-Korean Rivalry?

Predicting the future of inter-Korean relations, always hazardous, has never been more so than today, when both world politics and Northeast Asian politics are undergoing profound and long-term transformations. Indeed, it seems more unpredictable now than it did in the early to mid-1990s when a broad swath of academics and policy pundits were predicting the imminent collapse of North Korea followed by German-style reunification by absorption. Our understanding of the shape of things to come in inter-Korean relations is also greatly complicated by the fact that the countries involved in

Korean affairs (that is, the two Koreas plus the Big Four) have become moving targets on turbulent trajectories of their highly charged domestic politics, subject to competing and often contradictory pressures.

To say that the future of the two Koreas—particularly with anything involving North Korea—is unpredictable is to call it malleable, not predetermined. Herein lies the potential of various intervening peace strategies in reshaping inter-Korean relations in a more peaceful direction. However, it is worth noting here Marx's famous warning about our history-making power: "Men make their own history, but they do not make it just as they please; they do not make it under circumstances chosen by themselves, but under circumstances directly encountered, given, and transmitted from the past."[45] Indeed, there is a very large range of factors directly encountered, given, and transmitted from the past that are impacting and will continue to influence inter-Korean relations. These factors operate at four different levels in the strategic calculus of North and South Korea: domestically, dyadically, regionally, and internationally. The significance of the different levels will vary depending on the issue being examined at a particular historical moment.[46]

What is most striking about the inter-Korean rivalry, especially in the military and security domain, is the extent to which the United States has repeatedly functioned as Pyongyang's existential threat or critical life-support system, and sometimes both. Despite the habit-driven pronouncement about *songun* politics and *juche* ideology, North Korea's survival strategy is being shaped and reshaped as much in Washington's and Seoul's domestic politics, if not more, than in Pyongyang's Black Box.

That said, however, any effective security paradigm must address the legitimate security concerns and interests of all its members. Common security takes on special significance and urgency in the context of the divided Korean peninsula, given its position as a sensitive flashpoint and strategic pivot of Northeast Asia. In this environment, as elsewhere, true humanism (and common sense) recognizes the ineluctable truth that there has never been and never can be *absolute* security in human life. Because so much of the U.S. perceptions of other states' levels of cooperativeness have been viewed through the Manichean lens of September 11th, a view under which states are either for us or against us, there is a danger of speeding up security-dilemma dynamics, perhaps even transitioning Pyongyang into more irreversible nuclear trajectories. The quest for absolute security is a sure recipe for nuclear proliferation.

The common-security approach, by contrast, breaks away from the vicious and deadly logic of interactive security dilemmas and the dynamics of self-fulfilling prophecies via their impact on the behavior of other states. To follow a common-security approach that relies on recognizing the interrelations and interdependencies among countries, Washington—and the Lee Myung-bak administration—must step back and reassess the moral and practical implications of its foreign policy commandment, "Do as I say, Not as I do," when it comes to the subject of nuclear weapons. In place of this unidirectional fundamentalist posturing where all issues get conflated into one grand overarching goal as made manifest in President George Bush's "Axis of Evil" creed and President Lee Myung-bak's "Grand Bargain" approach, Washington and Seoul, must apply, as did Presidents Kim Dae Jung and Roh Moo-hyun, a simultaneous and synergistic approach—the functional "peace by pieces" approach. Given the half-century of mutual enmity and distrust, the issue of North Korea's nuclear program cannot be settled without addressing the country's legitimate security needs and fears in strategically and economically credible ways. In fact, this is more or less what the two Koreas and the Big Four agreed to do in the September 19, 2005, Joint Statement: "The Six Parties agreed to take coordinated steps to implement the aforementioned consensus *in a phased manner in line with the principle of 'commitment for commitment, action for action*" (emphasis added).

To bring about a long peace and stability—a scenario of unification by consensus—is to require that the two Koreas, especially the stronger South, continue to take a series of small but practical steps toward the creation of a "working peace system." While committed to a democratic and peaceful reunification as the ultimate end, such functional approach proceeds from the premises that (1) national unification per se does not automatically bring about peace, power, prosperity, and democracy; (2) Korean reunification without prior inter-Korean reconciliation—indeed without a prior working peace system—may be a sure recipe for catastrophe for all; and (3) the two Koreas must first initiate the politics of regional reconciliation with changes at home and then start the functional peace process by discussing areas of mutual interest on which they can most readily reach agreement.

Most ironic and revealing in the final analysis is that the reunification drive of the two Koreas resembles a Taoist paradox: doing less and less is really achieving more and more. To hold together different parts of a whole, one must first let them go their separate ways.

8 Asymmetric Rivals: China and Vietnam

Brantly Womack

IN MANY WAYS THE SINO-VIETNAMESE RELATIONSHIP IS A LIMIT case of China's relationships with its neighbors. As a durable relationship between settled states, only the Sino-Korean relationship is comparable, and no other border relationship has seen such wild swings from intimate support to hostility to normalcy in the past sixty years. Moreover, it is a relationship between the two largest remaining communist party-states, a fact that preempts many of the domestic political dimensions of two-level games existing elsewhere in Asia. It is necessary therefore to begin by asking how the concept of rivalry might apply to China and Vietnam and further how the idea of domestic differences influencing foreign policy might be applied to nonparliamentary political contexts. However, the case of the Sino-Vietnamese relationship has more to offer than merely being the outlier of a general comparative framework. The key to understanding the relationship lies in an appreciation of the role that the asymmetry of capacities has played in shaping the perspectives of both sides.[1] The role of asymmetry is enhanced in the Sino-Vietnamese relationship, but it has more general implications for the analysis of rivalries as well.

The term "rivalry" derives from the Latin for occupants of opposite sides of a river, and this fits well the long-term relationship of China and Vietnam. To the extent that a river both divides the populations on its banks and at the same time exposes each to the other, the etymology suggests a clear difference in identity and also a constant bilateral concern. However, the philology is considerably more broad and bland than the common usage of rivalry in international relations research.

We can tighten the meaning of "rivalry" somewhat to refer to competitive identities and interests, and with some squeezing and distortion, the general Sino-Vietnamese relationship can be fit within this narrower notion. Certainly Vietnam has had an attitude that the promotion of its interests required at least an unofficially critical and suspicious attitude toward China. The converse is far less true. Vietnam simply is not that important to China. Moreover, throughout much of the history of Sino-Vietnamese relations a stable asymmetric relationship has prevailed. Since 1999 the relationship can be characterized as one of normalcy, that is, one in which differences are subordinated to a bilateral framework built on the assumption that mutual interests will outweigh differences.

The most restrictive meaning of rivalry, that of a standing bilateral hostility, is most common in international relations literature and least applicable to the general Sino-Vietnamese relationship. Goertz and Diehl give three criteria for "enduring rivalries," competitiveness, time, and spatial consistency, and they clarify competitiveness to mean "the threat or actual use of military force."[2] Thompson presents a more nuanced analysis, distinguishing between territorial and positional (relative status) rivalries, and allowing that frequency of countable conflicts is not a reliable indicator of rivalries.[3] Moreover, he emphasizes that rivalries are mutual attitudes between particular states. But Thompson concurs that the other state must be identified as an opponent, not merely as a threat or a source of problems.[4]

China and Vietnam do not appear on the table of enduring rivalries produced by Goertz and Diehl, but the rivalry is found in one advanced by Thompson.[5] While the relationship was hostile in 1979–91, the search for previous major hostility would go back to the Ming occupation of Vietnam in 1407–27.[6] Positional conflicts have been important in the relationship, but they have been over Vietnam's autonomy (before 1427) and Vietnam's relationship to Laos and Cambodia (1975–91), not over supremacy in the bilateral relationship. With regard to spatial conflict, territorial disputes in the South China Sea are currently the most sensitive area of the relationship. However, the remaining land border disputes were resolved in principle in 2000 along the lines of the border as it has existed for the past thousand years and was further delineated by the French and the Qing Dynasty in the 1880s. The Spratly Island problem could better be characterized as a dispute rather than a rivalry since there are also conflicting territorial claims from the Philippines, Malaysia, and Brunei, and the Chinese claim is shared by Taiwan. The Paracel Islands are the only current bilateral territorial dispute, and they are a small cluster of reefs and flat islands inhabited only by Chinese garrisons.[7]

We are left, then, with the Sino-Vietnamese hostility of 1979–91, and that, too, is problematic as a rivalry. Clearly each was an enemy to the other. Both the military situation and their mutual diplomatic behavior provide sufficient evidence. But were they competing for the same goal? Vietnam was responding to a clear threat to its national security when it invaded Cambodia, though it is not unreasonable to assume that they wanted to assert permanent control over Indochina.[8] By 1985 Cambodia was secure and Vietnam's position shifted toward accepting military withdrawal. China's principal concern initially was Vietnam's alliance with the Soviet Union, though as its relations with Gorbachev improved, its hostility toward Vietnam remained.[9]

But there has been and remains a fundamental tension in the Sino-Vietnamese relationship. The tension would be admitted by both sides, and especially by Vietnam. Vietnam feels vulnerable to China; China is constricted by Vietnam. Even in the current era of increasing economic cooperation and political and military exchanges, the tension is there. But it is not the product of two competitors reaching for the same goal. Rather, it is the product of the asymmetry of capacities between China and Vietnam and the resulting differences of interests, attention, and perception.

The problem of domestic linkages to foreign policy in China and Vietnam is equally problematic, though for different reasons. While it would be a mistake to view the leadership of a party-state as indifferent to public opinion or to particular interests, there is little public spontaneity in politics and virtual uniformity of views in public media. Although there is increasing political diversity in both countries, it is growing from a comparatively tiny base and the basic party-state structures remain intact. Moreover, central control is strongest on sensitive issues such as international relations. That said, there have been differences among the Vietnamese leadership with regard to China, and there are discernable local and ministerial interests that affect China's policies toward Vietnam.

The applicability of the different categories of domestic influence suggested in this project is thus very faint indeed for China and Vietnam. In each there is only one governing party, so factional foreign policy is limited, and its public visibility is even more limited. In a Leninist party there is no legitimate, standing opposition, either within the party or (especially) on the outside. Thus the option of rivalry outbidding is precluded. The ploys of diversion and threat inflation are certainly available to party-state leaderships, though without the presence of independent media and opposition parties the judgment is in the eye of the beholder.[10] Perhaps the most appropriate category of domestic influences is that of governmental politics, though I will argue that these are more apparent in noncrisis situations. In sum, the party-state leaderships of China and Vietnam are closer to the stereotypical unitary national actor than are parliamentary regimes, even though party-states are not indifferent to domestic concerns.

The cases to be analyzed here are those of the developing Sino-Vietnamese hostility in 1975–79 and the movement from stalemate to normalization in 1986–91. I will argue that the leaderships of both countries were fairly uniform in their opinions of the other side in the former period, while in the latter there was significant diversity within the Vietnamese leadership. Ironically, in the 1970s the dynamics of the relationship were primarily bilateral, while external events were decisive in moving China and Vietnam to normalization. In order to support my argument that there is a more basic asymmetric tension in the relationship I will begin with a general discussion of the Sino-Vietnamese relationship.

The Context of the Sino-Vietnamese Relationship

The relationship between China and Vietnam has been one of substantive commonality on the one hand and identities defined by differences on the other. In cultural background, rural revolutionary experience, and current governance, there is no country more similar to China than Vietnam, and no country more similar to Vietnam than China. Nevertheless, Vietnam defines itself against China. Vietnam's name means "South Viet," and the northern Viet (Yue in Chinese) are the ancestral population of Guangdong and Guangxi. The name "Vietnam" was bestowed by the Chinese emperor in the early nineteenth century.[11] It was an improvement over the earlier name Annam (Pacified South). Conversely, one might also say that China's name *Zhongguo* (Central Kingdom) implies a periphery beyond its control.

Vietnam was a part of China for a thousand years, but from the tenth century to the present, the national self-consciousness of Vietnam has been one of being "not-China." Vietnam prides itself on its defensive patriotism, and the external object of its solidarity has usually been China. Vietnam plays a much smaller role in China's consciousness, but a major one in China's sense of its own limits. The defeat of the Ming occupation of Vietnam in 1427 was a watershed in China's inward turn for the next four hundred years. Vietnam defined the limits of China to the south, which was the natural direction of millennia of Chinese expansion.[12]

Despite the negative dimensions of mutual attitudes, China and Vietnam managed to have a stable, nonhostile relationship for most of the premodern period. The relationship was formalized in the tribute system, which provided for regular visits to Beijing by an official Vietnamese delegation.[13] Obeisance would be made to the Chinese emperor, gifts would be exchanged, and official recognition would be given to the Vietnamese ruler. The exchange of deference on Vietnam's part for recognition by China of Vietnam's legitimacy (implying a guarantee against invasion) was crucial for stabilizing the asymmetric relationship. China did not have to worry about Vietnam balancing against it, and Vietnam was free to pursue southern expansion and wars with its symmetric rivals, Champa, Cambodia, and Siam.

Western imperialism destroyed the framework of traditional East Asian diplomacy. What emerged was a more fraternal relationship of fellow sufferers that was particularly intimate for China and Vietnam. Ho Chi Minh taught rural revolution in China, and the nom de guerre of Truong Chinh, a top lieutenant, means "Long March." China was the first state to recognize the Democratic Republic of Vietnam in January 1950, and it provided unstinting assistance during its wars with France and the United States. But the very intimacy of the relationship created uneasiness. Ironically, Ho Chi Minh's most famous slogan, "Nothing is more precious than independence and freedom," was coined at the time of a mass rally in his honor at Tiananmen in July 1966.[14]

The illusions of victory that prompted post-1975 hostility will be discussed in detail below, but it is important to note that with the establishment of normal relations in 1991 asymmetric tensions still persist. The bilateral relationship is buffered by both states' general policies of reform and openness. More specifically, Vietnam's membership in ASEAN since 1975 and China's rapidly expanding multilateral relationship with ASEAN since 2002 have provided an encouraging context for cooperation. And China's strong performance in the current global economic crisis, as well as its available cash for investment, has made it more important for all of its neighbors. Nevertheless, Vietnam's sensitivities to China have been enhanced by feelings of increased dependency.[15] The Sino-Vietnamese relationship is likely to remain stable but not relaxed.

Illusions of Victory, 1976–1979

The collapse of the Thieu regime in January-April 1975, culminating in the peaceful entry into Saigon of the People's Army of Vietnam (PAVN), provided an unexpectedly swift conclusion to the colonial era of Southeast Asian history.[16] Although the United States had conceived of its mission in Vietnam as one of containing communism by supporting a postcolonial Saigon government, its withdrawal in 1973 and the subsequent collapse of the Republic of Vietnam (South Vietnam) marked the end of external powers and their dependent regimes in Southeast Asia.

The two happiest countries were Vietnam and China, but they marched in the same parade with different dreams. For Vietnam, Indochina's national liberation struggle had finally succeeded. Now it was free to reformulate its domestic and foreign policy without the constraints of war. Unified Vietnam was renamed the Socialist Republic of Vietnam, and the Fourth Party Congress in 1976 set an ambitious program of helping the South catch up with the socialist North. In foreign policy, the first task was "to endeavor to consolidate and strengthen the militant solidarity and relation of cooperation between our country and all the fraternal socialist countries."[17] Secretary Le Duan was careful to include China in his praise, but always after the Soviet Union and only in the context of international socialist solidarity.

While no other country could be as happy as the Vietnamese about their reunification, China had many reasons to be pleased. They had been Vietnam's strongest and most faithful supporter since 1950. The weakening and eventual defeat of the United States in Vietnam was the precondition for China's strategic shift from American imperialism as the principal threat to Soviet socialist imperialism. Moreover, supporting Vietnam during the war had been a considerable strain on China's resources, and it was looking forward to a more relaxed and less expensive relationship.

The Vietnamese and Chinese illusions of victory were not consciously opposed to one another, but they contained the tensions from which conflict quickly emerged. Vietnam mistook the reluctant cooperation of China and the Soviet Union during the war as socialist internationalism; China forgave Vietnam's acceptance of Soviet aid as a necessity of war. Vietnam assumed that victory strengthened its hand in arguing for aid from China; China figured that the end of the war meant the end of emergency aid. Vietnam assumed that the "common battleground" of Indochina had created a "special relationship" between Vietnam, Cambodia, and Laos that would last "forever";[18] China assumed that it could deal separately with independent states.

The deterioration of Sino-Vietnamese relations to the point of war in February 1979 passed through several stages.[19] The brief postvictory honeymoon lasted only until Le Duan's confrontational visit to Beijing in September 1975. Mao Zedong made it clear to Duan that the era of unstinting emergency aid was over: "Today you are not the poorest under heaven. We are the poorest."[20] Duan asserted Vietnam's independent foreign policy and left Beijing early and without holding the customary farewell banquet.[21]

From October 1975 to May 1978, mutual opposition hardened. China's sanctions against Vietnamese impertinence thinned out the veneer of official solidarity. China rejected new requests for aid and lagged in the implementation of existing agreements. Meanwhile Vietnam removed from its leadership all ethnic Chinese, those who were sympathetic to China, and even members of border-area ethnic minorities. Finally the third phase of open hostility began in May 1978 when China went public in its criticism of Vietnamese expulsion of ethnic Chinese, marking the period of open criticism that lasted until war in February 1979.[22] Vietnam joined COMECON in June 1978 and signed a treaty of friendship and cooperation with the Soviet Union in November. In December it invaded Cambodia and quickly pushed the Khmer Rouge to the Thai frontier. China responded with the invasion and destruction of Vietnam's northern provinces in February-March 1979. After the brief but bloody border war, officially a war to defend the border but unofficially an effort to teach Vietnam a "lesson," there was a cold war with border skirmishes from 1979 until official normalization in November 1991.[23]

Although China and Vietnam were each undergoing profound domestic transformations during the second half of the 1970s, there was no sustained or distinctive pattern of domestic differences related to the Sino-Vietnamese conflict itself. China provides the best demonstration of leadership consensus. The evolution of hostility was uninterrupted by the death of Mao in September 1976, the interregnum of Hua Guofeng from November 1976 to December 1978, and the beginning of the new era of reform and openness under Deng Xiaoping in December 1978. Had Vietnam been an issue within the top leadership, surely these shifts would have affected policy. Indeed, in Cambodia

Pol Pot was quite worried that the death of Mao and the fall of leftism would undermine China's support for the Khmer Rouge, but it did not.

In Vietnam, there was a purge of ethnic Chinese and of people connected with previous cooperation with China, but the purge was more ethnic cleansing than removal of a losing faction. Hanoi's fears of a "fifth column" of support for China among Vietnam's ethnic Chinese (Hoa) were certainly exaggerated.[24] Most Hoa were in the South, and they were part of the general pattern of urban, petty bourgeois ethnic Chinese throughout Southeast Asia. They had supported Sun Yat Sen and the Guomindang, their relatives had been persecuted during the Cultural Revolution, and they had little in common with socialist China.[25] In any case, they were outsiders to the politics of unified Vietnam.

Despite the lack of domestic factionalism, an argument could be made that the leaderships of China and Vietnam engaged in threat inflation for domestic purposes. After all, China's fear of a Soviet-Vietnam alliance turned out to be exaggerated, as was Vietnam's fear of Chinese domination. Was Deng Xiaoping consolidating his support by creating a foreign war? Was Le Duan trying to distract domestic attention from the failure of the economy after reunification? In both cases, the threat exaggeration hypothesis lacks explanatory value. Deng's political situation in January 1979 could hardly have been stronger. Almost everyone in China wanted to move beyond the bankruptcy of leftism. The demonstrations at Democracy Wall in December 1978 were in support of reform, not in opposition.[26] True, one dissident, Wei Jingsheng, was convicted of betraying the state secret of the number of casualties in the war, but he was not a typical voice, and he did not represent an antiwar faction. Moreover, the war ran against Deng's new trend of demilitarized foreign policy, and it did not win friends in Washington.

As for Duan, it can certainly be claimed that his aggressive attitude toward China was counterproductive, but the ultimate triggers for open hostility seemed unavoidable for Vietnam. Cambodia under the Khmer Rouge had become a serious and implacable threat to Vietnam's national security, and the prospect of vastly increasing Chinese aid to the Khmer Rouge increased the urgency of the Vietnamese invasion of December 1978.[27] Moreover, given the increasing likelihood of hostility with China, it seemed prudent that Vietnam enter into an alliance with the Soviet Union in November 1978. Meanwhile the first tactical adjustments of domestic policy began in 1979, but the strategic adjustment to reform (Doi Moi) was not initiated until 1986, after Le Duan's death. It would be difficult to argue that Deng started a war in order to mobilize for reform, while Duan did so in order to prevent it.

Bureaucratic politics had little to do with the war. One might say that the North and the military were its chief movers in Vietnam, but in the late 1970s, after a Northern victory ending thirty years of war, there no other significant government actors. The exception proving the rule was Nguyen Van Linh, Politburo member and Party secretary of Ho Chi Minh City. Linh disagreed with Duan concerning domestic policy and was removed from office in 1982. After Duan's death he became "Vietnam's Gorbachev" and father of Doi Moi. Linh's fate demonstrates that Duan was fully in control throughout the move toward war, and that the pressure to prioritize economic development and openness emerged rather slowly in the 1980s. In the case of China, Deng's bureaucratic ties were comprehensive, and he continued the move toward war at the same time that he ranked the military as the last of the "four modernizations."

In sum, the deterioration of Sino-Vietnamese relations in 1975–79 was grounded in the ambiguity of identities emerging from victory. China thought all was now quiet on the southern front, while Vietnam assumed that it was now a powerful new player that still deserved full support. The contradiction between Vietnam's assertiveness and China's resentment drove the relationship to the point where each could assume the other was an enemy. Neither domestic politics nor third parties played causal roles. Despite the seeming inevitability of conflict, Alexander Woodside was correct in his observation at the time that "since neither side can gain, it is obvious that each side has made catastrophic miscalculations about the other."[28]

Normalization, 1986–1991

Although Vietnam succeeded easily in occupying Cambodia and in installing a compliant government there, the strain of isolation led to serious rethinking of Vietnam's international posture in the second half of the 1980s. In 1990 China also shifted toward normalization, and so in November 1991 Party General Secretary Do Muoi and Chairman of the Council of Ministers Vo Van Kiet made their historic visit to Beijing and signed a joint communiqué reestablishing relations.

As one might expect with an internal change in policy direction, there were more signs of disagreement within the Vietnamese leadership in this phase of the Sino-Vietnamese relationship. Disagreement was less evident in China. However, for both states events external to the bilateral relationship played key causal roles in inducing policy change.

By 1985 Vietnam had cleared out the last bases of the Khmer Rouge inside Cambodia, and it began the process of turning over security responsibilities to the Cambodian government of Hun Sen. However, an exile government, the Coalition Government of Democratic Kampuchea (CGDK) had been formed with bases in Thailand, and it had support from ASEAN, China, and the United States. The groundwork for a prolonged stalemate had thus been laid: Vietnam controlled Cambodia, and opposition to Vietnam created an anti-Vietnam entente that was neither costly nor risky for its members.[29]

But Vietnam, the apparent winner, was in a weaker position. Its economy was desperately short of consumer goods and modern inputs.[30] It depended on the Soviet Union for economic and political support, and Gorbachev's dramatic change of direction in Asia policy announced in his Vladivostok speech of July 28, 1986, was a major shock to the Vietnamese leadership.[31] Although Gorbachev maintained support for Vietnam, he was clearly interested in normal relations with China, and the main obstacle from China's point of view was Vietnam's occupation of Cambodia.[32]

When Sihanouk met with Hun Sen in December 1987, the "Cambodia problem" moved from stalemate to endgame. With negotiations underway and Vietnam promising a unilateral withdrawal of its troops by 1990, regional actors began to think about life in a peaceful Southeast Asia. Thailand talked about turning Indochina from a battlefield into a marketplace, and Indonesia sponsored the Jakarta Informal Meetings to facilitate discussions among parties that denied each other's legitimacy. China and the United States were the slowest to move and were caught by surprise when Vietnam withdrew its troops in September 1989. Both then shifted their positions from demanding an end to Vietnamese occupation to demanding a guarantee of a peaceful and stable Cambodia.

For Vietnam, progress on Cambodia faced the leadership with a possible choice of two roads. On one side was the familiar ideological road of socialist internationalism and anti-imperialism.[33] But this path was now undermined by Gorbachev's reforms as well as by China's continuing hostility. The new side was a policy of international openness to complement the domestic reforms that began in 1986. The chief proponent of the new market-oriented path was Foreign Minister Nguyen Co Thach.[34] From 1988 until his dismissal as foreign minister in 2001, he led what might be called the pro-West faction of the leadership. He was particularly interested in normalization of relations with the United States, and he personally met with every American group visiting Vietnam in the late 1980s. There was little opposition in the leadership to improvement of relations with neighbors and with the capitalist world, but there were those who were less enthusiastic than Thach.

Thach's position was undermined by three events. First, the American reaction to his overtures was one of inertial hostility. New demands were raised about cooperation in the search for remains of soldiers missing in action (MIAs). The United States did not recognize Vietnam until July 1995, the month that Vietnam entered ASEAN, and Vietnam already had diplomatic relations with more than 160 countries by that time.[35] Second, the collapse of European communism in 1989–91 induced a resurgence of conservative anxieties about ideological and political security. Even Nguyen Van Linh, "Vietnam's Gorbachev," revived the old rhetoric of international class struggle and socialist solidarity. Third, in August 1990 China changed its Indochina policy. A secret summit was held Chengdu in September (Thach was not invited), and both sides reached agreement in principle concerning normalization.[36] Improving relations with China raised the conservative hope that the remaining socialist countries could band together.

China's change of policy regarding Vietnam was also catalyzed by events. It maintained an unyielding position of support for the CGDK (including the Khmer Rouge) until the United States suddenly dropped its support in July 1990. Then China was faced with the prospect of being isolated as the sole supporter of the Khmer Rouge, and it rethought its position. The secret summit occurred six weeks later. The second event, the Tiananmen Incident of June 1989, was not external, but it was incidental to the Sino-Vietnamese relationship. The shunning of China by developed countries after Tiananmen led to a reevaluation of China's relationships with its neighbors, including Vietnam. By cooperating with the UN-sponsored resolution of the Cambodian conflict China could start a new chapter in its general relationship with Southeast Asia as well as with Vietnam and Cambodia.

Although the two largest remaining communist countries normalized their relationship in 1991, China had no interest in a special and close relationship with Vietnam, to the disappointment of Vietnamese conservatives. China was still resentful of the unrequited efforts it had made on Vietnam's behalf during the wars, and the informal reaction to Vietnam's newfound friendship was that "anyone with milk is its mother." Official analyses argued carefully that socialist internationalism was a matter of each socialist country peacefully pursuing its own national interest rather than sharing resources.[37] For China, and eventually for Vietnam, the normal relationship between the two simply fit into larger strategies of good neighborliness and openness.

Although domestic factionalism in China between reformers and conservatives grew from 1986 and contributed to the catastrophe of Tiananmen, there are no signs of a significant policy difference regarding Vietnam or Cambodia. Deng Xiaoping was personally quite committed to teaching lessons to Vietnam, and other leaders kept contrary thoughts to themselves. Moreover, from June 1989 to July 1990, condemnation of Vietnam was one of the few things that China and the United States had in common. Even the post-1989 policy reassessment did not highlight differences because Jiang Zemin, Zhu Rongji, and Li Peng had seen the damage caused by factionalism. Thus the new policy of good neighborliness toward Southeast Asia in general and including Indochina was a group policy rather than a factional gambit or victory.[38]

Returning to our analytical categories of two-level policy influences, greater factionalism in both Vietnam and China distinguishes the end of Sino-Vietnamese hostility from its beginnings, but only in the case of Vietnam is factionalism directly relevant to policymaking. It should be noted that even Thach was originally a strong spokesman for the conservative position. Thach was a major source for Gareth Porter's presentation of the dying embers of Vietnam's illusions of victory in the early 1980s.[39] But as isolation began to break down in 1988–89, Thach fought mightily for a more Western option. While he did not oppose better relations with China, he was clearly not a friend of China's. One could accuse the conservatives of threat inflation with the collapse of European communism, but they do deserve some sympathy for their ideological trauma. From Confucianism and Buddhism to Catholicism and communism, all of Vietnam's major ideologies have come from abroad, and to have the source of one's orthodoxy fail can lead to desperate action. But the idea of holding tight to China was deeply repugnant to many Vietnamese, and had China been willing, the honeymoon would probably have been a short and mutually unsatisfactory one.

With regard to bureaucratic politics, one might expect that the resurgence of Ho Chi Minh City under reform might strengthen Thach's side, but in fact it would strengthen openness in any direction, including China. The army and security, associated with Le Duc Anh, were certainly more conservative than the Foreign Ministry. But the conservatives could not achieve a special relationship with China, so the final result for Vietnam was a general policy of reform and openness, China included. As for China, there is little evidence of a difference of opinion or interest despite the change in policy. Later on, the neighboring province of Guangxi developed special interests in promoting better relations, and naval expansion has complicated relationships with all of Southeast Asia and especially with Vietnam. But in 1986–91 there was little anticipated gain in normalization.[40]

Enduring Asymmetry

The complications that the Sino-Vietnamese relationship poses for a general understanding of rivalry can be illustrated by events in 2009.[41] By contrast, China's share in Vietnamese trade increased, and discussion continues regarding road and rail lines linking China through Vietnam to Singapore as well as regarding plans to make the Tonkin Gulf into a "mini-Mediterranean." On the other hand, there was a massive public outcry concerning Chinese investment plans for bauxite mining in Central Vietnam, with General Giap (Vietnam's preeminent military hero) playing a prominent role, and China's expansion of its submarine facilities in Hainan have led Vietnam to commit itself to purchasing six submarines from Russia. Chinese observers of Southeast Asia would agree that Vietnam is China's most problematic and least cooperative neighbor in the region, and Vietnamese would say that China is the country that most worries them. The China-ASEAN Free Trade Area (CAFTA) was launched in January 2010, which is also the sixtieth anniversary of Sino-Vietnamese relations, but the prospect of increased dependence on China fuels Vietnamese anxieties. The best guarantor for the stability of Sino-Vietnamese relationship is that it is embedded in the broader regional relations of both countries.

The general dilemmas of the current Sino-Vietnamese relationship also reflect a diversity of domestic pressures. In China, the strong nationalistic tone of "netizen" discussions sets a climate for policy that the leadership cannot ignore. Although Vietnam did not attract much attention in 2009, the Internet reaction to Burmese pressures on ethnic Chinese in the border area shows the sensitivity of the netizen trigger.[42] On the more peaceful side, Guangxi and Yunnan Provinces are clearly competing for leadership in developing pathways between China and ASEAN. The central government takes a back seat on these local initiatives so long as they do not conflict with overall national policy. Meanwhile the PLA's interest in a blue-water navy enhances the tensions in the South China Sea.

In Vietnam there is less segmentation of public influence on China policy, but it is more acute and effective. Deep-seated anxieties about China are pervasive, and the government has the delicate responsibility of preventing public expressions of anti-China sentiment from harming an important relationship.[43] In the case of the bauxite protests, there was a broad range of public criticisms, critical Web sites, and demonstrations, and eventually the government postponed indefinitely its decision on whether to allow Chinese investment to proceed. At the same time, it prevents discussion of the issue in the official media. The government's dilemma creates an opportunity for some politicians to play to the public's fears, and it creates an issue on which overseas Vietnamese can simultaneously vent their dislike of the government and show their patriotism. Less acute versions of the same phenomenon can be seen in ongoing criticisms of the border agreement and in demonstrations in late 2007 against Chinese policies regarding the Paracel and Spratly Islands. In sum, one could say that while at present China and Vietnam do not see their national interests as opposed in a zero-sum game and their governmental structures do not permit the oppositional conflict that highlights two-level games, there is a divergence of national perspectives, and evidence of differentiated domestic pressures can be seen. To return to the original meaning of rivalry, China and Vietnam are definitely on different sides of a river.

Rather than simply being a problem case for a general theory of rivalry, however, perhaps the Sino-Vietnamese relationship can be used to highlight a relational dimension that should be taken more seriously in other cases as well. While China and Vietnam are an uncomfortable squeeze into the category of enduring rivalries, the long and varied history of their relationship makes it an archetypal case of enduring asymmetry.

Certainly the difference in capacity between China and Vietnam was significant, multidimensional, and permanent. Traditional Vietnam did have symmetric rivalries with Champa, Cambodia, and Siam at various times, but not with China. China's traditional external relationships were never symmetric even though the Yuan (Mongol) and Qing (Manchu) dynasties were based on nomadic conquest of China.[44] Even when China fell apart, most recently in the warlord period (1916–27), its factions were more interested in competing among themselves for central control than in challenging neighbors. And Vietnam utilized the juncture between the Tang and Song dynasties to establish its independence, not to challenge China or to war with the part of China closest to it. Vietnam's highest priority vis-à-vis China is autonomy, not superiority.

Given China's relative invulnerability and Vietnam's exposure, it is not surprising that the asymmetric structure of the relationship influenced their perspectives. Even in peaceful and voluntary matters such as trade, China has proportionately less at risk than Vietnam. Vietnam can therefore be expected to be more alert to the opportunities and risks of the relationship and, as prospect theory teaches, the risks will be more vivid.[45] In ordinary times Vietnam is simply not as interesting to China as vice versa. Every leader in Vietnam watches China closely, while China's policies are less coordinated because they do not merit as high a priority in the national economy of attention. If Vietnam invested in a bauxite mine in China it would not become a national issue. Vietnam's greater exposure in the relationship is not created by China's policies but by its presence, and exposure is not restricted to security issues. It is the direct result of asymmetry.

Differences in perspective in an asymmetric relationship produce characteristic differences in perception, and these in turn influence reciprocal postures. For China, it is more convenient to fit policy toward Vietnam in more general categories, either as part of a larger strategy (reform and openness, good neighbor policy, China-ASEAN relations) or a general formula for the bilateral relationship (friendship or hostility). Underneath the strategic umbrella, however, various specific Chinese interests may pursue policies that from Vietnam's perspective suggest contradictory or ulterior motives. For instance, while Guangxi Province pursues trade links, Hainan Province announces a plan for tourism on the disputed Paracel Islands. Another problematic pair of initiatives would be China's 2002 agreement with ASEAN for peaceful settlement of disputes in the South China Sea and the construction of an advanced submarine base on Hainan across from central Vietnam. For Vietnam's part, it is constantly aware of its exposure to China, and therefore regardless of strategic commitments its China policies will be cautious. Its efforts to "connect the dots" of China's less coordinated behavior may lead its analysts to an unduly alarming picture of China as a malevolent and duplicitous schemer. Meanwhile China is tempted to view Vietnam's caution as the sign of an unwilling and unreliable partner. These structural misperceptions induced by asymmetry are most obvious in the emergence of hostility in the 1970s, but they are also clearly visible in the 1960s and 1990s. In the past ten years the strong diplomatic framework of normalcy has reduced the salience of mutual misperceptions, but it has not eliminated them.

Why, with its preponderance of power, has China not solved its Vietnam problem by force? David Kang argues that the strategic culture of East Asia is based on the acceptance of hierarchy and on reliance on an international order anchored by China.[46] It is certainly true that the interaction of China as a central power with its neighbors over the millennia has created a fundamentally different set of international expectations than the presumptions of competitive anarchy in the West.[47] But in fact culture in this case reflects a common habituation to the reality that a preponderance of power often does not translate into ease of domination. Vietnam's eventual defeat of China's occupation from 1407 to 1427 was a major reality test of the possibilities of domination. China learned to live within the limits of its reach, and its neighbors found that a stable, China-centered international order was more convenient than threatening. It is an open question whether China can restore a modernized version of the *pax Sinica* in East Asia, but the general success of its good neighbor policy in the past twenty years—especially in contrast to the results of American unilateralism in the same period—shows that the old approach is not irrelevant in a globalized world.

The underlying principles of the asymmetric relationship between China and Vietnam can be summed into "three Rs." First, asymmetry is "real." The difference of capacity is not a psychological or cultural construct, and it structures the material situation in which the relationship plays out. Second, asymmetry is "relational." Disparity of capacity creates differences of interest, of perspective, and of perception that create characteristic patterns of interaction. Not only does each relationship display its own path-dependent development, but also the larger and smaller positions within the relationship display structurally dependent, nontransposable characteristics. Third, asymmetry is "resilient." In times of peace, the different exposures in the relationship continually generate tensions that require diplomatic management. In times of hostility, China has found that it cannot impose its will on Vietnam, while Vietnam has experienced severe hardships and opportunity costs. Ironically, China's failure to dominate occurs not despite the asymmetry of capacities, but because of them. What to China is a "small war" with limited objectives is to Vietnam a mortal threat to its identity and existence. China has the option of withdrawing; Vietnam's only option is resistance.

Conclusion: Asymmetry Beyond the Archetype

An archetype has the strength of being the perfect illustration of a general principle. China and Vietnam have had a millennium of experience with stable asymmetry, and for all but a century of that experience there was no stronger third party distracting the bilateral relationship. But analysis by archetype has the weakness of not addressing the limits and conditionalities of its principle. Nevertheless, an archetypal analysis is useful in modifying the universality of contradictory claims and in adding analytical texture to the general picture of international relationships.

Returning to the initial question of the meaning of rivalry, Vasquez's argument that rivalries must be symmetric is acceptable if we limit the term to rivalries in which both sides attempt to achieve the same goal.[48] However, there are clearly significant situations of asymmetric international tension, and to exclude these from purview may provide too narrow a base for explicating the origins of conflict. Similarly, Vasquez's concentration on territorial disputes unduly restricts the search for contentious issues.

Rasler and Thompson cautiously allow the possibility of asymmetric rivalries, though as outliers to the general picture since the smaller state is by definition not an equal challenger.[49] More importantly, Rasler and Thompson add to the category of territorial rivalry that of positional rivalry, and they point out that territorial disputes often mask positional rivalry. However, they expect asymmetric rivalries to be primarily territorial. While it makes sense for two states who are close in the international pecking order to "make sure that the other state does not pull ahead," the only positional tension Rasler and Thompson see in an asymmetric relationship is resistance by the weaker to subordination.[50]

Asymmetry can be used to flesh out the linkage between territorial and positional rivalries, and it can add a new dimension to positional conflicts. As Rasler and Thompson suggest, tensions over territory and over relational standing are often connected. Indeed, since territory is the body of the state, a territorial dispute is at the same time a dispute over the boundaries of national identity. In an asymmetric relationship, the weaker side is necessarily more exposed and therefore is likely to be more sensitive to questions of physical boundary. By contrast, the stronger side can view the weaker's unwillingness to yield as a lack of proper deference. Thus the spatial dispute can become a synecdoche for the tensions of the general relationship, and they can each vow to fight to the death over land that in many cases (such as the Spratlys) is so inhospitable that it is not worth living in.

The notion of positional conflict implicit in asymmetric territorial disputes is somewhat different from that assumed by Rasler and Thompson. A territorial dispute appears to be the ultimate single-goal situation. The land belongs either to one state or the other. However, the implications of securing or losing the land are different for each side. If the weaker side loses territory by force, then it must wonder where the stronger side will stop. If it secures the disputed territory, then its autonomy has been confirmed by the stronger side. If the stronger side loses territory it loses face; if it gains territory the reality of its power is demonstrated. The positional conflict inherent in the territorial dispute is thus proportional rather than absolute. The weaker side does not want to be pushed into insignificance, and the stronger does not want to have its strength challenged, but neither seeks to displace the other and to occupy its position.

In the most general terms, the famous Athenian cynicism that "the strong rule when they can and the weak serve when they must" must be modified to cope with the realities of asymmetric relationships. In either war or peace—with rivalry in between—the weak and the strong may not want the same things. A "small war" to the strong is likely to be a mortal threat to the weak, and the desperate popular resistance of the weak may outlast the limited purposes and deployable resources of the strong. In peace, the strong want deference and the weak want acknowledgment of their autonomy. Deference and autonomy are not intrinsically incompatible, but when there is tension and the commitment of the other side is doubtful, a space for asymmetric rivalry is created.

Beyond an enrichment of general theory, asymmetry theory can contribute empirical questions to the investigation of other concrete cases of rivalry. I will suggest three ideas that might have "legs" that could reach elsewhere. First, symmetric rivalries are competitive for the same goals, but asymmetric rivalries concern incompatible but different goals. To what extent, for instance, does Pakistan's greater vulnerability to India create a divergence of goals? Does Kashmir mean the same thing to both countries? Second, rivalry between symmetric powers implies mortal risk for both, while asymmetric rivalry creates the temptation of "small wars" for the larger side, though of course these are extralarge, identity-threatening wars for the smaller side. To what extent, for example, is the interaction of North Korea and the United States a product of a disparity of risk? Perhaps greater risk makes North Korea's choice between compliance and challenge more dichotomous. Lastly, because of the standing difference in relative importance, the larger country's domestic pressures on policy are likely to be more diverse and less well coordinated at the top, while the smaller side is likely to be more alert to national opportunities and risks. If we review the relationship of the United States and Iran since the hostage crisis, Iranian policy has swung between national hopes and fears, while American policy has been more inertial, disengaged, and contradictory.

Perhaps Tolstoy would opine that happy international relationships are all alike, while every rivalry is unhappy in its own way. Nevertheless, it might be worth differentiating rivalries into those that are playing the same game for the same goal because they have (or believe they have) equal chances, and those in which one side sees itself as defending the obvious values of the international order (however it conceives them), and the other defends its identity against a mortal threat. In both cases domestic influences will surely be at work, but if the main game were like tennis in the latter case, then one side would be the permanent victor and the other would be the loser. To an American, or French, or Chinese audience, the name "Vietnam" suggests a more difficult and frustrating situation.

9 Two-level Games in Asian Rivalries

Sumit Ganguly and William R. Thompson

Examining interdependencies between domestic and international politics, two-level games, is not a new topic.[1] But, intermittently, analysts are reminded that it can be somewhat artificial to proceed as if domestic politics and international politics operate entirely independently. Putnam's 1988 article on two-level games provided one such reminder.[2] His focus was on bargaining in negotiations, and the main point was that it did not suffice for bargainers to work out arrangements successfully with their foreign counterparts. They also had to negotiate/bargain with their domestic constituencies. The international game could easily be constrained by the domestic game(s) just as the nature of international negotiations could influence the way in which domestic audiences evaluated the international bargaining process. The argument was not that domestic politics dictated how negotiators bargained internationally. Rather, negotiators had to appreciate that they were involved in making deals in international and domestic games more or less simultaneously.

Much of the subsequent writing on two-level games in international relations has continued to focus on the international bargaining theme. But that is not our interest. We wish to apply the two-level game metaphor to conflict situations that often do not possess the same structure as international negotiations in which agents have to make and sell outcomes to international and domestic audiences. Yet it is not inconceivable that decision-makers might find themselves in parallel situations in which, at least on occasion, national decision-makers act internationally (domestically) with one eye on domestic (international) audiences.

In Chapter 1, we had suggested some possible ways in which two-level games might be manifested. Factionalized struggles, rivalry outbidding, diversionary policies, governmental politics in which agencies compete for a piece of the policy pie, and threat inflation are some of the ways in which domestic political games can influence international policy games, and vice versa. But there is no guarantee that such processes can be found everywhere or all of the time. We should not start with the premise that two-level games are ubiquitous.

A combination of logic, a reading of the two-level game literature, and reflecting on how conflict interactions do and do not resemble conventional international bargaining situations can generate a number of hypotheses about when and where two-level games are more or less likely to be found.[3] Michael Colaresi, for instance, rules out two types of circumstances as unlikely to foster domestic-international linkages.[4] One case is the situation in which foreign policy acts are carried out by actors without decision-making authority. So long as the adversary recognizes the lack of authorization, a "loose cannon" clash is less likely to escalate internationally or develop domestic complications. Alternatively, brief and abrupt physical attacks that are either endured or responded to automatically are likely to take place too quickly for domestic implications to develop—unless, of course, the exchange escalates into something more dangerous via a protracted dispute (in which case, it is no longer a brief and abrupt physical attack).

Perhaps the most salient factor in determining whether two-level games are apt to be ongoing are situations in which the main decision-makers are fairly autonomous. If there are few domestic constituencies that must be placated or mobilized to support governmental activity, decision-makers may feel that they can safely ignore domestic politics while they concentrate on international interactions. In this respect, authoritarian regimes are likely to be in a better position than more open regimes. Authoritarian regimes, of course, are not always wholly autonomous. Dictators may have to answer to militaries, clergies, or wealthy landowners but not always and, often, not all at the same time. Authoritarian rulers also have to mobilize domestic support from time to time. More democratic regimes, nonetheless, are almost guaranteed to have multiple constituencies that require some level of attention and more often than in the case of authoritarian systems.

Similarly, if governments can control or restrict the amount of information that is available to domestic audiences, they may also be in a better position to focus exclusively on international interactions.[5] Military coffins from combat associated with foreign insurgencies returned home at night or with no media attention permitted, for example, create less need to appease public opinion—as Cuban, Soviet, and U.S. decision-makers have learned in different decades.

Other considerations may also constrain responses to adversarial initiatives. If the anticipated costs of a response to an attack are so great, avoiding an overt reaction may not require much deliberation. South Korean responses to North Korean provocations seem to possess this attribute. The North Korean ability to do serious damage to vulnerable Seoul is a valuable deterrent from South Korean counterresponses. External allies constitute another "game layer" and can also complicate and restrain counterresponses. By contrast, their involvement can be reassuring that a client state does not have to deal with a major security problem on its own. But the quid pro quo is that the major power ally must often be consulted before bellicose actions are taken. In most cases (but not all), major power allies prefer to stifle or restrain escalatory behavior to avoid conflict between major power patrons on opposing sides. To some extent then, we should expect situations involving serious major power involvement to dampen the probability of two-level games emerging.

Where might two-level games be expected to be most likely? Interactions between rivals with wide selectorates that are highly public and protracted affairs involving considerable threat intensity, in general, should be ideal breeding grounds. Wide selectorates are important for electoral considerations. It helps if decision-maker tenure is contingent on winning forthcoming elections. That does not mean that all decision-makers in political systems utilizing elections for elite circulation purposes will consult public opinion polls before acting or respond in a direction that promises winning the most votes, but neither approach is unknown.

Clashes need to be sufficiently public that most people cannot ignore or overlook them, as they tend to concentrate on their "backyard" concerns. Incoming or overhead missiles are dramatic and difficult to ignore. Submarine or maritime clashes that are kept secret are much easier to manage behind closed doors. Protracted affairs are much more difficult to manage as public demands that the government do something visibly to enhance national security rise. It is in these types of situations that rivalry outbidding can be encouraged with politicians and bureaucrats staking out more extreme positions due to ideological or electoral considerations.

Finally, another good petri dish for facilitating two-level games are political systems that are characterized by competing elite factions. Factional competition should encourage the adoption of different approaches to dealing with rivals. For that matter, different factions may perceive entirely different threat priorities leading to differential identification of which countries are genuine rivals. To respond to a rival, there needs to be some minimal consensus as to whether an adversary is an enemy. Disagreement over this basic fact could at least slow a response. It might also lead to calculated responses that are more, or at least as, sensitive to factional positioning considerations than they are to coping with an external adversary.

Figure 9.1 lists the factors hypothesized to push conflict situations toward or away from two-level games. If we are on the right track, what does that portend for our interest in Asian rivalries? By and large, we should expect limited two-level activity in most Asian rivalries if for no other reason than decision-maker autonomy is and has been quite high in this region. China is a central player in the Asian rivalry field and is notorious for managing or concealing elite disagreement over policy issues. Factions no doubt exist, but their behavior is difficult to discern from the outside. Vietnamese and North Korean politics operate on a similar basis. Electoral politics is still fairly new in states such as Taiwan and South Korea and only intermittent in states such as Pakistan. That leaves states such as India, Japan, and the United States as places where two-level games might be more common.

But even if circumstances appear to work against two-level games becoming prominent in a given region, it does not mean that situations cannot emerge that escape the normal constraints that suppress two-level gaming. Moreover, the factors listed in Figure 9.1 are only ad hoc hypotheses. They need to be tested to see how well they hold up. For that, we need to return to our case studies.

The Question of Two-level Games in Asia

In this volume on the principal Asian rivalries, the editors had requested that the contributors ascertain, to the extent applicable, if the logic of two-level

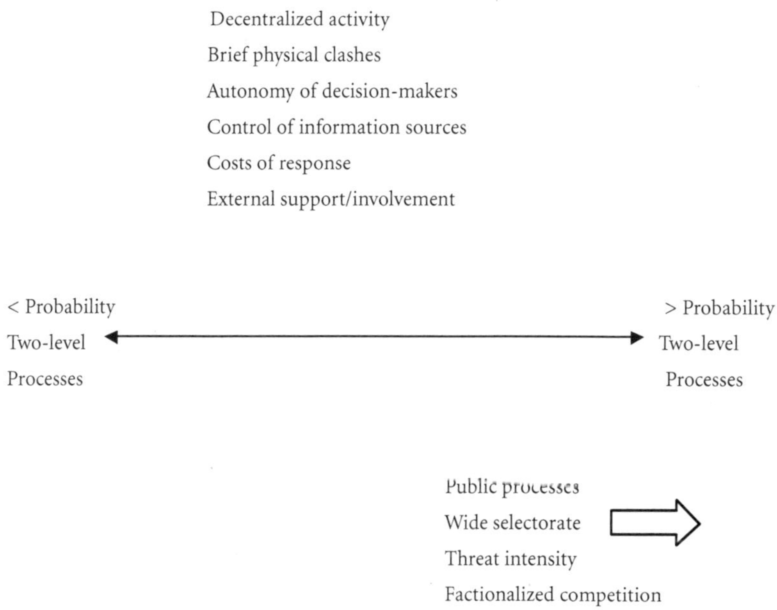

FIGURE 9.1 Some factors relevant to the likelihood of two-level games in interstate conflict.

games obtained in their particular cases. All of the authors, well-regarded specialists in their respective domains, have found only limited support for the interaction between domestic and international politics in the cases that they have examined. None of them explicitly rule out the significance of domestic politics and its interaction with international politics in shaping policy outcomes. However, in none of the cases under examination did domestic political coalitions, factions, and debates have a fundamental and determinative effect on policies toward rivals.

The case studies then all point toward a negative finding. Namely, that while the significance of domestic politics cannot be wholly dismissed, their impact appears to be distinctly limited. Based on this particular universe of cases we can then make a contingent generalization that in the recent past, domestic politics have not been of significant salience in shaping the course of a number of key Asian rivalries. It may be useful to test the robustness of this proposition in other rivalries in different geographic contexts.

In the section below we briefly summarize the key findings of the limited impact of domestic politics on the workings of these rivalries. One of the most important emerging rivalries in Asia obviously involves the United States and the People's Republic of China (PRC). Lyle Goldstein's chapter on the subject argues that "domestic politics are prominent, though not decisive, in determining whether cooperation or conflict will prevail." In his analysis, Goldstein focuses on two cases. The first deals with the decision of the Clinton administration to grant President Lee Teng-hui of Taiwan a visa to enable him to attend a function at his alma mater, Cornell University. In the first case, Goldstein reports that that domestic politics had a significant impact in contributing to Sino-U.S. tensions. In large part, Goldstein argues, domestic politics in both the PRC and in the United States became implicated because of the highly emotive nature of the Taiwan issue in Chinese domestic concerns and because of the role of Congressional conservatives on the visa issue in the United States. The second case involved the People's Liberation Army Navy's (PLAN) harassment of an unarmed U.S. oceanographic vessel in the South China Sea in 2009. Though fraught with the possibility of escalation, this event did not trigger a wider naval confrontation. Goldstein argues that the PLAN's aggressive actions stemmed largely from strategic imperatives, but the reporting on the incident in the Chinese media was quite muted. In the United States, in turn, he argues, the principal focus on the media was on the wars in Afghanistan and Iraq, so the event did not acquire much salience.

The emotive dimensions of the China-Taiwan rivalry are evident in Andrew Scobell's chapter on the rivalry. In his analysis he also finds limited support for a two-level game in one of the two illustrative episodes that he examines. His first case deals with the same episode involving the grant of an American visa to President Lee Teng-hui. However, he examines the issue from the standpoint of China-Taiwan relations. While at Cornell University Lee gave a speech that the PRC leadership found provocative because it focused on Taiwan's democratization and had emphasized the concept of "popular sovereignty." His speech led the PRC leadership to react with much vitriol and also a resort to missile tests in the Taiwan Strait in 1996. Despite this escalation in rhetoric and the threats emanating from the missile tests, Lee won the election handsomely. Beijing, Scobell argues, in all likelihood decided that while his election was no cause for celebration they could nevertheless live with the outcome, albeit grudgingly.

The second crisis stemmed from controversial rhetoric of the March 2004 presidential elections in Taiwan. Along with the election, the Democratic People's Party (DPP) presidential candidate, Chen Shui-bian, had included two potentially provocative items for a referendum. They involved the possibility of Taiwan acquiring more advanced antimissile systems if the PRC persisted with missile threats and whether Taiwan should negotiate with China to produce a "stable and peaceful framework" for cross-straits discussions. Despite these potentially troubling remarks, a crisis did not ensue. Scobell attributes the absence of a crisis to some explicit statements from the Bush administration, which sought to downplay the significance of the electoral platform and which affirmed the U.S. interest in maintaining the status quo in Sino-Taiwanese relations. From his examination of the two episodes Scobell concludes, "The primary stimuli in the cross-strait rivalry—at least in the period examined in this paper—are exogenous."

The PRC's fractious relationship with another of its neighbors, Vietnam, is the focus of Brantly Womack's chapter. Womack dwells on the growing hostility between the PRC and Vietnam between 1975 and 1979 and the normalization of their ties between 1986 and 1991. In the first case, Womack argues the crisis in the relationship emerged from a mismatch of mutual expectations in the aftermath of the Vietnamese victory in the Indo-China conflict. He holds that in this crisis neither domestic politics nor third parties played critical roles. In the second episode, he holds that domestic politics was only significant in Vietnam where party factionalism played a limited role in the resumption of normal diplomatic relations with the PRC.

The Sino-Russian rivalry, according to Lowell Dittmer, has now been transformed into a relationship that can be characterized as being one of "good neighbors." To this end, he examines two decades, those between 1949–59 and 1990–2000. According to Dittmer, the first period was an alliance and the second a phase of good neighborliness. For the first period he contends that neither domestic nor international factors could account for the Sino-Soviet alliance. Instead he holds that the origins of the alliance can best be traced to a "profoundly skewed ideological perspective." In the second phase, he argues that an amalgam of both domestic and international factors have contributed to an easing of tensions and the genesis of a limited strategic partnership.

While the PRC has managed to reach a rapprochement of sorts with at least two of its rivals, Russia and Vietnam, its dealings with India, its southern neighbor, remain highly contentious despite a growing trade and commercial relationship. In his chapter on the Sino-Indian rivalry, Manjeet Pardesi deals with two significant moments in the rivalry. They involve the PRC's ruthless suppression of the Tibetan uprising in 1959 and its repression of unrest in the same region in 1987–89. In the first case, Indian diplomatic and political choices led to a dramatic escalation of the rivalry and culminated in a short, harsh border war in 1962. In the second, India carefully avoided taking any actions that could have precipitated a wider conflict, and the rivalry de-escalated. In neither case does Pardesi find much evidence for domestic politics as a key variable in the escalation or de-escalation of the crises. In fact, he categorically states, "In sum, this study has demonstrated that in the two cases studies here—the consequences of instability in Tibet in 1959 and 1987–1989 and the Chinese military crackdown that followed it on the Sino-Indian rivalry—domestic political variables played no role."

The Indo-Pakistani rivalry remains the other enduring rivalry in the subcontinent. In his chapter on this rivalry, Paul Kapur examines three distinct periods in its evolution. To that end, he focuses on the highly conflictual period from 1947 to 1971, a relatively peaceful period between 1972 and 1989, and a final period of renewed tensions and conflict from 1990 to the present. He argues that during the periods under examination "the relevant domestic political factors remained fairly constant." Furthermore, he contends that domestic factors in this rivalry have played a mostly permissive role, facilitating the prospects of "both conflict and rapprochement, but not directly causing either development." The key dispute between the rivals remains their fundamental differences over the eventual status of the state of Jammu and Kashmir, an issue that stemmed from the process of British colonial disengagement from the region.

The final rivalry under discussion in this volume deals with the Korean peninsula and involves the North-South Korean rivalry. In his chapter, Samuel Kim examines eight periods where the roles of internal and external variables as well as their interaction evinced considerable variation. Yet Kim balks implicitly at comparing domestic and international influences in a rivalry that he views as, at least in part, a domestic rivalry from the outset. One society divided artificially by the cold war into a north and a south led to a rivalry over legitimation as the Korean government between the political systems located below and above the 49th Parallel. The grand strategies of these rival political systems oscillated over time with the North bent on conquest initially and then survival while the South argued over welcoming/hastening the collapse of the North and cringing from its implications. In some respects then, all PDRK-ROK interactions are domestic. Truly international are the interventions and involvements of the United States and China. From this perspective (although Kim does not take this position explicitly), everything in the rivalry of the two Koreas is a two-level game. But the two levels are not the conventional version of domestic and international politics. Korean interactions are domestic while major power intrusions are international.

Thus, the outcome of our "experiment" on two-level game hypotheses, the second motivation for this collection of essays, is rather easy to summarize. No one found much, if any, evidence supporting the idea that two-level games help to explain escalation and de-escalation in rivalry dynamics. That is not the same thing as saying no two-level games can be found in Asia. Electoral politics in places like India, Taiwan, Japan, and South Korea guarantee that decision-makers and politicians will say things that mean one thing to domestic audiences and another to foreign audiences. But, the seven case studies simply found no evidence that a sensitivity to two-level games were very helpful in explaining fluctuations in rivalry hostilities despite India, Taiwan, and South Korea being represented in the cases.

The case studies in this volume are simply interpretations of what transpired and why it transpired the way it did. Perhaps some or all are wrong. Analysts unaccustomed to looking for two-level games are less likely to find traces of them than are analysts who are suitably accustomed. Yet, until someone else demonstrates that these cases are misinterpreted or miss where the action "really" is, let us assume that the initial conclusion is correct. Two-level games are not rampant in Asian rivalries. What then? Does that mean we have learned nothing about Asian rivalry fluctuations?

The answer is no. The relative absence of two-level games in Asian rivalries is something that can be explained in general terms. It appears to be largely a function of how most political systems in the region operate—with considerable governmental insulation from public demands and with factional infighting suppressed or managed as best we can determine. Even in political systems with regular elections, substantial governmental autonomy appears to be the norm. Asian rivalries may not always be characterized by this type of domestic political environment. But they appear to have been characterized by limited domestic involvement to date.[6]

Being able to rule out one avenue of explanation most of the time is a positive finding. It alerts analysts to look elsewhere for their answers to rivalry behavioral puzzles. Yet there is something more that can be gleaned from the seven case studies in this volume. Instead of two-level games, we should be looking for nested games in which behavioral patterns are rendered more complex by games going on above the rivalry dyad.

Nested Games and Other Factors?

We began our inquiry by asking about two-level games. Yet posing the analytical question in the guise of a two-level game understates the nature of the problem. Analytically speaking, levels of analysis problems are ubiquitous in deciphering interstate interactions. Where should we look to find answers to our "why" questions? Do we look to system structure, international interactions, national characteristics, group decision-making, prominent personalities, or domestic politics in general? If only two levels were in action, the analytical problem would be more limited than it is. With multiple levels potentially in play, nested activities quickly become highly complex.

A case in point is the November 23 , 2010, shelling of Yeonpyeong Island by the People's Democratic Republic of Korea, the first shelling of South Korean territory and civilian populations in half a century. Initial reports indicate that the North Korean shelling followed the announcement of South Korean-U.S. plans to mount a naval exercise near North Korea in the Yellow Sea, North Korean warnings to stay away from the contested Korean maritime border, and a South Korean artillery shelling of the disputed area. The difference was that the South Korean shelling targeted open water while the North Korean response hit a populated island, leaving four dead and a number wounded. The North Korean shelling led to a second South Korean artillery response (with unknown casualties at the time of this writing).

What should we make of this artillery exchange? One very narrow interpretation would categorize it as a tit-for-tat military exchange with escalation. This international-level description is hard to deny, but it does not have much explanatory power. Several other possible interpretations have been floated. Another narrow interpretation is that North Korea wished to remind South Korea of its coercive powers and used this opportunity as an explicit demonstration. Some observers have called the shelling of the island an attempt to rally support for a tenuous political transition in North Korea, as an ill father gives way to a son with little experience or exposure. Or, it might be "a feeling one's oats" response related to the announcement of North Korea's progress in nuclear development matters. Then again, it could be more of what has been called a "mendicant" foreign policy in which North Korea periodically

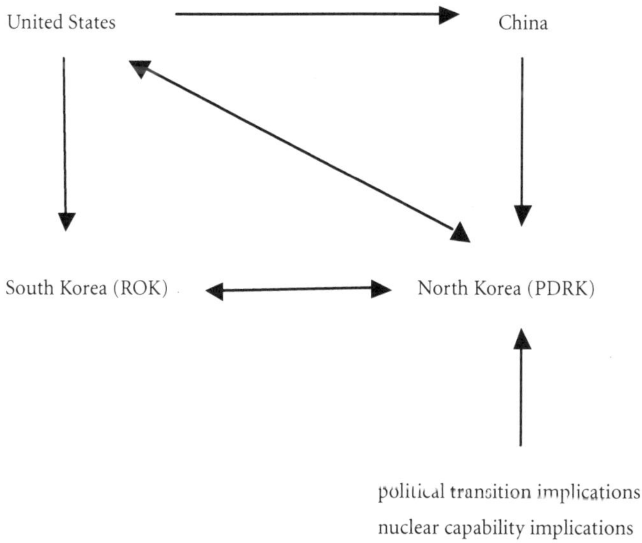

FIGURE 9.2 N-level games and nested rivalries interacting on the Korean peninsula.

needs to cause trouble in order to galvanize negotiations with, and concessions from, the United States and other states concerned with maintaining peace in Northeast Asia.

The affair is complicated further by the U.S. response of ordering an aircraft carrier into the area, a countermove presumably intended to signal resolve to both North Korea and its patron, China.[7] The clear message to China, made more explicit by a message sent by President Obama, is to restrain your client state if you do not wish more U.S. naval vessels in the immediate neighborhood.[8] But the U.S. move also signals military support for its client, South Korea. So, the question is just how many different games are going on here?

Figure 9.2 suggests at least six possible arrows or games taking place at three different levels (between the major powers, between the minor powers, and within one minor power). Of course, this reflects an aggregate translation of all (or at least most) of the possible things that might have been going on in the Korean peninsula that week in November 2010. There is no reason to assume that all of the possible interpretations are valid or equally supported. However, it is also conceivable that all of them are to varying extents. We offer no resolution of what precisely transpired in the Yeonpyeong affair.[9] Our only interest is in using the incident as an illustration of some of the problems inherent in analyzing interactions between rivals (in Asia and elsewhere). A one-game/one-level analysis is often difficult to defend.

Nonetheless, there is something striking about Figure 9.2. The most "robust" arrows—that is, the ones that are likely to be controversial, are above the line of the conventional, international-domestic, two-level game notion. There are multiple interstate games at play—U.S.-China, China-PDRK, U.S.-ROK, ROK-PDRK, U.S.-PDRK—that can be isolated and examined as complexities within the overlapping interactions of rivalries between two major powers and two minor powers, as well as two sets of patron-client relationships. What is left are speculations about North Korean motivations that may or may not be germane.[10] Perhaps the North Korean leadership feels especially vulnerable due to an ongoing transition in the Kim ruling family. Or, perhaps the North Korean leadership feels empowered by progress made in its development of nuclear capabilities. But, then again, these are mere hunches based in part on timing. Perhaps the Yeonpyeong incident was merely a tit-for-tat exchange that got out of hand or reflected an explicit decision to escalate solely due to the context of warnings about military exercises in or near North Korean waters. That is to say, the escalation might have happened whether a domestic political transition was underway or gains had been made in defensive capabilities.

Five studies emphasize triangular situations as important to conflict escalation. Scobell stresses a U.S.-Taiwan-China structure. What Taiwan does is less important than what China wants to communicate to Taiwan's external patron about Taiwan's behavior. In this case, two rivalries become intertwined although the major power-minor power one would seem to be subordinated to the one between the two major powers. One wonders, though, how hard and fast subordination in such a case is. Can we assume that a relationship that is subordinated at one point in time will always remain subordinated? Moreover, was it easier to subordinate the Chinese-Taiwan relationship to the U.S.-China relationship in the old days of KMT authoritarianism as opposed to the new days of electoral competition in Taiwan?

Kim posits a triangular structure (U.S.-South Korea-North Korea) that seems very similar to the one involving Taiwan except that it is not a two major and one minor power situation. Nor is the United States and North Korea relationship a rivalry. It also deviates from the Taiwanese case in that South Korea's external patron, at times, is more belligerent toward North Korea than its minor power client. But the similarity is paramount in the sense that the three actors do not have complete freedom of maneuver to act against its opponent without also taking into consideration the third member of the triangle. In an earlier period, Kim also notes the operation of a China-North Korea-Soviet Union triangle in which North Korea benefited from being able to encourage Chinese-Soviet competition in providing patronage to their mutual client. The structural complexity of Northeast Asia is made even more interesting by adding the China-U.S. rivalry and, formerly, the U.S.-Soviet rivalry to the subsystemic field. Clearly, the idea of a third party needs to be kept fairly flexible in what is at least a five-state ensemble.[11]

Pardesi also relies on a triangular conceptualization to account for India being more reluctant to take on China in 1987 without the Soviet support on which it once could rely. Dittmer's interpretation of the Sino-Russian relationship takes a similar position when he draws attention to Sino-Russian cooperation being more likely when they shared a mutual adversary in the United States. In both the China-India and China-Russia cases, the presence or absence of a third party works toward de-escalating conflict within the rivalry. In Womack's case, however, China is seen as being less interested in Vietnam than it was the Soviet-Vietnamese relationship. Once Vietnam could no longer count on Soviet support, China perceived less threat emanating from Vietnam.

Thus, the most common (five of seven) interpretation stresses the role of third parties in making dyadic dynamics both more complex and more conditional in the sense that third parties govern to varying degrees just how hostile (or cooperative) rivalry relationships can become. The two cases that did not stress third parties might well have done so if they had had different foci. The United States is frequently seen as a third party in Indo-Pakistani relations, with Pakistan formerly counting on U.S. intervention to salvage losing postwar positions. U.S.-Chinese relations were once difficult to interpret without injecting the Soviet Union as a third leg of the triangle.

One obvious question is whether we need to compare simple (no third parties) and complex (third parties) situations to see whether they work vastly differently. Of course, that assumes that we can isolate enough simple, two-party rivalries to make the comparison worthwhile. This observation leads to the corollary question of which rivalry field is more common—simple or complex? Do we do a disservice to rivalry analysis by stressing simple dyadic structures of conflict?

Another clue found in some of the case studies concerns capabilities. If rivals must be competitors by definition, relative capabilities should make some difference. Kapur argues that the Indo-Pakistani rivalry de-escalated considerably after Pakistan was defeated decisively in 1971. It only revived because local Kashmiri politics recreated a state of rebellion against India, and Pakistan had in the meanwhile developed a nuclear capability that protected it from being defeated as decisively as before. Womack contends that capability asymmetry is more important than rivalry in the China-Vietnam case. So long as the more powerful state fails to take the weaker state seriously, conflict is still conceivable but likely to be less intense than it might otherwise be. This might seem to be a curious case of a constant (asymmetry) explaining something that varies (conflict), but asymmetry can also be seen as acting as a governor (perhaps not unlike third parties) to just how hostile the relationship can become or how long it may persist.

Note, though, that Dittmer also stresses capability asymmetry but in an oscillating fashion.[12] In the first cooperative period (essentially the 1950s) in his case, China was extremely weak and that very weakness might be said to have destabilized the alliance and encouraged the resumption of rivalry.[13] China needed more than the Soviets were prepared to offer, which led to Chinese disgruntlement and hostility. In the second cooperative period (the 1990s onward), China has been growing stronger than Russia. To the extent that the Sino-Russian capability continues to expand, will Russia be willing to accept a subordinated position in the relationship? Or, will expanding asymmetry make a return to rivalry more probable?

Goldstein emphasizes issue salience in his U.S.-China case. Taiwan has been more important to China than monopolizing the South China Sea. The United States was distracted by Middle Eastern and Afghani problems. Hence, a crisis in the 1990s over Taiwan had much greater escalatory potential than a crisis in the South China Sea in 2009. Of course, one problem here is that issue salience is a variable that is likely to be subject to a fair amount of flux. It is not inconceivable that the South China Sea could take on more significance than Taiwan from a Chinese perspective, assuming some sort of quasi-resolution of Taiwan's status. The United States may not always be distracted by Middle Eastern and Afghan problems. These considerations make it more difficult to predict which issues will have high salience in the future. The advantages of hindsight are always welcome.

In some respects, Pardesi's emphasis on the threat environment shifting over time is a similar point of view, but it also bears some linkage to the parameter setting of asymmetrical capabilities. How and where decision-makers perceive threat is unlikely to take on constant features. In one case, decision-makers may feel trapped into escalating the ante because the stakes are seen as so high. In another situation, the same setting may offer more options for response because the stakes seem less great and the threat less acute. Here again, prediction is tricky and hindsight is most helpful.

Finally, external and internal shocks are likely to be important to shaping the course of rivalries, as is stressed in Kim's chronology of the rivalry between the two Koreas. Defining what constitutes a shock is more difficult than appreciating its effects. One consensus shock that runs through these cases explicitly and implicitly is the end of the cold war rivalry between the Soviet Union and the United States and the subsequent collapse of the Soviet Union (or vice versa). North Korea was forced to develop a new strategy to gain external resources and from different sources than before. Sino-Russian cooperation was more conceivable as the Soviet threat disappeared. Vietnam and India found themselves forced to reconsider their former reliance on the contingency of Soviet support when dealing with China. The foundation for U.S.-China cooperation in East Asia virtually evaporated with the collapse of the Soviet Union. The probability of a resumption of U.S.-Chinese rivalry was increased accordingly.

Conclusion

Seven case studies hardly qualify as a comprehensive and definitive examination of what makes rivalries "tick" in Asia. They represent only a preliminary foray that hopefully will be followed up by more studies of the questions raised but not completely answered. In the interim, what can we say? The maintenance and escalation/de-escalation of Asian rivalries, viewed collectively, do not appear to be strongly affected by two-level games of the domestic-international type. Two-level games are likely to be found in Asia, but so far, they have not been found to be significant factors in the fluctuation of hostility.

Other factors have been found to be more significant. Triangular complexities may be more important than strictly dyadic considerations. Third parties have been found to be important governors of conflict levels, either restraining or intensifying conflict. Relative capability calculations are likely to change over time. When they do, they can lead to differential incentives to conflict or cooperate. How issues and threats are perceived to be salient or otherwise are also subject to flux. Greater salience increases the likelihood of conflict; lesser salience decreases it. Shocks also deserve more thorough examination in changing contexts, the role of third parties, and possibly also influencing the variable salience of issues and threats.

The important thing is not whether we have captured adequately why Asian rivalries increase and decrease in intensity. We have definitely not captured it adequately, but then that was not one of our goals. We seek to raise the analytical profile of rivalries in Asian conflict (and peace) studies and to begin tackling the general question of how rivalries are maintained or fluctuate in hostility from year to year. We think both goals have been met but that does not mean that a great deal more work does not need to be done. Rivalry analysis, in Asia and elsewhere, remains in its infancy. Especially in Asia, though, we have compelling reasons to catch up in our ability to make sense of rivalry dynamics. Rivalries have strongly structured Asian international relations in the past sixty-five years. They are likely to continue doing so in the indefinite future.

Notes

Chapter 1

1. See, for example, the National Intelligence Council's perspective on the world in 2025, *Global Trends 2025: A Transformed World* (Washington, DC: Government Printing Office, 2008).

2. We recognize that it is more customary to refer to Asia as a continent, as opposed to a region. Increasingly, though, the regional distinctions among East, South East, Northeast, South, and Central Asia are blurring.

3. This definition is elaborated in William R. Thompson, "Identifying Rivals and Rivalries in World Politics," *International Studies Quarterly* 45, no. 4 (2001): 557–86; and to a greater extent in Michael Colaresi, Karen Rasler, and William R. Thompson, *Strategic Rivalry: Space, Position, and Conflict Escalation in World Politics* (Cambridge: Cambridge University Press, 2007). As such, it represents one approach to deciphering rivalry dynamics. In this approach, the identification and timing of rivalries is based on exploring decision-maker and analysts' discussions of who constitute a given state's primary competitive enemies. Enemy status requires some level of threat perception. Competitive status requires some rough equivalency in capability, but that does not preclude exceptions to the rule when stronger states perceive weaker states "not knowing their place" or weaker states behaving as if they were stronger than they actually were. For instance, Cambodia/Kampuchea, Vietnam, and China would not normally be competitors. For a few years in the 1970s and 1980s, however, Cambodia/Kampuchea and Vietnam and China and Vietnam competed for position and to a lesser extent territory in Southeast Asia. Both Cambodia/Kampuchea and Vietnam learned that they were not competitive with their rivals and were forced to change their behavior. However, there is a second approach to identifying and dating rivalries that is based less subjectively on requiring the satisfaction of some minimal level of

observed conflict within a specified time period. Thus, for instance, all pairs of states that have experienced X militarized interstate disputes within Y years qualify as rivals regardless of whether they view each other as competitors or enemies. For examples, see Paul F. Diehl and Gary Goertz, *War and Peace in International Rivalry* (Ann Arbor: University of Michigan Press, 2000); and Zeev Maoz and Ben D. Mor, *Bound by Struggle: The Strategic Evolution of Enduring International Rivalries* (Ann Arbor: University of Michigan Press, 2002).

4. Some notable exceptions of relatively explicit Asian rivalry analyses include Tun-jen Chang, Chi Huang, and Samuel S. G. Wu, eds., *Inherited Rivalry: Conflict Across the Taiwan Straits* (Boulder, CO: Lynne Rienner, 1995); Weiqun Gu, *Conflicts of Divided Nations: The Cases of China and Korea* (Westport, CT: Praeger, 1995); David P. Rapkin "The Emergence and Intensification of U.S.-Japanese Rivalry in the Early Twentieth Century," in William R. Thompson, ed., *Great Power Rivalries* (Columbia: University of South Carolina Press, 1999); Sumit Ganguly, *Conflict Unending: Indo-Pakistani Tensions Since 1947* (New York: Columbia University Press, 2001); John W. Garver, *Protracted Contest: Sino-Indian Rivalry in the Twentieth Century* (Seattle: University of Washington Press, 2002); Uk Heo and Shale A. Horowitz, eds., *Conflict in Asia: Korea, China-Taiwan and India-Pakistan* (Westport, CT: Praeger, 2003); T. V. Paul, ed., *The India-Pakistan Conflict: An Enduring Rivalry* (Cambridge: Cambridge University Press, 2005); and Ming Wan, *Sino-Japanese Relations* (Stanford: Stanford University Press, 2006).

5. On the utility of rivalry analysis, see William R. Thompson, "Why Rivalries Matter and What Great Power Rivalries Can Tell Us About World Politics," in William R. Thompson, ed., *Great Power Rivalries* (Columbia: University of South Carolina Press, 1999).

6. For the classic statement on the unitary conception of the state, see Kenneth N. Waltz, *Man, the State, and War* (New York: Columbia University Press, 2001).

7. We say "at least" two-level because it is certainly not unknown for agencies and elites within governments to compete with one another for control over policy outcomes.

8. On the issue of two-level games, see Peter B. Evans, Harold K. Jacobson, and Robert D. Putnam, *Double-Edged Diplomacy: International Bargaining and Domestic Politics* (Berkeley: University of California Press, 1993).

9. For an argument that high-level interactions are too serious to be influenced significantly by bureaucratic competition, see Stephen D. Krasner, "Are Bureaucracies Important? (Or Allison Wonderland)," *Foreign Policy* 7 (summer 1972): 159–79.

10. Rivalries, especially the ones of long duration, can seem to become constants in international relations. But all rivalries fluctuate from year to year in terms of intensity and hostility. When we say that we want to explain the variance in rivalry hostility, it is akin to saying that we are attempting to account for how rivalries manifest themselves in behavioral terms.

11. Friedberg's Asia stretched from Southwest Asia to Northeast Asia and the South Pacific. Our focus is similar although we are reluctant to add the South Pacific

to Asia at this time. See Aaron L. Friedberg, "Ripe for Rivalry: Prospects for Peace in a Mulitpolar Asia," *International Security* 18 (1993–94): 5–33.

12. More recent research demonstrates that democracies are less likely to fight one another but that democracies and autocracies are especially prone to fighting one another. See Nils Petter Gleditsch and Havard Hegre, "Peace and Democracy: Three Levels of Analysis," *Journal of Peace Research* 41, no. 2 (1997): 283–310; and Karen Rasler and William R. Thompson, *Puzzles of the Democratic Peace: Theory, Geopolitics and the Transformation of World Politics* (New York: Palgrave-Macmillan, 2005).

13. The reference is to Dehio's remarkable summarization of five hundred years of European geopolitics. See Ludwig Dehio, *The Precarious Balance* (New York: Vintage, 1962).

14. This point is made quite clearly in David C. Kang, *East Asia Before the West: Five Centuries of Trade and Tribute* (New York: Columbia University Press, 2010).

15. William R. Thompson and David R. Dreyer, *Handbook of Interstate Rivalries* (Washington, DC: Congressional Quarterly Press, 2011).

16. These rivalries are not missing from Thompson and Dreyer, *Handbook of Interstate*. The Anglo-Russian rivalry is categorized as a European major power rivalry and treated in a separate chapter. The U.S.-Soviet cold war is also treated separately.

17. China-Vietnam actually is a mixture of both types.

18. The variety of types means that we should not assume that all state populations are equally committed to the maintenance of interstate rivalries or, as in the Taiwanese and Korean cases, that the conflict is genuinely inter-state in format. For our purposes, it suffices if governments in different states act as if they are participating in an interstate rivalry. How deep the sense of rivalry is within a population is a different question and one, unfortunately, that has rarely been investigated.

19. The war data are taken from Meredith R. Sarkees and Frank W. Wayman, *Resort to War, 1816–2007* (Washington, DC: Congressional Quarterly Press, 2010).

20. Of course, there are other ways to terminate rivalries than issue resolution. A good number of rivalries end when one rival defeats another rival decisively. Alternatively, some rivalries end because new threats emerge that are viewed as greater than the threats associated with a traditional rival. Traditional rivals, especially if they are mutually threatened by the new source of trouble, have been known to settle old differences to better meet the new ones.

21. While all authors were asked to address the same questions, it is par for the course in this line of work that some liberties were taken in how authors chose to answer them. Some authors were so hard pressed to find occasions in which domestic politics made some difference along the lines for which we were looking that they deviated from the requested script.

22. Thomas J. Christensen uses the two-level game metaphor to good advantage in *Useful Adversaries: Grand Strategy, Domestic Mobilization, and Sino-American Conflict, 1947–1958* (Princeton, NJ: Princeton University Press, 1996). While he does not treat his cases as rivalry episodes per se, his argument is that decision-makers sometimes overreact or take harder lines with rivals than might otherwise be the case in order to build domestic support for major programs.

23. Graham Allison, *Essence of Decision: Explaining the Cuban Missile Crisis* (Boston: Little, Brown, 1971).

24. We initially had the China-Japan case covered, but the first author we had contacted defected late in the preparatory stage and the replacement for that individual failed to produce a paper.

25. Neither editor can be said to have a vested interest in finding evidence of two-level games in Asian rivalries. Neither of us has ever written about two-level games in previous work. Our only interest, as we have noted, is to (a) draw attention to the notion of rivalries and (b) see whether we can address specific and general reasons for fluctuations in rivalry hostility.

26. On this subject, see S. D. Muni, *Pangs of Proximity: India and Sri Lanka's Ethnic Crisis* (New Delhi: Sage Publications, 1993).

27. See Michael Colaresi, *Scare Tactics: The Politics of International Rivalry* (Syracuse, NY: Syracuse University Press, 2006), who develops a theory that the interaction between rivalry outbidding and expected future costs within a rivalry accounts for the probability of rivalry escalation, de-escalation or maintenance.

28. Allison, *Essence of Decision.*

29. Andrew Scobell, "Show of Force: Chinese Soldiers, Statesmen, and the 1995–1996 Taiwan Strait Crisis," *Political Science Quarterly* 115 (2000): 227–46.

Chapter 2

1. Roy Kamphausen, David Lai, and Andrew Scobell, eds., *Beyond the Strait: PLA Missions Other Than Taiwan* (Carlisle Barracks, PA: U.S. Army War College Strategic Studies Institute, 2009).

2. For comprehensive treatment of the China-Taiwan relationship as a rivalry, see Tun-jen Cheng, Chi Huang, and Samuel S. G. Wu, eds., *Inherited Rivalry: Conflict Across the Taiwan Straits* (Boulder, CO: Lynne Rienner, 1995).

3. The term was suggested to the author by David Strand of Dickinson College.

4. Andrew J. Nathan and Helena V. S. Ho, "Chiang Ching-kuo's Decision for Political Reform," in Shao-Chuan Leng, ed. *Chiang Ching-kuo's Leadership in the Development of the Republic of China on Taiwan* (Lanham, MD: University Press of America, 1995), 31–61.

5. Lowell Dittmer and Samuel S. Kim, "In Search of a Theory of National Identity," in Dittmer and Kim, eds., *China's Quest for National Identity* (Ithaca, NY: Cornell University Press, 1993), 13.

6. Dittmer and Kim, "In Search of a Theory of National Identity," 14.

7. David Kang, "Acute Conflicts in Asia After the Cold War: Kashmir, Taiwan, and Korea," in Muthiah Alagappa, ed., *Asian Security Order: Instrumental and Normative Features* (Stanford: Stanford University Press, 2001), 364.

8. These quotes come from Kang, "Acute Conflicts in Asia After the Cold War," and appear on pp. 366 and 352, respectively. In the latter quote Kang is summarizing the findings of other scholars.

9. In the past I have dubbed this "divided nation" aspect as an "ideology." Here it seems more appropriate to consider it part of the PRC's identity. For earlier consideration of this concept, see Andrew Scobell, "Making Sense of North Korea: Pyongyang and Comparative Communism," *Asian Security* 1, no. 3 (December 2005): 258–59.

10. Zhao identifies two other types of nationalism, "ethnic" and "liberal," but concludes that "state nationalism" dominates in modern China. He defines this third type as "the nation as a territorial-political unit and an organizational system to gather citizens of a given territory—voluntarily or not—to produce public goods for its members and make sovereign collective decisions." Suisheng Zhao, *A Nation-State by Construction: Dynamics of Modern Chinese Nationalism* (Stanford: Stanford University Press, 2004), 26. The quotations in the text come from pp. 281 and 289, respectively.

11. Thomas J. Christensen, "Posing Problems Without Catching Up: China's Rise and Challenges for U.S. Security Policy," *International Security* 25 (spring 2001): 15.

12. The balance of rivalry includes a variety of different "hard" and "soft" dimensions: military, economic, diplomatic, political, and identity. The concept was inspired by Stephen Walt's "balance of threat" conception. See his *Origins of Alliances* (Ithaca, NY: Cornell University Press, 1987).

13. See, inter alia, Chuck Downs and James R. Lilley, *Crisis in the Taiwan Strait* (Washington, DC: National Defense University Press, 1997); John W. Garver, *Face Off: The Taiwan Strait Crisis and Taiwan Democratization* (Seattle: University of Washington Press, 1997); Andrew Scobell, "Show of Force: Chinese Soldiers, Statesman, and the 1995–1996 Taiwan Strait Crisis," *Political Science Quarterly* (summer 2000) [a revised an expanded version appears in chapter 8 of Andrew Scobell, *China's Use of Military Force: Beyond the Great Wall and the Long March* (Cambridge: Cambridge University Press, 2003)]; Robert S. Ross, "The 1995–96 Taiwan Strait Confrontation: Coercion, Credibility, and the Use of Force," *International Security* 25 (fall 2000): 87–123.

14. Scobell, *China's Use of Military Force*, 176.

15. Richard Bush, "Lee Teng-hui and Separatism," in Nancy Bernkopf Tucker, ed., *Dangerous Strait: The U.S.-Taiwan-China Crisis* (New York: Columbia University Press, 2005), 84.

16. Bush, "Lee Teng-hui and Separatism," 85.

17. For astute analysis of whether or not Beijing "misperceived" Lee's rhetoric, see Bush, "Lee Teng-hui and Separatism," 92.

18. This episode has received far less attention than the 1995–96 one because the tensions did not escalate into a full-blown crisis. For one particularly interesting account, see James Mulvenon, "The PLA, Chen, and the Referenda: The War Dogs That Didn't Bark," *China Leadership Monitor*, no. 10 (spring 2004): 1–5.

For an excellent, thorough, and relatively recent treatment of Taiwan as an issue for China, see Richard C. Bush, *Untying the Knot: Making Peace in the Taiwan Strait* (Washington, DC: The Brookings Institution, 2005).

19. See Andrew J. Nathan and Andrew Scobell, *China's Search for Security* (New York: Columbia University Press, forthcoming), chap. 4.

20. Rigger, "The Unfinished Business of Taiwan's Democratization," in Tucker, *Dangerous Strait*, 19; and Bush, *Untying the Knot*, 69.

21. Rigger, "The Unfinished Business of Taiwan's Democratization," in Tucker, *Dangerous Strait*, 20.

22. Rigger, "The Unfinished Business of Taiwan's Democratization," 20. See also Bush, *Untying the Knot*, 71.

23. Rigger, "The Unfinished Business of Taiwan's Democratization," 20–21. For a careful analysis of the evolution of the referenda episode, see Jih-wen Lin, "Taiwan's Referendum Act and the Stability of the Status Quo," *Issues and Studies* 40, no. 2 (June 2004): 119–53.

24. For comprehensive discussion of China's international trade and foreign investment and Taiwan's role in both, see Barry Naughton, *The Chinese Economy: Transitions and Growth* (Cambridge, MA: MIT Press, 2007), pt. V.

25. These statistics are drawn from the International Institute for Strategic Studies, *The Military Balance*, various years.

26. Data in this paragraph were compiled by Cristine Salo.

27. On the New York summit meeting, see Robert L. Suettinger, *Beyond Tiananmen: The Politics of U.S.-China Relations, 1989–2000* (Washington, DC: The Brookings Institution, 2003), 241–43. On speculation about the lessons drawn from the crisis by Beijing and Washington, see ibid., 261–63. On Beijing's decision to adopt a less combative approach following the March 1996 election, see ibid., 264–65.

28. Scobell, "Show of Force," 235–36. The quotation is from p. 236.

29. This point is made in Andrew Scobell, "China's Rise: How Peaceful?" in Sumit Ganguly, Joseph Liow, and Andrew Scobell, eds., *Handbook of Asian Security Studies* (New York: Routledge, 2010), 17.

30. Kang, "Acute Conflicts in Asia After the Cold War," 366.

Chapter 3

1. "Obama Calls for Deeper U.S.-China Economic Relationship," *PBS Newshour*, July 27, 2009, on the Web at http://www.pbs.org/newshour/bb/politics/july-dec09/china_07–27.html.

2. The sale of F-16 fighters in 1992 caused tensions since it was the largest-ever arms sale by the United States to Taiwan. The Yinhe incident involved the boarding of a Chinese ship by the U.S. Navy in the Persian Gulf, in a mistaken attempt to halt chemical weapons precursors from going to Iran. This *Kitty Hawk* incident involved the harassment of a Chinese nuclear submarine by U.S. ASW aircraft flying from the USS *Kitty Hawk* in the vicinity of the Yellow Sea.

3. Another obvious case worthy of examination is the so-called EP-3 Crisis of April 2001. Recent studies of this crisis are available in Michael D. Swaine, Zhang Tuosheng, and Danielle Cohen, eds., *Managing Sino-American Crises: Case Studies and Analysis* (Washington, DC: Carnegie, 2006), 377–422. This case is not examined in this paper for two reasons. First, the case is unusual in that it involved a large group

of Americans being held temporarily in Chinese custody. The human dimensions of this "hostage situation" are so palpable that it likely forms an outlier for the study of domestic influence in crisis behavior. In other words, a typical Sino-American crisis likely does not generate this type of very intense domestic interest. A second and more simple reason is that the crisis has been examined by other analysts, whereas the March 2009 crisis involving American survey ships has not been explored in this academic context.

4. For an excellent description of U.S. military practice in China, see Rear Admiral Kemp Tolley, *Yangtze Patrol: The U.S. Navy in China* (Annapolis, IN: Naval Institute Press, 1971).

5. Thomas J. Christensen, *Useful Adversaries: Grand Strategy, Domestic Mobilization, and Sino-American Conflict, 1947–1958* (Princeton, NJ: Princeton University Press, 1996).

6. On role of Senator William Knowland, for example, see George C. Herring, *America's Longest War: The United States and Vietnam, 1950–1975*, 3d ed. (New York: McGraw-Hill, 1996), 43.

7. 钮俊 [Niu Jun] 1996, 年中苏边界冲突与中国外交战略的调整 [The Sino-Soviet Border Clash of 1969 and the Adjustment of Chinese Diplomatic Strategy] , in 当代中国史研究 [*Modern Chinese Historical Research*], no. 1 (1999): 66–77.

8. See my own analysis in Lyle Goldstein, "Return to Zhenbao Island: Who Started Shooting and Why It Matters," *China Quarterly* 168 (December 2001): 985–97.

9. James Mann, *About Face: A History of America's Curious Relationship with China, from Nixon to Clinton* (New York: Vintage, 1998), 268.

10. Interviews, Beijing, 2006.

11. In the view of this author, threat inflation among U.S. military and intelligence bureaucracies has not occurred chiefly because of acute consciousness of this deleterious phenomena in both the cold war case, as well as the more recent Iraq War case. Moreover, the "Global War on Terror" has created strong resource incentives to avoid focus on a peer competitor threat. Thus, Secretary of Defense Robert Gates has placed strict limits on the further production of the F-22 air superiority interceptor in April 2009, in the belief that this platform is not necessary for battles focused on countering terrorism.

12. Robert S. Ross, "The 1995–96 Taiwan Strait Confrontation: Coercion, Credibility, and the Use of Force," *International Security* 25, no. 2 (fall 2000): 99.

13. Ross, "The 1995–96 Taiwan Strait Confrontation," 104.

14. Mann, *About Face*, 336.

15. Ross, "The 1995–96 Taiwan Strait Confrontation," 91.

16. Mann, *About Face*, 322.

17. Ross, "The 1995–96 Taiwan Strait Confrontation," 93.

18. Robert L. Suettinger, "U.S. 'Management' of Three Taiwan Strait 'Crises'" in Michael D. Swaine, Zhang Tuosheng, and Danielle Cohen, eds., *Managing Sino-American Crises: Case Studies and Analysis* (Washington, DC: Carnegie, 2006), 279–80.

19. Suettinger, "U.S. 'Management' of Three Taiwan Strait 'Crises,'" 284.

20. Ross, "The 1995–96 Taiwan Strait Confrontation," 98.

21. To seriously investigate this hypothesis, one might examine Clinton's rhetoric (and that of his surrogates) during the 1996 campaign to see if he used this as an example of his toughness on national security issues.

22. Suettinger, "U.S. 'Management' of Three Taiwan Strait 'Crises,'" 284.

23. Ross, "The 1995–96 Taiwan Strait Confrontation," 122.

24. Michael Swaine, "Understanding the Historical Record," in Michael D. Swaine, Zhang Tuosheng, and Danielle Cohen, eds., *Managing Sino-American Crises: Case Studies and Analysis* (Washington, DC: Carnegie, 2006), 47.

25. Niu Jun, "Chinese Decisionmaking in Three Military Actions Across the Taiwan Strait," in Michael D. Swaine, Zhang Tuosheng, and Danielle Cohen, eds., *Managing Sino-American Crises: Case Studies and Analysis* (Washington, DC: Carnegie, 2006), 293.

26. Ibid., 308.

27. Andrew Scobell, "Show of Force: Chinese Soldiers, Statesmen, and the 1995–96 Taiwan Strait Crisis," *Political Science Quarterly* 115 (summer 2000): 4.

28. Ibid., 6, 11.

29. Ibid., 12.

30. Swaine, "Understanding the Historical Record," 43.

31. Ross, "The 1995–96 Taiwan Strait Confrontation," 108.

32. "Lost on China: A Bad Treaty Leads to a Naval Scrap," *Wall Street Journal*, March 11, 2009, on the Web at http://online.wsj.com/article/SB123672918272489143.html.

33. "Obama Calls for Improved Military Dialogue Between U.S. and China, After Naval Confrontation," *Foxnews.com*, March 12, 2009.

34. Thom Shanker and Mark Mazzetti, "China and U.S. Clash on Naval Fracas," *New York Times*, March 10, 2009, on the Web at http://www.nytimes.com/2009/03/11/world/asia/11military.html.

35. 陈家光, 陈浩 [Chen Jiaguang and Chen Hao], "中美船只南海对峙事件谁之过?" [Who Crossed Over the Line in the Confrontation Between U.S. and Chinese Vessels?], in 军事文摘 [*Military Digest*] (May 2009): 15.

36. 潘泽岗 [Pan Zegang], "碰撞: 从 '无瑕' 号事件看中美近海对抗" [Collision: A Look at the U.S.-China Confrontation in the Near Seas from the Vantage Point of the 'Impeccable' Incident], in 舰船知识 [*Naval & Merchant Ships*] (May 2009): 19. This point raises the issue that such incidents may happen with considerable regularity. Scholars are not privy to the interactions of ships on a day-to-day basis, so characterizing the March 2009 incident as a "crisis" may not be entirely accurate and could reflect certain biases inherent to media reporting in both countries on such events.

37. 周辉 [Zhou Hui], 机遇与挑战: 奥巴马时代的中美军事关系 [Opportunity and Challenge: U.S.-China Military Relations in the Obama Era], in 现代军事[*Contemporary Military Affairs*] (May 2009): 14–18.

38. "专家: 南海事件不足道中美战争可能性为零" [Expert: the Chance of the

South China Sea Incident Leading to a U.S.-China War is Zero], 环球时报 [*Global Times*], March 13, 2009.

39. Interviews, Beijing, April 2009.

40. 张文木 [Zhang Wenmu], 台海统一是中国建构西太平洋制海权的关键环节 [Taiwan Unification is the Key Link for China to Secure Sea Control in the Western Pacific] , in 领导者 [*Leader*] (April 2009): 27.

41. Interviews, Beijing, April 2009.

42. 陈家光, 陈浩 [Chen Jiaguang and Chen Hao], "中美船只南海对峙事件谁之过?" [Who Crossed Over the Line in the Confrontation Between U.S. and Chinese Vessels?], in 军事文摘 [*Military Digest*] (May 2009): 16.

43. Secretary of State Hilary Clinton's July statement regarding the South China Sea could be one such example of increased strategic competition, as might recent Pentagon discussions with Vietnam concerning enhanced military cooperation.

44. The author wishes to thank an anonymous reviewer of the chapter for pointing out this possibility. Still, there is no direct evidence of this alleged strategic behavior by the key actors.

45. Of the five different vessels involved in the March 2009 incident, only one was actually affiliated with the PLA. Still, there is ample evidence to suggest that both the State Oceanographic Administration as well as the Fisheries Law Enforcement Command have strong ties with the PLA Navy. See, for example, "Sea Patrol Force to Get More Muscle," *China Daily*, October 20, 2008, available at www.chinadaily.com.cn/china/2008–10/21/content_7123436.htm.

46. Swaine, "Understanding the Historical Record," 40.

47. Ibid., 45.

Chapter 4

1. Sumit Ganguly in Sumit Ganguly and S. Paul Kapur, *India, Pakistan, and the Bomb: Debating Nuclear Stability in South Asia* (New York: Columbia University Press, 2010).

2. One might argue that a state's behavior should always be coded as domestically caused when it results from internal political phenomena, even if those phenomena occurred within another state. For example, in this view, Pakistan's support for the Kashmir insurgency should be coded as having domestic political causes, since the insurgency resulted from political developments internal to India. The problem with this approach is that it would largely eliminate the division between domestic political and international strategic causes, rendering virtually all state behavior "domestic" in origin. This is the case because, aside from geography, most strategic variables, from civil wars to arms build-ups to quests for empire, have substantial roots in some state's internal politics. If a causal connection to internal political factors, regardless of location, made state behavior "domestic" in origin, little if any behavior would be internationally caused. A more useful approach is to consider political phenomena as

being domestic to the state in which they occur, but not to other states in the system; from the vantage point of other states, these phenomena are international in nature. Thus I code behavior resulting from a state's own internal politics as having domestic origins and behavior resulting from another state's internal politics as being caused by international strategic factors.

3. This is not to suggest that domestic politics in India and Pakistan remained wholly static on issues relevant to the Kashmir dispute. As Sumit Ganguly points out, the Bangladesh war badly discredited the two-nation theory upon which Pakistan was founded, and Indian secularism went into decline starting in the mid-1980s. Thus, over time, India and Pakistan's claims to Kashmir became rooted less in principle and more in real politik. See Ganguly, *Conflict Unending*, 5–6. Still, the point stands that ceding Kashmir remained incompatible with the claims of India and Pakistan's respective state-building projects. And, regardless of their precise motives, the two countries' domestic political preferences on Kashmir remained constant: Pakistan wished to undo the territorial status quo in the region, and India was determined to maintain it throughout the periods in question.

4. Ayesha Jalal, *Democracy and Authoritarianism in South Asia: A Comparative and Historical Perspective* (Cambridge: Cambridge University Press, 1995), 10.

5. Mohammad Ali Jinnah, "Presidential Address to the Constituent Assembly of Pakistan," August 11, 1947, in *Quaid-i-Azam Mohammad Ali Jinnah Speeches as Governor-General of Pakistan, 1947–1948* (Lahore, Pakistan: Sang-e-Meel Publications, 2004), 16.

6. Stanley Wolpert, *Jinnah of Pakistan* (New Delhi: Oxford University Press, 1984), 27, 35, 45.

7. Ian Talbot, *Pakistan: A Modern History* (New Delhi: Oxford University Press, 1998), 5.

8. See Mohammad Ali Jinnah, "Presidential Address," in *Mohammad Ali Jinnah Speeches*, 17.

9. Muhammad Iqbal, "1930 Presidential Address to the 25th Session of the All-India Muslim League," in Latif Ahmad Sherwani, ed., *Speeches, Writings and Statements of Iqbal* (Lahore: Iqbal Academy Pakistan, 2005), 178.

10. Hussain Haqqani, *Pakistan: Between Mosque and Military* (Washington, DC: Carnegie Endowment for International Peace, 2005), 5.

11. Ayesha Jalal, *The State of Martial Rule: The Origins of Pakistan's Political Economy of Defence* (Cambridge: Cambridge University Press, 2000).

12. Talbot, *Pakistan*, 85.

13. Ibid., 94.

14. Haqqani, *Pakistan*, 2–18; Mohammed Ayoob, "Two Faces of Political Islam: Iran and Pakistan Compared," *Asian Survey* 19, no. 6 (June 1979): 536–37.

15. Jalal, *Democracy and Authoritarianism*, 15–16, 25.

16. See S. Paul Kapur, "The Kashmir Dispute: Past, Present and Future," in Sumit Ganguly and Andrew Scobell, eds., *Handbook of Asian Security* (London: Routledge, 2009).

17. See Prem Shankar Jha, *Kashmir 1947: Rival Versions of History* (Delhi: Oxford University Press, 1996); H. V. Hodson, *The Great Divide: Britain-India-Pakistan* (Kara-

chi: Oxford University Press, 1985); Robert G. Wirsing, *India, Pakistan, and the Kashmir Dispute: On Regional Conflict and its Resolution* (New York: St. Martin's Press, 1994).

18. Stephen P. Cohen, *India: Emerging Power* (Washington, DC: Brookings, 2001), 219.

19. K. J. M. Varma, "Pak Not Ready to Sideline Kashmir: Musharraf," *Press Trust of India*, June 17, 2003.

20. "Excerpts from Pakistani President Pervez Musharraf's Address to the Nation," May 27, 2002, BBC monitoring, available at http://news.bbc.co.uk/1/hi/world/monitoring/media_reports/2011509.stm. Note that I am not suggesting that India's desire to maintain the status quo is in any way morally superior to Pakistan's desire to alter existing arrangements in Kashmir. My characterization of Indian and Pakistani preferences regarding the territory is purely factual in nature, not normative.

21. See Kapur, "Kashmir Dispute," in Ganguly and Scobell, *Handbook of Asian Security*.

22. See Sumit Ganguly, *The Crisis in Kashmir: Portents of War, Hopes of Peace* (New York: Cambridge University Press, 1997), 5, 140.

23. See, for example, Lyle J. Goldstein's discussion in Chapter 3 this volume of U.S. domestic political constraints during the 1995–96 Taiwan Straits crisis. For a contrasting case, in which domestic politics appear to have played little, if any role, see Brantly Womack's discussion of the Sino-Vietnamese rivalry in Chapter 8.

24. Other rivalries in this volume are, to a significant degree, also rooted in ideational conflict. See, for example, Samuel S. Kim's characterization of the rivalry between the two Koreas as a "legitimacy-cum-identity crisis" in Chapter 7. See also Lowel Dittmer's discussion in Chapter 6 of negative Russian and Chinese perceptions of each others' cultural and national identities.

25. See Kapur, "Kashmir Dispute," in Ganguly and Scobell, *Handbook of Asian Security*.

26. See Josef Korbel, *Danger in Kashmir* (Oxford: Oxford University Press, 1954), 98–100.

27. See Jawaharlal Nehru, "Facts Relating to Kashmir," Press Conference Statements in New Delhi, January 2, 1948, in *Jawaharlal Nehru, Independence and After: A Collection of Speeches, 1946–1949* (New York: John Day Company, 1950), 66, 69.

28. Sumantra Bose, *Kashmir: Roots of Conflict, Paths to Peace* (Cambridge, MA: Harvard University Press, 2003), 41. See also Sumit Ganguly, *Conflict Unending: India-Pakistan Tensions Since 1947* (New Delhi: Oxford University Press, 2002), 15–30.

29. Ganguly, *Crisis in Kashmir*, 57; Iffat Malik, *Kashmir: Ethnic Conflict International Dispute* (Oxford: Oxford University Press, 2002), 122.

30. See Ganguly, *Conflict Unending*, 31–50.

31. On these military operations, see ibid., 67–69.

32. Shahid Amin, *Pakistan's Foreign Policy: A Reappraisal* (Karachi, Pakistan: Oxford University Press, 2002), 72.

33. See Lawrence Ziring, *Pakistan: At the Crosscurrent of History* (Oxford: One-world Oxford Publications, 2003), 138–39; Amin, *Pakistan's Foreign Policy*, 76–78; Raza, *Zulfikar Ali Bhutto*, 227–36; Burke and Ziring, *Pakistan's Foreign Policy*, 422–24.

34. Ziring, *Pakistan*, 136; Burke and Ziring, *Pakistan's Foreign Policy*, 416–17.

35. Stephen P. Cohen, *The Pakistan Army* (Karachi, Pakistan: Oxford University Press, 1998), 73, 109, 139; Zulfikar Ali Bhutto, *If I Am Assassinated* (New Delhi: Vikas Publishing House, 1979), 116–17; Ziring, *Pakistan*, 135–36.

36. Quoted in Wolpert, *Zulfi Bhutto*, 194, 195.

37. Text of Simla Agreement, in P. R. Chari and Pervaiz Iqbal Cheema, *The Simla Agreement 1972: Its Wasted Promise* (New Delhi: Manohar, 2001), 204–6.

38. S. Paul Kapur, *Dangerous Deterrent: Nuclear Weapons Proliferation and Conflict in South Asia* (Stanford: Stanford University Press, 2007), 68–71.

39. Ibid., 22.

40. Note that the domestic political structures that produced these preferences remained essentially the same as well. Pakistan, at both the beginning and end of the "long peace," was a nominal democracy, headed by a civilian leader, but overshadowed by the military. And India, with the exception of a brief period of "emergency" between 1975 and 1977, remained a relatively robust democracy throughout this period. In fact, this pattern of military dominance or outright rule in Pakistan, and civilian democratic governance in India, was not limited to the "long peace"; it has remained essentially constant throughout the entire span of the two countries' histories. This divergence, despite a common colonial heritage, constitutes one of the region's most important political and developmental puzzles. On these issues see generally Jalal, *Democracy and Authoritarianism in South Asia*.

41. See Ganguly, *Crisis in Kashmir*, 65–73; Wirsing, *India, Pakistan, and the Kashmir Dispute*, 113–18; Bose, *Kashmir*, 107–35; Malik, *Kashmir*, 158–60, 283.

42. Wirsing, *India, Pakistan, and the Kashmir Dispute*, 115.

43. Bose, *Kashmir*, 126.

44. See Ahmed Rashid, *Taliban: Militant Islam, Oil, and Fundamentalism in Central Asia* (New Haven, CT: Yale University Press, 2000), 137, 186.

45. Note that the insurgency also allowed Pakistan to address the problem of its general strategic inferiority regarding India, attriting Indian resources over time, undermining Indian morale, and sullying India's international reputation. See John Lancaster and Kamran Khan, "Extremist Groups Renew Activity in Pakistan; Support of Kashmir Militants Is at Odds with War on Terrorism," *Washington Post*, February 8, 2003; Wirsing, *India, Pakistan, and the Kashmir Dispute*, 121.

46. See Wirsing, *India, Pakistan, and the Kashmir Dispute*, 121; Lancaster and Khan, "Extremist Groups Renew Activity in Pakistan," in Malik, *Kashmir*, 295–98.

47. Samina Ahmed, "Pakistan's Nuclear Weapons Program: Turning Points and Nuclear Choices," *International Security* 13, no. 4 (spring 1999).

48. Ziring, *Pakistan*, 152.

49. Kapur, *Dangerous Deterrent*, chap. 5. This is not to argue that Pakistan would have failed to support the Kashmir insurgency in the absence of nuclear weapons. The point, rather, is that a nonnuclear Pakistan would have been far less aggressive, and more circumspect in doing so, than was a Pakistan armed with a nuclear capacity.

50. Author interview of Benazir Bhutto, Dubai, United Arab Emirates, August 2004.

51. Author interview of Shireen Mazari, Islamabad, Pakistan, April 2004; Shireen Mazari, "Kashmir: Looking for Viable Options," *Defence Journal* 3, no. 2 (February–March 1999), http://defencejournal.com/feb-mar99/kashmir-viable.htm.

52. Ganguly, *Crisis Unending*, 92.

53. S. Paul Kapur, "Ten Years of Instability in a Nuclear South Asia," *International Security* 33, no. 2 (fall 2008).

54. S. Paul Kapur, "The Role of Deterrence in Indian Security Policy," *Seminar* (New Delhi), July 2009.

55. See Sumit Ganguly, "Will Kashmir Stop India's Rise?" *Foreign Affairs* 85, no. 4 (July/August 2006): 48; "India, Pakistan Agree on Opening of New Bus Link, Trade Routes," Press Trust of India, January 18, 2006.

56. Government of India, Ministry of Home Affairs, *Annual Report, 2006–2007*, 6, 143.

57. Ibid.

58. See "Pakistan, India Suspend Talks Indefinitely," December 8, 2008, available at http://www.expressindia.com/latest-news/Pakistan-India-suspend-talks-indefinitely/395690/

59. See Kapur, "Ten Years of Instability in a Nuclear South Asia," 91–92.

60. See Sumit Ganguly and S. Paul Kapur, "The Sorcerer's Apprentice: Islamist Militancy in South Asia," *Washington Quarterly* 33, no. 1 (January 2010).

Chapter 5

1. John W. Garver, *Protracted Contest: Sino-Indian Rivalry in the Twentieth Century* (Seattle: University of Washington Press, 2001).

2. More importantly, 1959 set the stage for the short but bitter border war between the two countries in late 1962.

3. Charles Tilly and Robert E. Goodin, "It Depends," in Robert E. Goodin and Charles Tilly, eds., *The Oxford Handbook of Contextual Political Analysis* (New York: Oxford University Press, 2006), 13.

4. On Mill's "method of difference," see Alexander L. George and Andrew Bennett, *Case Studies and Theory Development in the Social Sciences* (Cambridge, MA: MIT Press, 2005), 153–60.

5. Ibid., 156.

6. Deborah Welch Larson, "Indeterminacy and Causal Mechanisms in International Relations Theory," Paper presented at the 104th Annual Meeting of the American Political Science Association, Boston, MA (August 28–31, 2008). Available online at http://www.concepts-methods.org/working_papers/20080908_05_PM%2015%20Larson.pdf [accessed November 1, 2009], 11.

7. Charles Tilly, "Why and How History Matters," in Goodin and Tilly, "It Depends," 422–23.

8. John Gerring, "Is There a (Viable) Crucial-Case Method?" *Comparative Political Studies* 40, no. 3 (2007): 231–53.

9. Ibid., 233.

10. Jack S. Levy, "An Introduction to Prospect Theory," *Political Psychology* 3, no. 2 (1992): 171–86.

11. See Graham T. Allison and Philip Zelikow, *Essence of Decision: Explaining the Cuban Missile Crisis*, 2d ed. (New York: Longman, 1999).

12. Stephen D. Krasner, "Are Bureaucracies Important? (Or Allison Wonderland)," in G. John Ikenberry, ed., *American Foreign Policy: Theoretical Essays*, 5th ed. (Boston: Houghton Mifflin Company, 2005), 447–59.

13. For example, see James M. Lindsay, "Congress, Foreign Policy, and the New Institutionalism," *International Studies Quarterly* 38, no. 2 (1994): 281–304; and William G. Howell and Jon C. Pevehouse, "Presidents, Congress, and the Use of Force," *International Organization* 59, no. 1 (2005): 209–32.

14. For example, Gaddis has argued that during the cold war the Democrats and the Republicans favored different strategies and force structures. See John Lewis Gaddis, *Strategies of Containment: A Critical Appraisal of American National Security Policy During the Cold War*, rev. and exp. ed. (New York: Oxford University Press, 2005). Also see Yuen Foong Khong, "Neoconservatism and the Domestic Sources of American Foreign Policy: The Role of Ideas in Operation Iraqi Freedom," in Steve Smith, Amelia Hadfield, and Tim Dunne, eds., *Foreign Policy: Theories, Actors, Cases* (New York: Oxford University Press, 2008), 251–67.

15. Piers Robinson, "The Role of Media and Public Opinion," in Smith, Hadfield, and Dunne, *Foreign Policy*, 137–53.

16. Jeffrey W. Legro, "Military Culture and Inadvertent Escalation in World War II," *International Security* 18, no. 4 (1994): 108–42.

17. Kurt Dassel, "Civilians, Soldiers and Strife: Domestic Sources of International Aggression," *International Security* 23, no. 1 (1998): 107–40.

18. This section is not intended as an exhaustive treatment of these issues but only as they pertain to India and China along the lines discussed above.

19. Jonathan D. Spence, *The Search for Modern China*, 2d ed. (New York: W. W. Norton, 1999), 494.

20. Frederick C. Teiwes, "The Chinese State During the Maoist Era," in David Shambaugh, ed. *The Modern Chinese State* (New York: Cambridge University Press, 2000), 105.

21. Tony Saich, *Governance and Politics of China*, 2d ed. (New York: Palgrave Macmillan, 2004), 25.

22. Teiwes, "Chinese State During the Maoist Era," 113–14.

23. Carol Lee Hamrin, "Elite Politics and the Development of China's Foreign Relations," in Thomas W. Robinson and David Shambaugh, eds., *Chinese Foreign Policy: Theory and Practice* (Oxford: Clarendon Press, 1995), 83.

24. Ibid., 83.

25. Liu was one of Mao's chosen heirs and the second-most important leader in the PRC after Mao. Liu was followed by Zhou who was the number-three leader in the regime. See Teiwes, "Chinese State During the Maoist Era," 117.

26. Deng was then a powerful leader in the regional government of the Southwest

Bureau. At its inception, the PRC was divided into six massive regions, with each having its own unified military command. See Spence, *Search for Modern China*, 497–98.

27. Roderick MacFarquhar, "The End of the Chinese Revolution," *The New York Review of Books*, July 20, 1989, 10; emphasis added.

28. Hamrin, "Elite Politics," 83.

29. John P. Burns, *The Chinese Communist Party's Nomenklatura System* (Armonk, NY: M. E. Sharpe, 1989). Also see Cheng Li, "University Networks and the Rise of the Qinghua Graduates in China's Leadership," *The Australian Journal of Chinese Affairs* no. 32 (1994): 1–30.

30. Saich, *Governance and Politics of China*, 121–54.

31. Ibid., 121.

32. See Kenneth G. Lieberthal and David M. Lampton, eds., *Bureaucracy, Politics, and Decision-making in Post-Mao China* (Berkeley: University of California Press, 1992).

33. Hamrin, "Elite Politics," 89–93.

34. Lu Ning, "The Central Leadership, Supraministry Coordinating Bodies, State Council Ministries, and Party Departments," in David M. Lampton, ed., *The Making of Chinese Foreign and Security Policy in the Era of Reform, 1978–2000* (Stanford: Stanford University Press, 2001), 50.

35. Ching-chang Hsiao and Timothy Cheek, "Open and Closed Media: External and Internal Newspapers in the Propaganda System," in Carol Lee Hamrin, Suisheng Zhao, and A. Doak Barnett, eds., *The Decision-making in Deng's China: Perspectives from Insiders* (Armonk, NY: M. E. Sharpe, 1995), 76.

36. A *xitong* is a grouping of bureaucracies that deals with the tasks that the top leadership wants to implement. See Kenneth Lieberthal, *Governing China: From Revolution Through Reform* (New York: W. W. Norton, 1995), 192–208.

37. See David Shambaugh, "The Soldier and the State in China," *The China Quarterly* no. 127 (1991): 527–68; and Ellis Joffe, "Party-Army Relationship in China: Retrospect and Prospect," *The China Quarterly* no. 146 (1996): 299–314.

38. Tai Ming Cheung, "The Influence of the Gun: China's Central Military Commission and its Relationship with the Military, Party, and State Decision-Making Systems," in Lampton, *Making of Chinese Foreign and Security Policy in the Era of Reform*, 62.

39. Liu and Zhou—the only other civilians in the CMC—served only until 1954. The remaining half dozen or so members of the CMC were military generals. See Teiwes, "Chinese State During the Maoist Era," 121.

40. In fact, if not for its political sensitivities, Deng might even have been granted the title of marshal in 1955. Ibid., 122.

41. MacFarquhar, "End of the Chinese Revolution," 8.

42. At different times in the Mao era, this small group included Liu Shaoqi, Zhou Enlai, Lin Biao, Deng Xiaoping, and Hua Guofeng. In the Deng era, this small group included Chen Yun, Hu Yaobang, Zhao Zhiyang, Jiang Zemin, Yang Shangkun, and Li Peng. See Lu Ning, "Central Leadership, Supraministry Coordinating Bodies, State

Council Ministries, and Party Departments," in Lampton, ed., *Making of Chinese Foreign and Security Policy*, 41.

43. David Shambaugh, "Chinese State in the Post-Mao Era," in Shambaugh, ed., *The Modern Chinese State*, 161–87.

44. J. N. Dixit, *Makers of India's Foreign Policy: Raja Ram Mohun Roy to Yashwant Sinha* (New Delhi: HarperCollins Publishers, 2004), 77.

45. Jayantanuja Bandyopadhyaya, *The Making of India's Foreign Policy: Determinants, Institutions, Processes, and Personalities*, 3d ed. (New Delhi: Allied Publishers, 2003), 83.

46. Stephen P. Cohen, *India: Emerging Power* (Washington, DC: The Brookings Institution Press, 2001), 68.

47. Raju G. C. Thomas, *Indian Security Policy* (Princeton, NJ: Princeton University Press, 1986), 91–92.

48. Raju G. C. Thomas, *The Defense of India: A Budgetary Perspective of Strategy and Politics* (Bombay: Macmillan, 1978).

49. Cohen, *India: Emerging Power*, 68.

50. Thomas, *Indian Security Policy*, 93.

51. Cohen, *India: Emerging Power*, 69.

52. Thomas, *Indian Security Policy*, 94.

53. The Janata Party—a coalition of parties which were only united by their opposition to the Congress Party—did manage to form a government in 1977 under the leadership of Desai. However, the Janata government fell just two years after its creation due to its internal contradictions as well as a consequence of its weak majority in the Parliament. There was no significant departure in India's foreign and security policy under the Janata government and the Congress Party resumed power in 1980 under the leadership of Indira Gandhi. See Robert L. Hardgrave Jr. and Stanley A. Kochanek, *India: Government and Politics in a Developing Nation*, 7th ed. (Boston, MA: Thomson Wadsworth, 2008), 315–21.

54. For an example of the impact of the Indian foreign policy bureaucracy on policy implementation, see Jeffrey Benner, *The Indian Foreign Policy Bureaucracy* (Boulder, CO: Westview Press, 1985).

55. For details, see Nicolas Blarel and Manjeet S. Pardesi, "Indian Public Opinion and the War in Iraq," in *International Public Opinion and the Iraq War*, Richard Sobel, Peter Furia, and Bethany Barratt, eds. (Potomac, forthcoming).

56. There have been a few international public opinion surveys on Indian sentiments toward the United States and its foreign policy since the late 1980s. However, the impact of these opinions on Indian decision-making remains unclear.

57. Given the fraught history of partition of the Subcontinent in 1947, India's Pakistan policy has always been an issue of national concern. Furthermore, India's South Asian policy is often influenced by regional politics within India itself. For example, developments in Bangladesh and Sri Lanka impact developments in the Indian states of West Bengal and Tamil Nadu respectively (and vice versa).

The influence of regional public opinion within India on such issues cannot be dismissed.

58. For more on public opinion and India's nuclear policy, see David Cortright and Amitabh Mattoo, *India and the Bomb: Public Opinion and Nuclear Option* (Notre Dame, IN: University of Notre Dame Press, 1996).

59. See Garver, *Protracted Contest*, 57.

60. See J. K. Baral, Pramod Panda, and Nilanchal Muni, "The Press and India-China Relations," *China Report* 25 (1989): 373.

61. Cohen, *India: Emerging Power*, 77.

62. Lloyd I. Rudolph and Susanne Hoeber Rudolph, "Generals and Politicians in India," *Pacific Affairs* 37, no. 1 (spring 1964): 5–19 (p. 8).

63. The military proved its nationalist credentials only in 1947–58 during the first Kashmir War. See K. M. Panikkar, *Problems of Indian Defence* (London: Asia Publishing House, 1960), 36.

64. Sumit Ganguly, "From the Defense of the Nation to Aid to the Civil: The Army in Contemporary India," *Journal of Asian and African Studies* XXVI, nos. 1–2 (1991): 11–26.

65. The Defense Committee of the Cabinet sought inputs from the Defense Minister's Committee, which in turn sought inputs from the Chiefs-of-Staff Committee. See Thomas, *Defense of India*, 70.

66. Rudolph and Rudolph, "Generals and Politicians in India," 8.

67. Instead, she relied on the police and the paramilitary forces to maintain her authoritarian rule. See Stephen P. Cohen, "The Military and Indian Democracy," in Atul Kohli, ed., *India's Democracy: An Analysis of Changing State-Society Relations* (Princeton, NJ: Princeton University Press, 1988), 129, n 41.

68. See Sumit Ganguly and Devin T. Hagerty, *Fearful Symmetry: India-Pakistan Crises in the Shadow of Nuclear Weapons* (Seattle: University of Washington Press, 2005), 77.

69. Carole McGranahan and Elliot Sperling, "Introduction: Tibet, India, and China," *India Review* 7, no. 3 (2008): 161–63 (p. 161).

70. Strategic rivalries are fought over position, territory, ideology, or a combination of these factors. See Michael P. Colaresi, Karen Rasler, and William R. Thompson, *Strategic Rivalries in World Politics: Position, Space, and Conflict Escalation* (Cambridge: Cambridge University Press, 2007), 79–83.

71. Wu Xingbo, "China: Security Practice of a Modernizing and Ascending Power," in *Asian Security Practice: Material and Ideational Influences* (Stanford: Stanford University Press, 1998), 115.

72. On China's quest for great power status between 1912 and 1949, see William C. Kirby, "The Internationalization of China: Foreign Relations at Home and Abroad in the Republican Era," *The China Quarterly*, no. 150 (June 1997): 433–58.

73. On historical influences on China's foreign and security policy, see John W. Garver, *Foreign Relations of the People's Republic of China* (Englewood Cliffs, NJ: Prentice Hall, 1993), 2–30.

74. On the Sinocentric world order, see John King Fairbank, ed., *The Chinese World Order: Traditional China's Foreign Relations* (Cambridge, MA: Harvard University Press, 1968). For a view that a rising China will attempt to reestablish this Sinocentric world order in East Asia, see David C. Kang, *China Rising: Peace, Power, and Order in East Asia* (New York: Columbia University Press, 2007).

75. On China's "national humiliation," see Peter Hays Gries, *China's New Nationalism: Pride, Politics, and Diplomacy* (Berkeley: University of California Press, 2004), 43–53.

76. On the Chinese civilization and its history, see Jacques Gernet, *A History of Chinese Civilization*, 2d ed. (New York: Cambridge University Press, 1996).

77. The Treaty of Nanjing signed between Britain and Qing China in 1842 traditionally marks the beginning of the period of "unequal treaties" and "national humiliation." See Spence, *Search for Modern China*, 160–66.

78. Gries, *China's New Nationalism*, 47.

79. Garver, *Foreign Relations of the People's Republic of China*, 8.

80. For details, see Tsering Shakya, *The Dragon in the Land of the Snows: A History of Modern Tibet Since 1947* (New York: Penguin, 1999), 33–91.

81. For details, see Anne-Marie Blondeau and Katia Buffetrille, eds., *Authenticating Tibet: Answers to China's 100 Questions* (Berkeley: University of California Press, 2008).

82. On Qing-Tibet relations, see Chusei Suzuki, "China's Relations with Inner Asia: The Hsiung-Nu and Tibet," in *The Chinese World Order*, 192–97.

83. Melvyn C. Goldstein, *A History of Modern Tibet, 1913–1951: The Demise of the Lamaist State* (Berkeley: University of California Press, 1989), 59–62. The Tibetan declaration of independence was in accordance with its own traditional politics, not as independence is understood in the Western context.

84. Quoted in Karunakar Gupta, *The Hidden History of the Sino-Indian Frontier* (Calcutta: Minerva, 1974), 100–1.

85. See A. Martin Wainwright, "Regional Security and Paramount Powers: The British Raj and Independent India," in Marvin G. Weinbaum and Chetan Kumar, eds., *South Asia Approaches the Millennium: Reexamining National Security* (Boulder, CO: Westview Press, 1995), 41–62.

86. See Lorne Kavic, *India's Quest for Security: Defence Policies, 1947–1965* (Berkeley: University of California Press, 1967), 8–20, on this "ring fence" system.

87. A complete discussion of British India's grand strategy and its inheritance and modification by independent India is beyond the scope of this study. Only those aspects of this strategy as they relate to Tibet and China will be discussed here. For a detailed analysis of this geostrategic inheritance by independent India, see the relevant sections in Ashley J. Tellis, "Securing the Barrack: The Logic, Structure, and Objectives of India's Naval Expansion," *Naval War College Review* (1990): 79–83. For the continuation of this strategy, albeit with significant modifications in the context of Pakistan, see Manjeet S. Pardesi and Sumit Ganguly, "The Rise of India and the India-Pakistan Conflict," *The Fletcher Forum of World Affairs* 31, no. 1 (winter 2007): 131–45.

88. Menon was Panikkar's predecessor and independent India's first ambassador to Nationalist China.

89. K. P. S. Menon, *Many Worlds: An Autobiography* (London: Oxford University Press, 1985), 270.

90. Garver, *Protracted Conflict*, 35.

91. Yun-yuan Yang, "Controversies over Tibet: China Versus India, 1947–49," *The China Quarterly* 111 (September 1987): 414.

92. Shakya, *Dragon in the Land of Snows*, 12–13.

93. Ibid., 32.

94. Garver, *Protracted Conflict*, 49–50.

95. Hugh E. Richardson, *Tibet and its History*, 2d ed. (Boulder and London: Shambhala, 1984).

96. For the details of these three agreements, see Goldstein, *History of Modern Tibet*, 74–76.

97. See A. W. Stargardt, "The Emergence of the Asian System of Powers," *Modern Asian Studies* 23, no. 3 (1989): 562–65; and A. Appadorai, "The Asian Relations Conference in Perspective," *International Studies* 18, no. 3 (1979): 275–85.

98. It was expected that the Chinese delegation at the ARC would have been led by Dai Jitao, a senior Guomindang (KMT) leader who had visited India in November 1940. However, suspecting an "ulterior motive" behind India's separate invitation to Tibet, Dai declined to lead the Chinese delegation at the ARC. See Yun-yuan Yang, *Nehru and China, 1927–1949* (University of Virginia, unpublished PhD dissertation, 1974), 103–11.

99. Werner Levi, *Free India in Asia* (Minneapolis: University of Minnesota Press, 1952), 38.

100. Yang, "Controversies over Tibet," 418–19.

101. "India and Anglo-American Imperialism," *World Culture*, September 16, 1949. For the extracts of this article, see Document 10 in R. K. Jain, ed., *China: South Asia Relations, 1947–1980*, vol. 1 (New Delhi: Radiant Publishers, 1981), 7–9.

102. On the expulsion of the Chinese from Tibet and Richardson's possible involvement, see B. R. Deepak, *India and China, 1904–2004: A Century of Peace and Conflict* (New Delhi: Manak, 2005), 108–16.

103. Richardson, *Tibet and its History*, 178.

104. See Qiang Zhai, "Tibet and the Chinese-British-American Relations in the Early 1950s," *Journal of Cold War Studies* 8, no. 3 (2006): 34–53.

105. To be sure, the Qing dynasty had launched a military expedition against Nepal in 1793 and had established a "tributary relationship" with Nepal that lasted until 1908. However, this was mostly symbolic and no permanent Chinese military garrison was established in Nepal. See Vijay Kumar Manandhar, *A Comprehensive History of Nepal-China Relations up to 1955 AD*, vols. 1 and 2 (New Delhi: Adroit, 2004). Furthermore, during the Tang Dynasty, China wielded limited but significant politico-military influence in the northwestern regions of the Indian subcontinent. See Tansen Sen, "Kasmir, Tang China, and Muktapida Lalitaditya's Ascendancy Over the South-

ern Hindukush Region," *Journal of Asian History* 38, no. 2 (2004): 141–62. Finally, during the Tang Dynasty, there was also a minor Chinese-led military foray into northern India. See Tansen Sen, "In Search of Longevity and Good Karma: Chinese Diplomatic Missions into Middle India in the Seventh Century," *Journal of World History* 12, no. 1 (spring 2001): 1–28. However, none of these episodes presented a sustained Chinese politico-military pressure on India.

106. Patel's note to Nehru (dated November 7, 1950) can be found in Durga Das, ed., *Sardar Patel's Correspondence, 1945–50*, vol. X (Ahmedabad, Pakistan: Navajivan Publishing House, 1974), 335–41.

107. See Document 39 titled "Prime Minister Nehru's note on China and Tibet forwarded to Vallabhai Patel," dated November 18, 1950 in Jain, *China: South Asia Relations*, 44.

108. On the strategic rationale behind India's policy of nonalignment, see Raju G. C. Thomas, "Nonalignment and Indian Security: Nehru's Rationale and Legacy," *Journal of Strategic Studies* 2, no. 2 (1979): 153–71.

109. Jawaharlal Nehru, "A Monroe Doctrine for Asia," a public speech delivered on August 9, 1947. For the full text, see *Selected Works of Jawaharlal Nehru*, Second Series, vol. III (New Delhi: Oxford University Press, 1985), 133–35.

110. Jawaharlal Nehru, *The Discovery of India* (New Delhi: Penguin Books, 2004 [1946]), 597.

111. Judith M. Brown, *Nehru: A Political Life* (London: Yale University Press, 2003), 245.

112. Charles H. Heimsath and Surjit Mansingh, *A Diplomatic History of Modern India* (Calcutta: Allied Publishers, 1971), 56.

113. Document 39, in Jain, *China: South Asia Relations*, 45.

114. Sumit Ganguly, "India and China: Border Issues, Domestic Integration, and International Security," in Francine R. Frankel and Harry Harding, eds., *The India-China Relationship: What the United States Needs to Know* (New York: Columbia University Press, 2004), 108–9, and 128, n 23.

115. Dawa Norbu, "Tibet in Sino-Indian Relations: The Centrality of Marginality," *Asian Survey* 37, no. 11 (November 1997): 1080.

116. See Document 55 titled "India-China agreement on trade and intercourse between Tibet Region of China and India," in Jain, *China: South Asia Relations*, 61–67.

117. Norbu, "Tibet in Sino-Indian Relations," 1081.

118. Under the British, three different boundary lines were proposed between Kashmir and Tibet—the Ardagh-Johnson line, which was the most extensive of the three and included the Aksai China region (an extension of the Tibetan plateau), the Macartney-Macdonald line which placed Aksai Chin in Sinkiang/Xinjiang (another region of ambiguous international status), and the Trelawney-Saunders line that placed the borders of the Ladakh region of Kashmir along the Karakoram mountains. However, there was no clear consensus on where this border lay at the time of the departure of the British from India. See Steven A. Hoffman, *India and the China Crisis* (Berkeley: University of California Press, 1990), 9–16.

119. The following section is drawn from Garver, *Protracted Contest*, 80–88.

120. Ibid., 80.

121. *History of the Conflict with China, 1962* (New Delhi: History Division, Ministry of Defence, 1992), 36. This restricted report of the government of India was leaked and is now available online at http://www.bharat-rakshak.com/LAND-FORCES/Army/History/1962War/PDF/1962Main.pdf [accessed on November 10, 2009].

122. Ibid., 36–37.

123. Hoffman, *India and the China Crisis*, 13–28, 35–36.

124. Garver, *Protracted Contest*, 89–90.

125. Steven A. Hoffman, "Rethinking the Linkage between Tibet and the China-India Border Conflict: A Realist Approach," *Journal of Cold War Studies* 8, no. 3 (summer 2006): 174.

126. See "Tawang: A Brief Sum-up," in Parshotam Mehra, *Essays in Frontier History: India, China, and the Disputed Border* (New Delhi: Oxford University Press, 2007), 136–39.

127. On the importance of the southern Himalayan slopes for India's defense, see Garver, *Protracted Contest*, 98–100.

128. Randeep Ramesh, "Last Vestige of Old Tibetan Culture Clings on in Remote Indian State," *The Guardian*, November 20, 2006. Available online: http://www.guardian.co.uk/international/story/0,1952122,00.html [accessed November 10, 2009].

129. Garver, *Protracted Contest*, 51.

130. For a text of this agreement, see Shakya, *Dragon in the Land of the Snows*, 449–52.

131. Jampa Panglung, "What Caused the 1959 Rebellion in Tibet?" in Blondeau and Buffetrille, *Authenticating Tibet*, 75.

132. Ibid., 75.

133. On "ethnographic" and "political" Tibet, see Chen Jian, "The Tibetan Rebellion of 1959 and China's Changing Relations with India and the Soviet Union," *Journal of Cold War Studies* 8, no. 3 (2006): 61–70.

134. Panglung, "What Caused the 1959 Rebellion in Tibet?" 76.

135. Chen Jian, "Tibetan Rebellion of 1959," 68.

136. Panglung, "What Caused the 1959 Rebellion in Tibet?" 77.

137. Garver, *Protracted Contest*, 56.

138. M. Taylor Fravel, *Strong Borders, Secure Nation: Cooperation and Conflict in China's Territorial Disputes* (Princeton, NJ: Princeton University Press, 2008), 78.

139. Shakya, *Dragon in the Land of the Snows*, 207.

140. Hoffman, "Rethinking the Linkage Between Tibet and the China-India Border Conflict," 188–89.

141. Shakya, *Dragon in the Land of the Snows*, 207.

142. Ibid., 213.

143. Garver, *Protracted Contest*, 54.

144. Chen Jian, "Tibetan Rebellion of 1959," 85.

145. Mark Kramer, "Introduction," *Journal of Cold War Studies* 8, no. 3 (2006): 12.

This is a special issue of this journal on *Great-Power Rivalries, Tibetan Guerilla Resistance, and the Cold War in South Asia.*

146. See Shakya, *Dragon in the Land of the Snows,* 185–211.

147. Quoted in Chen Jian, "Tibetan Rebellion of 1959," 85.

148. Ibid., 91.

149. John Kenneth Knaus, *Orphans of the Cold War: America and the Tibetan Struggle for Survival* (New York: Public Affarirs, 1999).

150. Carole McGranahan, "Tibet's Cold War: The CIA and the Chushi Gangdrug Resistance, 1956–1974," *Journal of Cold War Studies* 8, no. 3 (summer 2006): 102–30.

151. Garver, *Protracted Contest,* 55–58. India and the United States did carry out several joint espionage expeditions in Tibet. However, meaningful collaboration between India and the United States began only after the 1962 Sino-Indian War. Most of these joint expeditions took place between 1965 and 1968. See M. S. Kohli and Kenneth Conboy, *Spies in the Himalayas: Secret Missions and Perilous Climbs* (Lawrence: University Press of Kansas, 2002).

152. See Document 110 titled "Dalai Lama's statement in Tezpur (India), in Jain, *China: South Asia Relations,* 115–17.

153. Quoted in Jian, "Tibetan Rebellion of 1959," 85.

154. Ibid., 89.

155. *History of Conflict with China, 1962,* 33–35.

156. Until then Nehru had kept the Indian Parliament in the dark about Chinese military activities along the border (that began at least as early as 1955). Nehru was of the opinion that the border between India and China was settled and accepted by both sides as such barring some minor issues regarding different perceptions of its exact location along a few points. However, Zhou's letter "greatly surprised" and "distressed" Nehru. For Zhou's letter see Document 121 titled "Chou En-lai's reply to Nehru's letter of 22 March 1959, 8 September 1959," in Jain, *China: South Asia Relations,* 138–40. And for Nehru's reply to this letter, see Document 128 titled "Nehru's reply to Chou En-lai's letter of 8 September 1959, 26 September 1959," in Jain, *China: South Asia Relations,* 147–51.

157. Due to poor connectivity with the rest of China, India was Tibet's main gateway for import and export of essential commodities.

158. On domestic political developments in India after 1959 and their impact on Sino-Indian relations, see Srinath Raghavan, *The War and Peace in Modern India: A Strategic History of Nehru Years* (Ranikhet, Uttarakhand: Permanent Black, 2010), 287–92; and Srinath Raghavan, "Civil-Military Relations in India: The China Crisis and After," *Journal of Strategic Studies* 32, no. 1 (2009): 149–75.

159. For details of the decision that led to the formulation of the forward policy, see Hoffman, *India and the China Crisis,* 92–111.

160. Ganguly, "Border Issues, Domestic Integration, and International Security," 114. Also see Allen S. Whiting, *The Chinese Calculus of Deterrence: India and Indochina* (Ann Arbor: University of Michigan Press, 1975).

161. For details, see Hoffman, *India and the China Crisis,* 163–210.

162. See John W. Garver, "China's Decision to Wage War with India in 1962," in Alastair Iain Johnston and Robert S. Ross, eds., *New Directions in the Study of China's Foreign Policy* (Stanford: Stanford University Press, 2006).

163. Ganguly, "Border Issues, Domestic Integration, and International Security," 115.

164. Baldev Raj Nayar and T. V. Paul, *India in the World Order: Searching for Major-Power Status* (New Delhi: Cambridge University Press, 2004), 150.

165. John Lewis and Litai Xue, *China Builds the Bomb* (Stanford: Stanford University Press, 1991).

166. A. G. Noorani, "India's Quest for a Nuclear Guarantee," *Asian Survey* 7, no. 7 (1967): 490–502.

167. Sumit Ganguly, "Why India Joined the Nuclear Club," *Bulletin of the Atomic Scientists* 39, no. 4 (April 1983): 30-33.

168. Santosh Mehrotra, *India and the Soviet Union: Trade and Technology Transfer* (Cambridge: Cambridge University Press, 1990).

169. See Linda Racioppi, *Soviet Policy Towards South Asia Since 1970* (Cambridge: Cambridge University Press, 1994).

170. On the details of the Sino-Pakistani border demarcation, see W. M. Dobell, "Ramifications of the China-Pakistan Border Treaty," *Pacific Affairs* 37, no. 3 (autumn 1964): 283–95.

171. Ganguly, "Border Issues, Domestic Integration, and International Security," 118.

172. T. V. Paul, "China-Pakistani Nuclear/Missile Ties and the Balance of Power," *The Nonproliferation Review* (summer 2003).

173. Garver, *Protracted Contest*, 187.

174. C. V. Ranganathan, "India-China Relations," *World Affairs* 2, no. 2 (April-June 1998). Available online: http://www.ciaonet.org/olj/wa/wa_apr98rcv.html [accessed August 29, 2009].

175. On the Chinese dimension in Siachen, see V. R. Raghavan, *Conflict Without End* (New Delhi: Viking, 2002), 19–28.

176. Mahnaz Z. Ispahani, *Roads and Rivals: The Political Uses of Access in the Borderlands of Asia* (Ithaca, NY: Cornell University Press, 1989), 205–6.

177. Georges Tan Eng Bok, "How Does the PLA Cope with 'Regional Conflict' and 'Local War'?" in Richard H. Yang, *China's Military: The PLA in 1990/91* (Kaohsiung: National Sun Yat-sen University, 1991), 151.

178. Sumit Ganguly, "The Sino-Indian Border Talks, 1981–1989: A View from New Delhi," *Asian Survey* 29, no. 12 (December 1989): 1130–31.

179. Fravel, *Strong Borders, Secure Nation*, 199.

180. Sanjoy Hazarika, "India and China Cite Each Other for Massing Troops in the Himalayas," *The New York Times*, May 8, 1987.

181. Stephen P. Cohen, *India: Emerging Power* (Washington, DC: Brookings Institution Press, 2007), 148.

182. Georges Tan Eng Bok, "How Does the PLA Cope with 'Regional Conflict,'"150.

183. Ibid., 151.

184. Shakya, *Dragon in the Land of the Snows*, 416–25.

185. Robert Barnett, "What Caused the Riots, and Did It Have Anything to with the Dalai Clique," in Blondeau and Buffetrille, *Authenticating Tibet*, 317–18.

186. Per Kvaerne, "What Is the Chinese Government's Attitude Toward the Five-Point Proposal Put Forward By the Dalai Lama in the United States During September 1987?" in Blondeau and Buffetrille, *Authenticating Tibet*, 119–21.

187. Shakya, *Dragon in the Land of the Snows*, 412–16.

188. Ibid., 412.

189. Shakya mentions that no Indian official accompanied the Dalai Lama to the United States unlike his other foreign travels. Ibid., 414–15. It is in fact possible that the Indians knew what was about to happen and in not having an Indian governmental official accompany him, the Indians distanced themselves from the proposal.

190. Anne-Marie Blondeau, "How Does the Chinese Government View the Dalai Lama's 'New Proposal on Tibet he put forwards in Strasbourg, France, in June 1988?'" in Blondeau and Buffetrille, *Authenticating Tibet*, 121–23.

191. Shakya, *Dragon in the Land of the Snows*, 424.

192. See Salamat Ali, "India Plays It Cool," *Far Eastern Economic Review* 22 (October 1987).

193. Devin T. Hagerty, "India's Regional Security Doctrine," *Asian Survey* 31, no. 4 (1991): 351–63.

194. K. Natwar Singh, *My China Diary, 1956–1988* (New Delhi: Rupa, 2009). Singh had accompanied Gandhi to China in 1988.

195. T. Karki Hussain, "India's China Policy: Putting Politics in Command," in Satish Kumar, ed., *Yearbook on India's Foreign Policy, 1989* (New Delhi: Sage, 1990).

196. John W. Garver, "The Indian Factor in Recent Sino-Soviet Relations," *The China Quarterly* no. 125 (1991): 80.

197. Ibid., 81.

198. Surjit Mansingh and Steven I. Levine, "China and India: Moving Beyond Confrontation," *Problems of Communism* 38, nos. 2–3 (1989): 40.

199. Baral, Panda, and Muni, "Press and India-China Relations," 361.

200. Li Li, *Security Perception and China-India Relations* (New Delhi: Knowledge World, 2009), 41.

201. Ibid., 41.

202. Xuecheng Liu, *The Sino-Indian Dispute and Sino-Indian Relations* (Lanham:University Press of America, 1994), 136.

203. Ibid., 137.

204. Timo Kivimäki, "'Reason' and 'Power' in Territorial Disputes: The South China Sea," *Asian Journal of Social Science* 30, no. 3 (2002): 525–46.

205. Tun-jen Cheng, "Democratizing the Quasi-Leninist Regime in Taiwan," *World Politics* 41 (July 1989).

206. Daniel Markey, "Developing India's Foreign Policy 'Software,'" *Asia Policy* 8 (July 2009).

207. Linda Jakobson and Dean Knox, "New Foreign Policy Actors in China," *SIPRI Policy Paper*, no. 26, September 2010.

208. For example, see "Uproar in Lok Sabha Over Tibet Unrest," *The Times of India*, March 17, 2008. Available online at http://timesofindia.indiatimes.com/Uproar_in_Lok_Sabha_over_Tibet_unrest/articleshow/2873817.cms [accessed November 10, 2009].

209. "No change in Tibet Policy: Mukherjee," *Business Standard*, March 17, 2008.

210. Phunchok Stobdan, "An Indian Perception of the Tibetan Situation," *Asia Pacific Bulletin* no. 31 (March 20, 2009).

211. Dennis Woodward, "The People's Liberation Army: A threat to India?" *Contemporary South Asia* 12, no. 2 (2003): 229–42.

212. Abanti Bhattacharya, "Explaining China's India Policy," *IDSA Comment*, September 17, 2008. Available online at http://www.idsa.in/idsastrategiccomments/ExplainingChinasIndiaPolicy_ABhattacharya_170908 [accessed November 10, 2009].

213. "India Left ends coalition support," *BBC News*, July 8, 2008. Available online at http://news.bbc.co.uk/2/hi/7494795.stm [accessed November 10, 2009].

214. "China Poses New Challenges to India," *Rediff*, November 4, 2008. Available online at http://www.rediff.com/news/2008/nov/04chindia.htm [accessed November 10, 2009].

215. See Jyoti Malhotra, "Military Upgradation Plan along China India Border finally takes wing," *Business Standard*, June 17, 2009. Available online at http://www.business-standard.com/india/news/military-upgradation-plan-along-china-border-finally-takes-wing/361282/ [accessed November 10, 2009].

216. See Richard McGregor, Jamil Anderlini, and Tom Mitchell, "China Seals off Tibetan Capital," *Financial Times*, March 16, 2008. Available online at http://www.ft.com/cms/s/0/b0713f2e-f353–11dc-b6bc-0000779fd2ac.html [accessed November 10, 2009].

217. For example, see Cheng Ruisheng, "Trend of India's Diplomatic Strategy," *China International Studies* (spring 2008): 20–40; and Ding Ying, "The Mounting Nuclear Imbalance," *Beijing Review*, September 6, 2007.

Chapter 6

1. Yet the Mongols also contributed to the development of a postal road network, census, fiscal system, and Russian military organization. They actually did not interfere much in social life; as Shamanists (at that time) they were quite broadminded about religion and permitted subject populations to retain their own customs and culture, also assigning Russian elites to collect taxes on their behalf. Donald Ostrowski, *Muscovy and the Mongols: Cross-cultural Influences on the Steppe Frontier* (Cambridge: Cambridge University Press, 1996), 109ff.

2. On July 25, 1919, the new Bolshevik regime issued the First Karakhan Declaration in support of Chinese national self-determination disavowing all secret treaties with Japan and China and promising to return "to the Chinese people everything that has been seized from them by the tsarist government," including restoration without

compensation of the Chinese Eastern Railway. But later the People's Commissariat of Foreign Affairs argued that the text that had been wired to its Chinese counterparts was inauthentic. In a later presentation of the official text this paragraph was no longer there.

3. Seeking disciples on the Left, Moscow provided military and financial assistance to any number of dubious confederates—to Wu Peifu, to the "Revolutionary Armies" of Feng Yuxiang, and to the "left-wing" KMT under Wang Jingwei. Alexander Lukin, *The Bear Watches the Dragon: Russia's Perception of China and the Evolution of Russian-Chinese Relations Since the 18th Century* (Armonk, NY: M.E. Sharpe, 2003), 87.

4. Moscow's treaty with Nanking was a matter of considerable shock and dismay to the CCP, who had not been consulted or even informed. See Dieter Heinrich, *Die Sowjetunion und das kommunistische China 1945–1950: Der beschwerliche Weg zum Buendnis* (Baden-Baden, Germany: Nomos Verlagsgesellschaft, 1998), 99–117.

5. David Wolff, "'One Finger's Worth of Historical Events': New Russian and Chinese Evidence on the Sino-Soviet Alliance and Split, 1948–1959" (Woodrow Wilson International Center for Scholars, Washington, DC, August 2000), Cold War International History Project, Working Paper No. 30, 73. Available online at http://www.wilsoncenter.org/topics/pubs/ACFB14.pdf

6. According to Conquest's estimate, revised after securing access to Soviet archives at the end of the cold war, fifteen to twenty million died in Stalin's purge and collectivization movements. Robert Conquest, *The Great Terror: A Reassessment,* 40th Anniversary ed. (New York: Oxford University Press, 2007), xvi.

7. See Chen Jian, *Mao's China and the Cold War* (Chapel Hill: University of North Carolina Press, 2001); and Lorenz M. Luethi, *The Sino-Soviet Split: Cold War in the Communist World* (Princeton, NJ: Princeton University Press, 2008). Sergey Radchenko, *Two Suns in the Heavens: The Sino-Soviet Struggle for Supremacy, 1962–1967* (Stanford: Stanford University Press, 2009) attributes more importance to national interest and power-political considerations, but Radchenko's study focuses on the height of the conflict rather than its origins, when the dispute had already become institutionalized and path-dependent.

8. Jacques Levesque, *Le conflit sino-sovietique et l'Europe de l'Est: Ses incidences sur les conflits sovieto-polonzis et sovieto-roumain* (Montreal: Les Presses de l-Universite de Montreal, 1970), 24.

9. See Lowell Dittmer, *Sino-Soviet Normalization and its International Implications, 1945–1990* (Seattle: University of Washington Press, 1992), chap. 2.

10. As Khrushchev put it in a December 1963 Plenum: "On what question do we have disagreements with China? Ask me! I don't know, don't know." Nikita Khrushchev's speech at the December 1963 CC CPSU Plenum (December 13, 1963), as cited in Radchenko, *Two Suns*, 91, n 78.

11. Although Washington refused publicly to endorse China's 1979 "pedagogical war" against Vietnam—a costly strategic error from Beijing's perspective, with some twenty thousand casualties and an indeterminate outcome—the United States did provide satellite photos of Soviet troop deployments along China's northern borders.

12. It is fairly clear that Gorbachev's visit played some role in stimulating the Tiananmen protest, but China also played an important if indirect role in the collapse of Soviet and Eastern European communism, essentially by eliminating mass repression as a morally acceptable option. Although there were Eastern European attempts to emulate the "Chinese solution" (for example, Romania), all failed. Cf. Nancy Bernkopf Tucker, "China as a Factor in the Collapse of the Soviet Empire," *Political Science Quarterly* 110, no. 4 (winter 1995): 501–19.

13. 37: The Chinese apparently contacted Prime Minister Evgenii Primakov about a treaty shortly after the NATO bombing of their embassy in Belgrade. Cf. "vos'maia vstrecha" (the 8th meeting), *Rossiiskaia Gazeta,* July 14, 2001, 1, as cited in Jeanne L. Wilson, *Strategic Partners: Russian-Chinese Relations in the Post-Soviet Era* (Armonk, NY: M. E. Sharpe, 2004), 37.

14. Bobo Lo, *Axis of Convenience: Moscow, Beijing, and the New Geopolitics* (Chatham House; Washington, DC: The Brookings Institution Press, 2008).

15. RFE/RL Newsline, vol. 9, no. 125, part 1, July 1, 2005; as cited in Wilson, *Strategic Partners,* 114. More recent surveys indicate some improvement in the Chinese popular image.

16. The Sino-Soviet border was some 7,000 kilometers long. Since the disintegration of the USSR, it has contracted to 3,484 km, while the Sino-Kazakh border stretches for about 2,000 km, the Sino-Kyrgyz border for 1,000 km, and the border with Tajikistan is about 500 km long.

17. The sudden drop was clearly a result of a drastic reduction of Chinese imports, also reversing the previous trade imbalance in China's favor: according to Chinese figures, Russian imports increased by 12.1 percent (since 2006) while Chinese exports to Russia increased 79.9 percent; according to Russian figures (which exclude shuttle trade), Russian exports to China increased from US$15.8 billion to a mere US$15.9 billion while Chinese imports nearly doubled, from US$12.9 billion to US$24.9 billion. John Garnaut, "Russia on Edge as China Grows," *Sydney Morning Herald,* Business Day, June 9, 2008, 1. On Chinese weapons export complaints see Nikita Petrov, "Chinese Border Action," Moscow RIA *Novosti,* September 20, 2007.

18. In 2006, China's CNPC and Russia's state-run oil firm Rosneft agreed to build a 200,000 bpd refinery and jointly operate three hundred or more petrol stations, and to construct a large oil refinery in Tianjin. In February 2009 Rosneft and state oil pipeline monopoly Transneft agreed a US$25 billion loan from the Chinese Developmental Bank, secured by twenty years of oil supplies. Thus Russia will start shipping crude to China in 2010 via the country's first oil pipeline to Asia, which should supply ca. 4 percent of China's annual crude demand. In 2006, the Russian gas export monopoly Gazprom announced it would build two major pipelines to China, though this project has been delayed due to disagreements over gas pricing. Reuters, June 15, 2009. In 2006, the Russian gas export monopoly Gazprom announced it would build two major pipelines to China, though this project has been delayed due to disagreements over gas pricing. Michael Richardson, "Loans-for-Oil Deal Should Seal Sino-Russian Ties," *Straits Times* (Singapore), February 5, 2009.

19. Russia's export of tanks in 1992 dropped 79–fold, sales of combat aircraft fell 1.5 times in comparison to 199, leaving warehouses of the military-industrial complex overstocked with unsold weapons. China was the principal buyer of Russian weapons in 1992, making purchases worth US$1.8 billion. Pavel Felgengauer, "Arms Exports Continue to Fall," *Sogodnya* (Moscow), July 13, 1993, 3.

20. Sharif M. Shuja, "Moscow's Asia Policy," *Contemporary Review* 272, no. 1587 (April 1998): 169–78.

21. Cf. Peggy Falkenheim Meyer, "Russia's Post-Cold War Security Policy in Northeast Asia," *Pacific Affairs* 67, no. 4 (winter 1994): 495–513.

22. The Institute of the Far East (IDV, in its Russian initials) in the Russian Academy of Sciences, previously led by Oleg Rakhmanin, now by his former deputy Mikhail Titorenko, still the largest Moscow research center for Chinese studies, has shifted from its critical stance toward Maoist ideology to an ardent embrace, largely the CCP has avoided privatization and political reform while successfully regenerating socialist economic performance. Alexander Lukin, "Russia's Image of China and Russian-Chinese Relations," *East Asia: An International Quarterly* 17, no. 1 (spring 1999): 5ff; see also Evgeniy Bazhanov, "Russian Perspectives on China's Foreign Policy and Military Development," in Jonathan Pollack and Michael Yang, eds., *In China's Shadow: Regional Perspectives on Chinese Foreign Policy and Military Development* (Santa Monica, CA: Rand Corp., 1998), 70–91.

23. The first, modest shipment of oil from Kazakhstan to China—a shipment of 1,700 metric tons of Kazakh crude oil by rail to refineries in Xinjiang—was sent in late October 1997.

Chapter 7

1. Nicholas Eberstadt and Richard J. Ellings, eds., *Korea's Future and the Great Powers* (Seattle: University of Washington Press, 2001).

2. Michael P. Colaresi, Karen Rasler, and William R. Thompson, *Strategic Rivalries in World Politics: Position, Space and Conflict Escalation* (New York: Cambridge University Press, 2007), 79.

3. For discussion on the role of systemic shocks in the initiation or termination of strategic rivalry, see Paul F. Diehl and George Goertz, *War and Peace in International Rivalry* (Ann Arbor: University of Michigan Press, 2000), 12.

4. Robert Jervis, "The Impact of the Korean War on the Cold War," *Journal of Conflict Resolution*, 24, no. 4 (1980): 563–92.

5. Chae-sung Chun, "The Cold War and Its Transition for Koreans: The Meaning from a Constructivist Viewpoint," in Chung-in Moon, Odd Arne Westad, and Gyoo-hyoung Kahng, eds., *Ending the Cold War in Korea: Theoretical and Historical Perspectives* (Seoul: Yonsei University Press, 2001), 115–45; Roland Bleiker, *Divided Korea: Toward a Culture of Reconciliation* (Minneapolis: University of Minnesota, 2005); and

Samuel S. Kim, *The Two Koreas and the Great Powers* (New York: Cambridge University Press, 2006), 2–3.

6. Kim, *Two Koreas and the Great Powers*, 345.

7. Bleiker, *Divided Korea.*

8. *Rodong Sinmun* (Worker's Daily) (Pyongyang), June 25, 2000, 6; emphasis added.

9. Diehl and Goertz, *War and Peace,* 12; emphasis added.

10. David E. Sanger, "Allies Hear Sour Notes in 'Axis of Evil' Chorus," *New York Times,* February 17, 2002. See also Clay Chandler, "Koreans Voice Anti-American Sentiments," *Washington Post,* February 21, 2002.

11. For further discussion on South Korean perceptions of the United States, see Eric Larson, Norman Levin, Seonhae Baik, and Bogdan Savych, *Ambivalent Allies? A Study of South Korean Attitudes Toward the U.S.* (Santa Monica, CA: Rand Corporation, March 2004).

12. Kang Choi and Joon-Sung Park, "South Korea: Fears of Abandonment and Entrapment," in Muthiah Alagappa, ed. *The Long Shadow: Nuclear Weapons and Security in 21st Century Asia* (Stanford: Stanford University Press, 2008), 386.

13. Joint New Year Editorial of *Rodong Sinmun, Joson Inmingun, Chongnyong Jonwi,* "Let Us Fully Demonstrate the Dignity and Might of the DPRK Under the Great Banner of Army-based Policy," January 1, 2003 at http://www.kcna.comjp/item2003/200301/news01/01.htm.

14. Chung-in Moon, "Comparing the 2000 and 2007 Inter Korean Summits," *Global Asia* 2, no. 3 (2007): 76–88.

15. It is beyond the scope of this chapter to fully evaluate all the competing claims and explanations of the cause of the Cheonan incident.

16. Peter Hayes and Stephen Noerper, "The Future of the U.S.-ROK Alliance," in Young Whan Kihl and Peter Hayes, eds. *Peace and Security in Northeast Asia* (Armonk, NY: M. E. Sharpe, 1997), 266.

17. See "DPRK Proposes to Start of Peace Talks," Korean Central News Agency (KCNA), January 11, 2010.

18. President Roh's Address at the 53rd Commencement and Commissioning Ceremony of the Korea Air Force Academy, March 8, 2005, available at http://english.president.go,kr/warp/app/en_speeches/view?group_id=en_ar.

19. See Chung-in Moon, *Arms Control on the Korean Peninsula: International Penetrations, Regional Dynamics, and Domestic Structure* (Seoul: Yonsei University Press, 1996), 56.

20. Ministry of National Defense, *Defense White Paper 2008* (Seoul: Ministry of National Defense, December 31, 2008), 316.

21. John Feffer, "Ploughshares into Swords: Economic Implications of South Korean Military Spending," *Academic Paper Series* 4, no. 2 (February 2009): 2.

22. For South Korea's figure and North Korea's figure in 2006, see *Defense White Paper 2008*, 315; and *Vantage Point* (April 2008), 29.

23. For further analysis, see Feffer, "Ploughshares into Swords."

24. Jae-Jung Suh, "The Imbalance of Power, the Balance of Asymmetric Terror:

Mutual Assured Destruction (MAD) in Korea," in John Feffer, ed. *The Future of U.S.-Korean Relations: The Imbalance of Power* (New York: Routledge, 2006), 69.

25. Hamm Taik-young, *Arming the Two Koreas* (London: Routledge, 1999), 166.

26. David C. Kang, "International Relations Theory and the Second Korean War," *International Studies Quarterly* 47, no. 3 (2003): 306.

27. Quoted in Andrew Mack, "The Nuclear Crisis on the Korean Peninsula," *Asian Survey* 33, no. 4 (1993): 342.

28. Muthiah Alagappa, "Introduction: Investigating Nuclear Weapons in a New Era." In Muthiah Alagappa, ed., *The Long Shadow: Nuclear Weapons and Security in 21st Century Asia* (Stanford: Stanford University Press, 2008), 23.

29. Victor D. Cha, "Making Sense of the Black Box: Hypotheses on Strategic Doctrine and the DPRK Threat," in Samuel S. Kim, ed., *The North Korean System in the Post-Cold War Era* (New York: Palgrave, 2001), 181.

30. Suh, "Imbalance of Power," 64.

31. David C. Kang, "International Relations Theory and the Second Korean War," *International Studies Quarterly* 47, no. 3 (2003): 304.

32. (North) Korean Central News Agency (KCNA), October 29, 2008; see also *Rodong Sinmun* (Workers' Daily), October 29, 2008.

33. See *The Korea Times,* "Operation Plan 5029: Don't Let Contingency Scenario Become Self-Fulfilling Prophesy," editorial, November 2, 2009.

34. "Seoul Overhauls N. Korea Contingent Plan," *Chosun Ilbo* (Seoul), January 21, 2010.

35. See "Preemptive Strikes Needed to Prevent N.K. Nuclear Attack," *The Korea Herald* (Seoul), January 20, 2010; and Choe Sang-Hun, "South Korea Warns North on a First Nuclear Strike," *New York Times,* January 21, 2010.

36. David Kang, "North Korea's Military and Security Policy," in Samuel S. Kim, ed., *North Korean Foreign Relations in the Post-Cold War Era* (New York: Oxford University Press, 1998), 168–69.

37. Marcus Noland, *Avoiding the Apocalypse: The Future of the Two Koreas* (Washington, DC: Institute for International Economics, June 2000), 96.

38. Immanuel Kant, *Perpetual Peace: A Philosophical Sketch.* Reprinted in *Kant's Political Writings*, ed. Hans Reiss (Cambridge: Cambridge University Press, 1970 [originally published in 1795]), 114; italics in original.

39. Bruce Russett and John R. Oneal, *Triangulating Peace: Democracy, Interdependence and International Organizations* (New York: W. W. Norton, 2001); John R. Oneal, Frances Oneal, Zeev Mao, and Bruce Russett, "The Liberal Peace: Interdependence, Democracy and International Conflict, 1950–1986," *Journal of Peace Research* 33, no. 1 (1996): 11–28.

40. See Solomon W. Polachek, "Conflict and Trade," *Journal of Conflict Resolution* 24, no. 1 (1980): 57–78.

41. Albert O. Hirschman, *National Power and the Structure of Foreign Trade*, expanded edition (Berkeley: University of California Press, 1980), chap. 1.

42. Kenneth Waltz, *Theory of International Politics.* Reading (Reading, MA: Ad-

dison-Wesley, 1979); Joseph M. Grieco, "Anarchy and the Limits of Cooperation: A Realist Critique of the Newest Liberal Institutionalism," *International Organization* 42 (summer 1988): 485–529; James D. Morrow, "When Do 'Relative Gains' Impede Trade?" *Journal of Conflict Resolution* 41, no. 1 (1997): 12–37.

43. Bradley O. Babson, "Inter-Korean Economic Relations in a Regional Context," *Asian Perspective* 26, no. 3 (2002): 71–89.

44. For a more detailed analysis, see Samuel S. Kim and Abraham Kim, "Conflict Management," in Mary Hawkesworth and Maurice Kogan, eds., *Encyclopedia of Government and Politics*, 2d ed. (London and New York: Routledge 2004), 980–93.

45. Karl Marx, "The 18th Brumaire of Louis Napoleon," in Lewis Feuer, ed., *Basic Writings on Politics and Philosophy: Karl Marx and Friedrich Engels* (New York: Doubleday, 1959), 320.

46. For detailed multilevel and multidimensional analysis, see Samuel S. Kim, ed. *Inter-Korean Relations: Problems and Prospects* (New York: Palgrave, 2004).

Chapter 8

1. Brantly Womack, *China and Vietnam: The Politics of Asymmetry* (New York: Cambridge University Press, 2006).

2. Gary Goertz and Paul F. Diehl, "Enduring Rivalries: Theoretical Constructs and Empirical Patterns," *International Studies Quarterly* 37, no. 2: 154

3. See William R. Thompson, "Principal Rivalries," *Journal of Conflict Resolution* 39, no. 2 (1995): 195–223; and Karen Rasler and William R. Thompson, "Explaining Rivalry Escalation to War," *International Studies Quarterly* 44, no. 3 (2000): 503–30.

4. Thompson, "Principal Rivalries," 201.

5. See William R. Thompson, "Identifying Rivals and Rivalries in World Politics," *International Studies Quarterly* 45 (2001): 557–86.

6. The Chinese invasion of 1788 was too brief and too much related to Vietnamese dynastic politics to count as a rival hostility. See Buu Lam Truong, "Invention Versus Tribute in Sino-Vietnamese Relations, 1788–1790," in John King Fairbank, ed., *The Chinese World Order: Traditional China's Foreign Relations* (Cambridge, MA: Harvard University Press, 1968).

7. The Chinese claim is shared by the PRC and the Republic of China (Taiwan), but unlike the Spratlys, there is no Taiwan presence. See Greg Austin, *China's Ocean Frontier* (St. Leonards, NSQ, Australia: Allen and Unwin Australia, 1998).

8. Nayan Chanda, *Brother Enemy: The War After the War* (New York: Macmillan, 1986).

9. Quichen Qian, *Ten Episodes in China's Diplomacy* (New York: Harper Collins, 2005), 1–32.

10. For example, Christensen and Chen argue that Mao's 1958 confrontation over Taiwan and the 1965 increase in support for Vietnam were attempts to mobilize the population for domestic purposes, but this is not the only possible interpretation. See Thomas J. Christensen, *Useful Adversaries* (Princeton, NJ: Princeton University Press,

1996); and Jian Chen, *Mao's China and the Cold War* (Chapel Hill: University of North Carolina Press, 2001).

11. Alexander Woodside, *Vietnam and the Chinese Model: A Comparative Study of Vietnamese and Chinese Government in the First Half of the Nineteenth Century* (Cambridge, MA: Harvard University Press, 1971).

12. C. Patrick Fitzgerald, *The Southern Expansion of the Chinese People* (New York: Praeger, 1972).

13. See John E. Wills, "Great Qing and Its Southern Neighbors, 1760–1820: Secular Trends and Recovery from Crisis," *in Interactions: Regional Studies, Global Processes and Historical Analysis,* March 28–February 3, 2001 (Washington, DC: Library of Congress, 2001); and John K. Whitemore, "Vietnamese Embassies and Literati Contracts," paper presented at the annual meeting of the Association of Asian Studies, 2005.

14. Ho Chi Minh, *Selected Works* (Hanoi, Vietnam: Foreign Languages Publishing House, 1977).

15. Brantly Womack, "China and Vietnam: Managing an Asymmetric Relationship in an Era of Economic Uncertainty," *Asian Politics and Policy* 2, no. 4 (2010): 583–600.

16. William Turley, *The Second Indochina War*, 2d ed. (Lanham, MD: Rowman and Littlefield, 2009).

17. Communist Party of Vietnam, *Fourth National Congress Documents* (Hanoi: Foreign Languages Press, 1977), 150.

18. Ibid., 151.

19. Brantly Womack, "Asymmetry and Systemic Misperception: The Cases of China, Vietnam and Cambodia during the 1970s," *Journal of Strategic Studies* 26, no. 2 (2003): 91–118.

20. Mao Zedong, "Mao Zedong to Le Duan, September 24, 1975," in Odd Arne Westad, Chen Jian, Stein Tonnesson, Nguyen Vu Tung, and James Herschberg, eds., *Conversations Between Chinese and Foreign Leaders on the Wars in Indochina, 1964–1977*, Cold War International History Project Working Paper, no. 22 (Washington, DC: Woodrow Wilson Center, May 1998), 195.

21. Kay Moeller, *China und das weidervereinte Vietnam* (Bochum: Studien verlag Brockmayer, 1984), 277–83.

22. Pao-min Chang, *Beijing, Hanoi and the Overseas Chinese*, China Research Monograph, no. 24 (Berkeley, CA: Center for Chinese Studies, 1982).

23. Chanda, *Brother Enemy*, 323.

24. *Vietnam Courier*, 1978.

25. Pao-min Chang, *Beijing, Hanoi and the Overseas Chinese.*

26. Andrew Nathan, *Chinese Democracy* (Berkeley: University of California Press, 1986).

27. Biao Geng, "Keng Piao's [Geng Biao's] Report of the Situation of the Indochinese Peninsula," *Issues and Studies* (January 1981): 78–96.

28. Alexander Woodside, "Nationalism and Poverty in the Breakdown of Sino-Vietnamese Relations," *Pacific Affairs* 52, no. 3 (1979).

29. Brantly Womack, "Stalemate in Indochina: The Case for Demilitarization," *World Policy Journal* 4, no. 4 (1987): 675–93.

30. Melanie Beresford and Dang Phong, *Economic Transition in Vietnam: Trade and Aid in the Demise of a Centrally Planned Economy* (Cheltenham, UK: Edward Elgar, 2000).

31. Gail W. Lapidus, "The USSR and Asia in 1986: Gorbachev's New Initiatives," *Asian Survey* 27, no. 1: 1–9.

32. Qichen Qiang, *Ten Episodes in China's Diplomacy.*

33. Eero Palmujoki, "Ideology and Foreign Policy: Vietnam's Marxist-Leninist Doctrine and Global Change, 1986–96," in Carlyle A. Thayer and Ramses Amer, eds., *Vietnamese Foreign Policy in Transition* (New York: St. Martin's Press, 1999).

34. See Gareth Porter, "Hanoi's Strategic Perspective and the Sino-Vietnamese Conflict," *Pacific Affairs* 57, no. 1: 7–25; and Alexander Vuving, "Strategy and Evolution of Vietnam's China Policy," *Asian Survey* 46, no. 6: 805–24.

35. Bui Thanh Son, "Vietnam-US Relations and Vietnam's Foreign Policy in the 1990s," in Carlyle Thayer and Ramses Amer, eds., *Vietnamese Foreign Policy in Transition* (New York: St. Martin's Press, 1999).

36. Vuving, "Strategy and Evolution of Vietnam's China Policy."

37. Guo Ming, 1992. Zhong Yue guanxi yanbian sishi nian 中越关系演变四十年 [Forty Years of the Evolution of Sino-Vietnamese Relations] (Nanning: Guangxi Renmin Chubanshe).

38. Brantly Womack, "China's Southeast Asia Policy: A Success Story for the Third Generation," *Cross-Strait and International Affairs Quarterly* 1, no. 1: 161–84.

39. Porter, "Hanoi's Strategic Perspective and the Sino-Vietnamese Conflict."

40. Brantly Womack, "Sino-Vietnamese Border Trade: The Edge of Normalization," *Asian Survey* 34, no. 6: 495–512.

41. Womack, "China and Vietnam . . . "

42. Drew Thompson, "Border Burdens: China's Response to the Myanmar Refugee Crisis," *China Security* 5, no. 3: 11–21.

43. A. Carlyle Thayer, "Political Legitimacy of the One-Party State," Paper presented at Vietnam Update 2009, the Australian National University, Canberra, November 19–20, 2009.

44. Brantly Womack, *China Among Unequals: Asymmetric Foreign Relations in Asia* (Singapore: World Scientific Press, 2010).

45. Daniel Kahneman and Amos Tversky, "Prospect Theory: An Analysis of Decision Under Risk," *Econometrica* 47 (1979): 263–91.

46. See David Kang, "Getting Asia Wrong," *International Security* 27 (2003): 57–85; "Hierarchy, Balancing, and Empirical Puzzles in Asian International Relations," *International Security* 28, no. 3: 165–80; and David Kang, *China Rising* (New York: Columbia University Press, 2007).

47. Womack, *China Among Unequals.*

48. John A. Vasquez, *The War Puzzle* (Cambridge: Cambridge University Press, 1993).

49. Rasler and Thompson, "Explaining Rivalry Escalation to War."

50. Ibid., 508.

Chapter 9

1. Even in the case of Asian rivalries, as the Christensen book that we noted in chapter 1 demonstrates. See Thomas J. Christensen, *Useful Adversaries: Grand Strategies, Domestic Mobilization, and Sino-American Conflict, 1947–1958* (Princeton, NJ: Princeton University Press).

2. Robert D. Putnam, "Diplomacy and Domestic Politics: The Logic of Two-Level Games," *International Organization* 42 (1988): 427–60.

3. In addition to the Putnam 1988 article, which is reprinted in Peter B. Evans, Harold K. Jacobson, and Robert D. Putnam, eds., *Double Edged Diplomacy: International Bargaining and Domestic Politics* (Berkeley: University of California Press, 1993), along with thirteen original articles on two-level game applications, see Howard P. Lehman and Jennifer L. McCoy, "The Dynamics of the Two-Level Bargaining Game: The 1988 Brazilian Debt Negotiations," *World Politics* 44, no. 4 (1992): 600–44; Jeffrey W. Knopf, "Beyond Two-Level Games: Domestic-International Interaction in the Intermediate-Range Nuclear Forces Negotiations," *International Organization* 47, no. 4 (1993): 599–628; Davd Carment and Patrick James, "Two-Level Games and Third Party Intervention: Evidence from Ethnic Conflict in the Balkans and South Asia," *Canadian Journal of Political Science* 29, no. 3 (1996): 521–54; Peter F. Trumbore, "Public Opinion as a Domestic Constraint in International Negotiations: Two-Level Games in the Anglo-Irish Peace Process," *International Studies Quarterly* 42 (1998): 545–65; Andreas Schedler, "The Nested Game of Democratization by Elections," *International Poltiical Science Review* 23, no. 1 (2002): 103–22; and Jacob Shamir and Khalil Shikaki, "Public Opinion in the Israeli-Palestinian Two-Level Game," *Journal of Peace Research* 42, no. 3 (2005): 311–28.

4. See Michael Colaresi, *Scare Tactics: The Politics of International Rivalry* (Syracuse, NY: Syracuse University Press, 2006).

5. This is another caveat found in Colaresi, *Scare Tactics.*

6. This question is thus one that needs to be asked again as the region continues to evolve. Some authoritarian states have become less authoritarian. States that currently manage or conceal elite disagreements have not always done so in the past. Nor may they continue to do so in the future.

7. The aircraft carrier seems to have been heading for the area in any event as part of the planned naval exercise.

8. The Chinese public response seems to have been restricted to warning states to stay away from the area in which the U.S.-South Korean naval exercise was scheduled to be held.

9. The Yeongpyang affair is still in motion as this chapter is being written.

10. There is also a domestic politics aftermath of the incident on the South Korean side. The defense minister resigned, voluntarily or otherwise, over political re-

criminations concerning the slow and relatively weak South Korean military response to the shelling of Yeonpyeong. But, unless an increasing domestic demand for revenge forces a stronger South Korean military response—something that does not seem to be developing at the time of this writing—the domestic response in South Korea is not really part of the Yeongpyang puzzle. What happens after the shelling does not appear to contribute anything to explaining why the shelling occurred in the first place.

11. Adding Japan, of course, would make it a six-state ensemble, which has encompassed as many as five interstate rivalries, although not all of them were operational at the same time.

12. The history of Korean rivalry is also characterized by a switch in capability asymmetry. The North initially was more industrialized. Gradually, the South caught up and definitively surpassed the North in this dimension. In this respect, the conflict changed from one that asked whether the more powerful North would absorb the weaker South by force to one of how much Southern economic absorption of the North would cost (and if it could be avoided).

13. If one pushed the Sino-Russian rivalry back to its origins in the seventeenth century, China was initially the stronger partner in the relationship.

Index